Bendelow and Kidd's
Dictionary
of Football

Ian Bendelow

Jamie Kidd

Oakamoor
Publishing

Published in 2015 by Oakamoor Publishing, an imprint of Bennion Kearny Limited.

Copyright © Oakamoor Publishing

ISBN: 978-1-910773-12-3

Published by Oakamoor Publishing, Bennion Kearny Ltd
6 Woodside
Churnet View Road
Oakamoor
Staffordshire
ST10 3AE

www.BennionKearny.com

Dad and John - you sparked my interest in football and for that I'll be ever grateful. Mum and Megan, you both deserve awards for patience and understanding. Peter Reid - you made me fall in love with the game the day John Mullin slotted it under Peter Schmeichel at the Fulwell End, so thanks for that.

Melanie Michael-Greer's enthusiasm about the project helped to really get it off the ground and also thanks to James Lumsden-Cook at Bennion Kearny for his excellent guidance during the editing process.

And of course how can I forget Jamie and all those games of table football back in sixth form?

Ian

My part in our book is dedicated to my father Billy, who played for 24 consecutive years for Morpeth Town FC without ever being booked or sent off. He instilled in me a love for football and although I could never ping it in from 30 yards like he did (and probably still can) he continues to offer his unconditional support in everything I do. Thank you Dad.

Jamie

Ian Bendelow and Jamie Kidd are from Morpeth in Northumberland. Their days of sixth form college spent playing table football first birthed the fledgling idea for this book, due in the most part to their running commentary on the proceedings and the jubilant scenes that followed. They are Sunderland and Everton fans respectively.

Preface

"Hey look, obviously the boo-boys have had their say but it's a minority of fans, and from my point of view we'll continue to give it 110% to try and break this barren spell. You know, rolling our sleeves up and getting back to basics in training is the best way to answer the critics, so, in all honesty, no one inside that dressing room will be pressing the panic button anytime soon. And I'm not worried about this so-called dreaded vote of confidence – I really don't fear the axe – I'm the manager of this football club until the chairman tells me otherwise. I've seen some absolute rubbish printed in the papers this week about my future... not that I read them."

*

Football parlance is a lexicographer's dream, and very often a fan's nightmare. There are thousands of words and expressions which are wonderfully obscure, yet to those who understand them – they are as clear as a *stonewall* penalty.

The reality is that football fans appreciate what *losing the dressing room* is all about, nod knowingly when a defence is at *sixes and sevens* and, although contrary to physics, are privy to the knowledge that a ball can actually be hit *too well*. Rather inadvertently, we have all become fluent in another language: that of football.

*

"The first goal has a tonic effect in a game like this and Millwall are all out to get that goal."

Not the words of a modern day commentary wordsmith such as Clive Tyldesley or Jonathan Pearce but Raymond Glendenning, one of the pioneers behind the microphone. Although not laden with platitude-ridden phraseology, the quote from 1945 does offer a flavour of what might emerge over the next 70 years. Just what is a *tonic effect*? And what exactly is meant by going *all out* for the goal?

Of course, in the era of flat caps and referees wearing jackets, nobody would have a clue what a *great advert for the Premier League* was, would laugh at the thought of the *hairdryer treatment* being dished out, and in those halcyon days of two points for a win, a *relegation six-pointer* would be completely alien.

For a while, Mr Glendenning enjoyed something of a monopoly on football commentary, being the go-to man for many of the big occasions. He was also one of the forerunners of horse racing and boxing commentary, such was his oratory prowess; perhaps it was because he sounded like he was genuinely excited. However, the creeping expansion of the media into football, and the transformation of footballers into *Champagne Charlies* meant there was a clamour for further access to the beautiful game, including increased coverage, in-depth analysis, and more column inches. This development heralded a contemporary era of football, which required a new vocabulary: one of linguistic excess, glorification and romanticism. Henceforth, this fledgling vernacular has exploded, ensuring football would never be the same again.

The 1960s and 1970s saw an increase in the amount of specialist footballing terminology, particularly with the introduction of *Match of the Day* and *On the Ball* to our screens. Co-commentators and studio pundits became commonplace as the nation's appetite for football grew to greater heights in the aftermath of England's 1966 World Cup triumph. Some became known for their vice-like grip on the language of football; David Coleman was a notable proponent, coining such pearlers as, *"If that had gone it, it would have been a goal."* Thanks, David.

Players too needed an expanded linguistic catalogue with which to express and articulate their thoughts as they were increasingly thrust in front of the camera post-match or into the TV studio as pundits. It so happened that trite platitudes and banal observations became the vehicle of choice and there is no doubt that, for many, this formula has stuck. It is not to say that this is a book of the trite and banal; on the contrary, the following pages will seek to demonstrate how the language of football is so much more than that.

Fast forward to the 90s and the birth of Sky, and its juggernaut of pomp, ceremony and endless hours of coverage. Sky transformed the football landscape, ushering in a new era of modern punditry. Mark Lawrenson (more of him later), Alan Hansen and Ron Atkinson became regular fixtures on our television screens, with the latter famed for creating a language all of his own; *back stick, early doors* and *little eyebrows* all became part of a staple stock of phrases affectionately dubbed *Ronglish*.

Without doubt, the unique language of football has developed exponentially, being used from the pubs to the terraces, and the pitch to the manager's office by pundits, fans, players and officials as a tool to explain the seemingly inexplicable. Strange little quirks and phrases unique to the game gradually found themselves used more frequently, and with ever-greater fervour. Why say *"the goalkeeper has exaggerated that save there"* when *"I'll tell you what, that was one for the cameras, Clive"* is far more appealing?

Some people are renowned for their aptitude in creating new words and phrases, finding their curious take on the English language adopted into wider use and the development of football's dictionary. Sir Alex Ferguson's *squeaky bum time* is now commonplace on the terraces, while Jose Mourinho introduced the world to the concept of *parking the bus*. Some have made up new words entirely; who could forget the day Iain Dowie coined *bouncebackability*? Perhaps this is the lexicographer's equivalent of a 25-yard *howitzer*.

So where do all of these terms come from? Religion, mythology and rhyming slang, to name but a few, have played their part in the construction of a language any sociolinguist would find worthy of study. From Wembley's *hallowed turf* to Plymouth Argyle's *herculean effort* and Paul Merson's *beans on toast* to the *barnstorming run* of a *marauding* full back, football's lexicon has been drawn from influences far and wide over many years.

The United Kingdom is not alone in developing a unique vocabulary. Our German friends, in particular, have a wide range of terminology reserved for the beautiful game. If Steven Gerrard was one of *Die Mannschaft*, he would not be known for the *Hollywood pass*; instead he would excel at the *bananenflanken*, (banana pass). A German Jim White would undoubtedly shout *"Transfer-Hammer!"* on receipt of news that Bayern had just announced a deadline day record deal. Meanwhile, the basement dwellers of a division are derided as the *gurkentruppe* (cucumber troop). What is clear is that the desire to explain things in football's own indomitable way transcends cultures and nations; it is a requirement no matter where you are in the world. In the UK, we might see a player get *nutmegged*, whereas in Brazil this would translate to *dar um ovinho* (to give a small egg). Our American cousins have also developed their own idiomatic way to describe the action. A good position to shoot from, for example, would be said to be *right in your wheelhouse*.

It should be noted the book's authors are not detractors of the curious language of football. Indeed, we see it as something to be cherished, developed and studied. Many football figures are quoted in the following pages and while some are direct quotations, others have been created with a degree of artistic license. We believe that there are many ways to tell this tale, and this one is ours.

1-9

0-0 written all over it

A game seemingly destined for a *stalemate* as both sides have the measure of each other, whilst at the same time showing absolutely no attacking intent. It is often a scoreline predicted by pundits in the opening half, only for a *goal fest* to ensue. *"Well that game had 0-0 written all over it from about 20 minutes Gary… how wrong was I?"*

Etymology: A commonly held opinion throughout the ages is that humans have six basic emotions: happy, sad, surprised, afraid, disgusted and angry. When something is said to be 'written all over your face' it's almost certain that the person in question is displaying one of these emotions. The ease with which a pundit, fan or manager can detect a game has 0-0 written all over it suggests this scoreline is one of the most easily detectable results of all.

1-0 to the referee

Chanted by fans who believe a *shocker* of a refereeing decision has directly led to their side going behind. Accusations are made about him being on the payroll of the opposition when, in reality, the aggrieved set of supporters have their *blinkers on*, as preceding the decision was a defensive slip, a *suicidal backpass* and a clanger from the 'keeper.

Etymology: It was only in 1891 that the Football Association decreed that one official should have control over a whole game. They were usually members of different football clubs; however, this spawned a number of claims that they were being unduly influenced by their perceived loyalties. In the 1906 book 'The Much Abused Referee', the principal whistle blower of the age, John Lewis said, "for myself, I would take no objection to hooting or groaning by the spectators at decisions with which they disagree. The referee should remember that football is a game that warms the blood of player and looker-on alike, and that unless they can give free vent to their delight or anger, as the case may be, the great crowds we now witness will dwindle rapidly away."

110%

The required percentage expected of all footballers and managers; although it is of course a mathematical impossibility. This is necessary to prove that they are fully committed to the cause. The *extra 10%* may contain, but is not limited to:
1. Staying late for extra shooting practice.
2. Going *full blooded* into tackles.
3. Leaving everything on the pitch.
4. Volunteering to take one of the first five shootout penalties, despite having severe cramp.

11th hour

The most treacherous time for many a transfer deal due to the sheer number which fall down at this time. Examples include Loic Remy to Liverpool, the initial Ruud van Nistelrooy to Manchester United agreement, and of course Demba Ba's move to Stoke, which was *vetoed* by an eagle-eyed Potters doctor. Deals may also be rushed through at the 11th hour, particularly on deadline day, much to the excitement of Sky Sports News viewers.

Etymology: Biblical phrase, referenced in Matthew 20:6, which told of workmen who were hired late in the day. "And about the eleventh hour he went out, and found others standing idle, and saith unto them, why stand ye here all the day idle?"

20-goal a season man

Somebody who is worth his weight in gold. The type of player every promoted club looks to *unearth* in a bid to establish themselves in the league. Can also be a *10- or 15-goal a season man*, but the key thing is they provide goals on a consistent basis.

2-0 is a dangerous lead to have

Possibly the most perilous of leads. Worse even than 1-0, because everyone in football from Jeff Stelling to Sir Trevor Brooking knows the *third goal is crucial*.

38-game season

Managers say this to remind players and fans alike that it's a *marathon not a sprint*. This also applies to 46-game seasons. Before 1995/96, it was known as a 42-game season.

40-point mark

Hallowed points total for the perennial relegation battler. *"Monk: We won't let up until the 40 point mark is smashed."* Whoever deigned 40 was the required number of points is unknown, but obviously didn't see West Ham in 2002/03 coming or indeed Sunderland in 1996/97.

40 years of hurt

A period of time, which began in 1966 and is ever expanding. Works on the assumption that the period of hurt began straight after England won the World Cup, leaving them no time whatsoever to enjoy their success. No doubt they were *back into training on Monday morning*.

Etymology: Originally '30 years of hurt', a line found in the Baddiel & Skinner & The Lightning Seeds' Three Lions.

50-50 challenge
Two players *going for the same ball*. One often *comes off worse*, leading to the referee calling for the physio and possible invisible card waving from the injured players' teammates. There is usually *no malice intended* in these challenges, however those on a yellow would be wise to keep their studs firmly on the ground.

50 years of hurt
Phrase to be used in advance of England's Euro 2016 *campaign*.

A

Abductor & adductor
Known in layman's terms as a groin or hip strain respectively. The injuries are difficult to identify, and only once the player has been *sent for a scan* will the extent become clear. If it's a grade one tear then the player in question might be doing shuttle runs within the week. If it is grade three, a short spell in a specially designed hyperbaric chamber followed by a warm weather break in Dubai might be in order.

Accolade
An award of some sort. It is usually a shorter-term one, such as manager or player of the month as opposed to an end of season *gong*. To be given an accolade often means taking the *plaudits* for the team's success during that period, but it may also be to recognise the individual in question is something of a local legend: *"Gareth Ainsworth has had a new bus named after him as local operator Aviva honour Buckinghamshire icons which also include former Prime Minister Benjamin Disraeli."*

They do however have the ability to be negative. *"Richard Dunne has the unwanted accolade of being the Premier League's top own goal scorer; with nine to his name, he really is someone who just loves to find the back of his own net."*

Etymology: The conferral of a knighthood during the middle ages, i.e. the highest honour.

Ace
During times of transfer speculation, these most coveted of players will be *eyed*. Ability doesn't always come into it as any level of the game can have an *ace* plying their trade; they are just as likely to turn out for Biggleswade Town as they are for Manchester United. Players may also be described as the *ace in the pack*.

Achilles heel

The weak point of a side. Usually a *carthorse* in the Phil Babb mould. The bumbling player is often advocated as the main reason why a team *shipped* five goals last Saturday. Entire areas of the pitch might also be described as such, as is the propensity to concede at certain times. *"Tranmere's issues seem to stem from the fact they have let in so many goals in the final 10 minutes of matches."*

Etymology: Trojan War hero and the central character of Homer's Iliad, Achilles was reputed to have been killed after being shot in the heel by his rival Paris. Legend had that when he was baptised in the river Styx to make him immortal; the only part of his body not immersed in the water was his heel, and was hence his only weak point.

Activity on the bench

The suggestion a substitution is imminent. *"There's activity on the bench, with Gary Rowett readying a change, Adam McGurk the player who is going to be sacrificed."* There are numerous types of activity, including:
1. A player getting *stripped*.
2. The manager deep in discussion with his *number two*.
3. Various non-playing staff *dishing out* the instructions to the player going on with accompanying notepad and hand gestures.

Any sort of *ding dong* necessitates much stronger lexicon, such as *uproar* on the bench, or potentially, *fireworks,* as was the case with Carlos Tevez' *bench-gate* furore after he refused to come on for Manchester City in a Champions League tie against Bayern Munich.

Add-ons

Extras on top of a transfer fee. May include:
1. International cap bonuses.
2. Appearance fees. Not going over the appearance threshold has been a common reason in the past as to why players have inexplicably been jettisoned from the first team… clearly the club do not want to pay the extra amount. It may also make a loan deal permanent: *"Aruna Dindane can only make one more appearance for Portsmouth before the club have to pay £4 million to French club Lens to sign him permanently, sparking a stand-off on the south coast."*
3. Extra payments due to the number of minutes played. Southampton allegedly had a clause in the transfer of Alex Oxlade-Chamberlain stating extra payments if he played 20 minutes or more in the game. The teenage sensation unsurprisingly had a number of 71st minute introductions into

the game; although the Gunners failed to realise the 20 minutes also included stoppage time.

Adjudged
Players are *adjudged rightly* or *wrongly* in a number of situations. Almost always used in the past tense, being adjudged offside, to have committed an infringement, fouled, dived or handled are common examples. In football, this legal term takes precedence over the more commonly used *judged.*

Adjustment period
Required when a side makes a *raft* of pre-season signings, the often scattergun nature of signings must take time to gel, perhaps with the back four all being required to attend English classes. *"Watford's busy summer in the transfer market means players may need time to bed in."*

Advanced talks
Akin to moving to second base, advanced talks have moved on from simple *talks.* Indeed, a deal may be close to completion, and it's just the sunbed for Gazza's sister, which gets the move to Spurs over the line.

Advert for the Premier League
The humdinger of a match, which provides sure-fire confirmation that the Premier League is the best in the world. The phrase *great advert for the Championship* is also used, although it does have more patronising connotations, as if the commentator is surprised at the standard of football being served up.

Even further down the proverbial food chain, when non-league sides face more illustrious opponents in the cup, they could prove themselves a *great advert for non-league football* owing to their *plucky* performance. *"I'll tell you what Guy, Worcester City have really played out their skins at the Ricoh today."*

Aerial
1. *Ability.* The goalkeeper who has the ability to catch (and never elects to punch) a ball from a corner time after time. Is the hallmark of the gloveman who possesses the ultimate *safe pair of hands.* Alternatively, this is the defender who would head away a breeze block if required.
2. *Battle.* The type of match where dominance is asserted through supremacy in the air. *"They're playing the game up in the sky here at Sixfields."*
3. *Bombardment.* Tactic used by a team, which likes to *pump the ball into the box* to try to find the *target man.* Other plane analogies are often used in the same breath, such as a ball being *flighted* into the area. Nautical terms may

also make an appearance; poor crosses into the box are often said to *sail* over everyone.

A family affair for...

A situation that arises usually when Lee and Gary Johnson face each other in a *managerial matchup in the lower reaches* of the football league. An on-field scenario that sadly never materialised between Teddy and Charlie Sheringham. Also refers to when siblings are on the same pitch together, such as Rio & Anton Ferdinand, Phil & Gary Neville and, of course, Brian and Mark Stein at Luton Town. Perhaps the biggest family affair was when the three Wallace brothers (Rod, Danny and Ray) lined up for Southampton in the 1980s.

Afforded

1. When the referee is deemed too quick to penalise a side for a soft foul they are accused of affording the opposition *far too much protection*. This usually applies to goalkeepers. Managers may also be seen to call for more protection for some of their players. Particularly those who are *targets*, such as *silky wingers* or those *made of glass*. Complainants to such incidents are the midfield enforcers (e.g. Graeme Souness) who love to let their talented yet fragile counterparts know they are there, often leaving their *calling card*. This is usually achieved by smashing into their quads like a freight train before the clock has ticked past five minutes. Such challenges are very likely to hamper the victim for the rest of the match.

2. A player is afforded *legendary status* after being with the same club for a period of time, or if they score a particularly *crucial* goal. *"Jimmy Glass' last gasp goal for Carlisle afforded the 'keeper legendary status in these parts."* Someone who *writes their name into the history books*.

Afters

Continuation of an ongoing feud between two warring players. *"Lazaridis goes in hard on Hinchcliffe… with a bit of afters there too! Tensions really starting to run high at Goodison now, the ref needs to get a grip… and fast."* Invariably follows a *tasty* challenge.

'A' game

The level of performance needed on the big occasions. *"If we don't bring our A-game to the table, there's no doubt Droylsden will come away with the points."* It indicates:

1. The defence must be mean.
2. The midfield must create.
3. The attack must be deadly.

It is not clear what 'B' games consist of but it is generally thought to be slack marking, wayward passes and profligate finishing.

A game of two halves

1. The quintessential cliché. Quoted when a) reflecting upon how a team's fortunes *altered dramatically* in the *second period* or b) when looking ahead to the second half in an attempt to say, "*It's not over until the fat lady sings.*"
2. A short-lived Irish sporting quiz show, fronted by Trevor Welch.

Against all odds

1. A team who is faced with such a difficult game, no odds can truly sum up the magnitude *of the task*, not even 1,000,000,000/1. Odds that even bookmakers would consider unrealistic. E.g. Accrington Stanley *romping to victory* in a *packed* Camp Nou.
2. 1980s song by hit-maker Phil Collins, and latterly Westlife featuring Mariah Carey; although her knowledge of the footballing connotations is thought to be limited.

Against the run of play

The run of play is an important monitoring device in football, as it is the indicator as to which side deserves *all three points*. If a goal is scored by the team who has been defending for the majority of the game up until that point, it can be said to have come *against the run of play*. If the team who were on top don't get back into the match, allegations of a serious injustice might be made, depending on just how *one sided* an *affair* it was. It may also be a *game changer. "Preston's opener came very much against the run of play, but it was one-way traffic after that."*

Agents

1. Pantomime villains of *the game*. Almost universally disliked, they are seen as people who look to make money off the back of football clubs, and therefore the fans. Managers despise them for *turning player's heads*, demanding *exorbitant signing on fees, inflating the market* and *holding clubs to ransom*. The name suggests they carry some level of expertise in advising players, but they may just as likely be a rotund Essex wide boy with a Volvo and access to a fax machine.
2. The term *agent* is placed before the surname of player or manager who has such woeful abilities they must be some sort of double agent, looking to bring down a team from the inside. This often applies to those who have ties to a rival club.

Agricultural challenge

A mud-and-stud, earthy tackle. Generally perceived to be one of a *clumsy* nature, which usually sees the offender get away with it. *"Lee Frecklington with what could be termed an agricultural challenge on Mike Wilde, but the referee deems it fair."*

Aimless ball

A big long punt to no one in particular. The opposite of a *searching* ball over the top, even though to all intents and purposes they are exactly the same; the crucial difference being if the player in question is of international pedigree or not, in which case it is the former. If you are Clint Hill, it is a directionless *punt*.

Air shot

An effort regularly found on the school playground and Sunday league pitches; when produced on the professional stage the only reaction from the stands will be howls of derision, with both sets of supporters usually able to see the funny side. Air shots carry the most severe consequences when committed by a goalkeeper – as Paul Robinson can confirm.

All

1. *Action.* A footballer who throws himself into *the mix,* contributing to defence, midfield and attack. He looks to *dictate play* at every opportunity, passing, tackling and generally *covering every blade of grass.* Often at the heart of *everything that is good* about a side. See also *fully functioning footballer.*

2. *Day long.* For an accomplished player, their *bread and butter* tasks can be dealt with *all day long.* Defenders are able to head away unimaginative long balls into the box, and goalkeepers will save shots *straight down their throat* with consummate ease. *"If that's the level of firepower Spurs have then they are in trouble; Begovic will save those all day long."* An alternative is that they will be able to deal with such duties *in their sleep.* See also *meat and drink.*

3. *At sea.* A defence who invites the opposition to drive a coach and horses through it due to a complete lack of organisation. The phrase is trotted out whenever Andre Marriner is the man in black, causing seafaring pun aficionados to have a field day. *"The Shrimpers were all at sea before Andre Marriner took centre stage."*

   Etymology: Nautical term, which pre-dates reliable maps and navigational equipment, with a ship in this position in danger of being lost.

4. *Ends up.* Being beaten in a manner almost as humiliating as it is absolute. Goalkeepers are afflicted with this occurrence on the most regular of bases, however for them it is to let in a shot considered *unsaveable.* A defender who is beaten all ends up by an attacker could – and arguably

should – have done more to combat the attacking threat. *"Korkmaz tied himself in knots trying to keep up with the marauding Rivaldo; it was to no avail as the mercurial Brazilian beat the hapless Turk all ends up."*

5. *Guns blazing.* Sides beginning at a *furious pace* in the hope of *nicking an early goal.*

6. *Over the shop.* As Alan Hansen would say: *"No positional sense, no tactical awareness, no first touch, no composure, no confidence, no nothing."* The list could go on, but these are all signs of a performance of a player who is all over the shop. *"Diabolical."*

7. *Square.* An evening up of the score line, i.e. back to *level pegging:* *"You couldn't get a fag packet between Raith and Dundee at Stark's Park. All square here."*

   Etymology: Reputed to originate from one of two sources meaning back to square one. This is either:
   a) *During radio commentaries, football commentators would divide the pitch up into squares. When a move broke down or the ball went back to the 'keeper, it went to square one.*
   b) *Square one of a games board, for example Snakes and Ladders.*

8. *-ticket affair.* Matches for which tickets can only be bought in advance. You won't be able to *pay on the gate* or try to *sneak in round the back*; although you could stand on the grassy knoll overlooking the ground and take in the action with a pair of binoculars and a bottle of *20/20* if at a lower league/non-league ground.

All about the team performance
Post-match interviews with the scorer of the match winner usually contain this phrase. It is a show of false modesty, as he will certainly be lapping up the praise *in the confines of the dressing room.* *"Getting on the scoresheet was nice, but it was all about the team performance today."*

Already on the beach
With their league status assured and nothing left to play for except pride, these teams have their flip flops on and deckchairs out, and will usually take *two points out of a possible eighteen* at the end of the campaign. *"With their Scottish Premier League status secure, Killie couldn't be blamed for already being on the beach."* Conversely, slow starts to a new season are another matter altogether. *"Sluggish Royals playing as if they are still poolside in Fuerteventura."*

Already walking

A player who already knows his fate. He won't even wait for the referee to produce the red card, as it was *a stick-on second bookable offence*, or alternatively a *horror tackle*. *"He's apologised to the lads in the dressing room."*

Amateur dramatics

Play acting which would not look out of place in a Chepstow theatre group production of Hamlet. Players who roll around on the floor as if they have been shot manage to con the referee into believing the pain they are feeling is genuine. Not that it would fool the wily commentators, who would no doubt suggest this kind of play-acting certainly wouldn't earn a six-month contract as Barry Evans' brother on *Eastenders*.

Ambassador

Ex-players or club *veterans* who have achieved almost *legendary status* are seen as *great ambassadors* for the game. They help to expand the *football family* across the globe. Pele will play five-a-side with villagers in Botswana, Michel Platini may visit a power plant in South Korea, and Carlos Alberto takes in a visit to schoolchildren in Cambuslang.

Ambitious

This trait applies in particular to managers who have a point to prove to fans, themselves, and most importantly the media - who are seen by many as the kingmakers in the pantomime of football. Cocksure gaffers have an unshakeable self-belief born of their stellar performance at the A-licence badge school, and their hallmark is achieving promotion then *jumping ship* when one of the *big boys* come calling the following season.

Ammunition

Alternatively known as *service* – which is essentially the football. A lack of ammunition, or ammo, going to the front-line is seen as one of the reasons for a paucity of goals in a side. *"The boy Rhodes has a nose for goal, but he still needs the ammunition from his midfield."*

Anchorman

1. The *linchpin* of a midfield. Someone who provides a defensive solidity to an attacking outfit. E.g. Roy Keane, Gennaro Gattuso, Karl Henry.
2. Oft-quoted moustachioed newsman played by Will Ferrell.

Etymology: The last man of a tug of war team traditionally was known as the anchorman. In a news context, the first anchorman is thought to have been legendary US newshound Walter Cronkite.

And into the net!
What Alan Green says after every goal he sees scored.

Anonymous
1. Someone who *goes missing* during a game, having no effect whatsoever *on proceedings*. Usually ends up being hauled off after 60-minutes. Often asked if he has *"even had a touch of the ball?"* or was he *"even on the pitch?"*
2. Most of the texters into 6-0-6.

Anti-football
Proponents of the long ball game; teams who put 11 men behind the ball or play a 4-6-0 formation to *shut up shop* have this accusation levelled against them. Managers may complain the opposition, *"had no intention of coming to play football."* Whereas slick passing games are seen as a *philosophy*, the kick and thump school is seen as more of a *system*.

Aplomb
A composed method of scoring a goal. Forwards who normally finish with *aplomb* are usually high on confidence, and in the *midst of a hot goalscoring streak*. *"Midson raced clear of the defence and finished with aplomb into the corner of the net."*

Etymology: From the French phrase à plomb meaning poised, upright and balanced.

Appeal for hands
A handball *shout*, which isn't usually successful as the referee isn't interested. *"Appeal for hands by the Rotherham defence, but the referee says there's nothing doing."* A co-commentator might add, *"Well it's going to take a lot more for him to point to the spot than that."* Can also be made in full voice by the fans, who from 100 yards away claim to have seen it perfectly.

Archetypal
Footballer who exhibits all the stereotypical attributes expected of a player in his position. Rock solid defenders with zero pace or dexterity, midfielders who can orchestrate a game from the middle of the park, and strikers who have a real nose for goal (i.e. Wes Morgan, Michael Thomas and Alan Shearer are often afforded this tag).

Armband
This has long been a colloquialism for the role of captain. The England *armband* is perhaps the most talked about award of them all, the destination of which is always the subject of much speculation, particularly when Sol Campbell gives his two pennies on the England grudge he harbours.

Armchair fan

An overweight pint swiller, who despite never having kicked a ball in his life still offers expert opinions on the game. He is guaranteed to shout *"shoot"* as his side advances over the halfway line, but will rarely see the full ninety. This is because he will either a) be too busy polishing off their tenth *John Smith's extra cold*, or b) have switched off in disgust.

They are the first to ring *Call Collymore* or *text 6-0-6*, simply because they weren't there. Once on air, *armchairs* espouse numerous viewpoints without actually having seen the game, unless of course they catch it in the *Dixons* window.

Arsenal

A store of weapons a team has in reserve, which will be *brought out* with the intention of inflicting maximum damage. *"It's going to be interesting to see what Oldham's players have in their arsenal to deal with the Dale."*

A sea of [X colour shirts]

Usually seen when a team crowds its own penalty area in anticipation of a corner or a free kick that is about to be fired into the *danger zone*. It can only work when the team plays in one predominant colour, for example Barnsley, Dover or Wigan. Can also be termed *massed ranks*.

As well as they have played, they aren't that good

Mildly patronising statement made towards the *underdogs* who have beaten English opponents in the Champions League. Commentators insist that the English team are still favourites to progress. *"As well as Olympiakos have played Clive, they are not that good and I fully expect Manchester United to advance."*

Ask

These are always *huge* and other varying synonyms. *"Colchester, down to ten men since the 30th minute have been well and truly beaten here. And once that second went in it really was a huge ask for them to get anything out of the game."* Alternatively, this may be of a player. *"It's some ask to expect Guillem Bauzà to replace the goals of Jason Scotland."*

Asking real questions of

Such questions stem from the attacking team giving their opponents a *stern examination* by *probing* at every opportunity. They are not simply *knocking the ball around in* the *middle of the park* but attempting to make *real inroads* into opposition territory in search of a goal.

Assignment

Often *tricky* in nature. *"The Bluebirds will look to negotiate another tricky assignment as Mike Walker's Norwich outfit come to town."* Unkind cup draws throw these up: *"If Cambridge thought that the last tie was a test, they've now been assigned a trip to Elland Road."*

A top, top player

Phrase favoured by Harry Redknapp, not long after he has refused to talk about other club's players. See also *triffic lad* and *top job*.

At the double

Often two quick-fire goals. See also bagging a brace. *"Tavernier at the double in Robins romp."*

Attacking principles

A team that has come through adversity over the course of a season by virtue of a forward thinking philosophy. *"Charlton have garnered much admiration for sticking to their attacking principles, because now they are reaping the rewards."* The defensive variant is more of a *mindset, outlook* or *philosophy*.

Audacious

A willingness to try something unlikely to come off. On the pitch, it is almost exclusively an *audacious lob, which* players will attempt, although the *backpass* variant also exists.

It is also possible to get an *audacious takeover attempt*, often by a billionaire tycoon or alternatively an ex-player fronting up a consortium. It's usually a *club legend*, such as Gary Lineker at Leicester. Additionally a *transfer bid* of this type might be made by footballing minnows, such as Basingstoke Town's attempt to sign Ronaldinho.

Auspicious clearance

Usually a hump upfield from a centre half who believes he is the new Franz Beckenbauer. Pioneered by the likes of Bobby Moore and Thiago Silva, this pass fortuitously finds a man and the commentator heralds it a pass of real quality. Can additionally be anything of quality on the pitch. *"Maierhofer rifled home a Matthew Jarvis corner at the death to begin his Premier League career in auspicious style."*

Authorities

1. FIFA. Protectors of the modern game, vanquishing corruption and spreading the football word the world over, protecting the little people along the way. Members get the really *posh seats* at big events.

Outgoing President Sepp Blatter has undoubtedly carved out a reputation as a visionary through the years. Many of his ideas and thoughts have been put into practice; and some have not. Some, which may or may not have been realised are:
a)   The ill-fated silver goal.
b)   Handshakes to combat racism.
c)   Tighter shorts for women footballers.
d)   The blockbuster film *United Passions*.

2.   The FA. Does - or *did* - the stuff FIFA tells it to.
3.   The Premier League. Does the stuff Sky tells it to.
4.   The Football League. Used to be chaired by Brian Mawhinney. Main tasks include sampling *Johnstone's Paint* tester pots on the exterior walls of FL HQ.

AWOL
A player can go AWOL in a number of circumstances.
1.   To *go missing* during a game.
2.   To not turn up for training for some unspecified reason, possibly a night out on the sauce.
3.   Returning late from international duty. The reason given for this is usually to *"receive further treatment for an injury sustained while with the national squad"* but it then turns out this was not sanctioned by his club.
4.   To flee the country, having released a statement on Twitter stating reasons for refusing to return. Possibly, because of some sort of perceived witch-hunt, such as Nicolas Anelka's self-imposed exile at West Brom.
5.   To open unauthorised negotiations with other clubs and driving down to said team for talks, leaving the parent club none the wiser as to the player's whereabouts. Peter Odemwingie famously did this in 2013, when he turned up at Loftus Road to speak to QPR; his excitement turned to horror when a) Jeremy Peace slammed the brakes on any deal and b) he realised he'd run out of 20p pieces for the parking meter. He was subsequently left to *rot* in the reserves.

Axe
Getting the sack. A chairman can *swing the managerial axe*, or the *axe may fall*. One thing is certain – no manager fears it, despite their head being on the chopping block. *"I'm not worried about what might or might not happen. I've never walked away from a challenge in my life and I don't intend to do so now."*

B

Back in to training on Monday morning
Phrase used to appease furious fans after a weekend *shellacking*. *"Rest assured we will be back into training, Monday morning, to put this right."* Not as bad as being *called in on a Sunday morning.*

Back-pedalling
  1. Frantic running by a defender who is under pressure from a marauding attacker. It is the kind of thing done when *backing off* the opposition, or a goalkeeper trying frantically not to be lobbed; see David Seaman v Nayim & Ronaldinho.
  2. Rectifying statement made by broadcaster during the programme after comments made by one of their pundits ignites a *Twitter storm.*

      "They are pulling at each other like a bunch of girls."
      [60 minutes later] *"Like Robbie, like everyone here at the BBC, we are fully in favour of women's sport."*
      "I apologise."

Back stick
The back post of the goal frame. Is interchangeable, depending on what *flank* the *set-play* is being delivered from.

Etymology: Forms part of Ron Atkinson's Ronglish lexicon.

Back to basics
Teams who have had a *bad day at the office* must return to these principles of football in an attempt to get results back on track. It can be assumed, therefore, that they were not concentrating on areas such as passing, defending and tactics. It is not known what so-called *basics* are, however scholars maintain that it involves a football and giving it *110%*.

Etymology: In 1993, John Major launched the Conservative Government's back to basics campaign, which aimed to return the United Kingdom to some of its traditional values including neighbourliness, decency and courtesy. The campaign was to be relatively short-lived, however, with a number of Conservative ministers caught up in scandals over the next few years; something subsequently satirised by Viz comics' Baxter Basics character.

Backs to the wall

Teams who are under relentless pressure from the start can expect to undertake a *backs to the wall job* for most of the afternoon, as Ben Foster once experienced when playing for Birmingham: *"I'm going out for a few beers. I've never been put under that much pressure. That was a major backs-to-the-wall job. The second half especially was an onslaught."*

Etymology: Field Marshall Haig released his famous 'Backs to the Wall' communique during the First World War when British forces were being bombarded by German counterparts in the spring of 1918. In it, he said, "there is no other course open to us but to fight it out. Every position must be held to the last man: there must be no retirement. With our backs to the wall and believing in the justice of our cause each one of us must fight on to the end."

Bad boy image

Many footballers over the years have gained the reputation for being a bad boy. This can be achieved through but is not limited to:

1. Participation in orgies or production of sex tapes.
2. Smoking in public.
3. Brawling in public.
4. Multiple red cards.
5. Reacting badly to being subbed.

It is an image that players will profess to have *shed* as they gain more experience. Henceforth the casual class-A drug habit has to go, as does kicking toys out the pram when the DJ won't play said players favourite record in the nightclub. Also out goes anything to do with cars, headlights, bonnets and undercover newspaper reporters.

Etymology: The origin of the phrase is unclear; however, it may have musical roots, with many artists inserting the phrase into song titles since the 1960s including Inner Circle, Marty Wilde, The Jive Bombers and Catatonia.

Bag

Three points are put in here.

Bagged a brace

Scoring twice in one game. Players can also help themselves to a brace, be *at the double,* or even provide *double trouble* for the opposition.

Ball to hand
Players who appear to have got away with one will often argue *ball to hand*, although it might often be ball to arm, *hand* is the catchall phrase. *"That's not ball to hand Martin, he's got no right doing that. Stonewall penalty for me."*

Ball watching
One of the *cardinal sins* of football. As pundits nationwide will tell you, you never take your eyes off the man. The consequences of *ball watching* are the *hairdryer treatment*, lampooning from Robbie Savage (if you're really unlucky Garth Crooks) and/or a fine. *"The backline was guilty of ball watching as midfielder Helmi Remeli reacted first to fire the ball into an empty net."*

Bamboozle
1. A player who produces something unexpected or skilful that ties a defender in *knots*. *"Adel Taarabt bamboozles the defence with a beautiful turn, inside and out before knocking one out wide right off the laces. Majestic stuff."*
2. Popular daily quiz featured on Teletext with Bamber Boozler. Weekend children's version featured Buster.

Banana skin
"And that concludes the FA Cup Third round draw. What do you think Ray [Clemence, England legend] and Ricky [from the Kaiser Chiefs]… any potential banana skins there?" Jim Rosenthal asks those charged with drawing the balls in this banana skin environment on a now-yearly basis from the FA's headquarters at Wembley or some other footballing establishment. *"Well Jim, I think that Brighton could cause Spurs a few problems at the Amex"* Ray might respond. Note that *banana skins* are always *potential*, and never guaranteed.

Those charged with drawing the balls will always be either praised or chastised for giving their side a *tough* or *favourable* draw.

Barely touched
A common protestation by a player whose teammate has been penalised is *"come on ref, he barely touched him!"* This statement is countered by a member of the opposition who gestures to his prone teammate with arms outstretched, mimics the *pushing motion* or perhaps indicates a *flailing elbow*.

Bargain basement
Teams who go shopping in the lower reaches of a division or the Football League, hoping to *unearth the next* Joe Hart or Glenn Murray. It is akin to finding *Die Hard* for £3 in the bargain bin outside *Blockbusters*, or the second season of *Grafters* starring Geordie heartthrob Robson Green for £1.50 on VHS.

Etymology: While now a synonym, bargain basement was literally the basement of a department store selling sale items.

Barnstorming run

Powerful surge, which gets the crowd *on their feet*. *"Jose Dominguez, certainly living up to his price tag there, producing a barnstorming run which was only ended by the studs of Chippo. Scintillating stuff here at Highfield Road."*

Barracked

1. Receiving abuse from a section of the crowd. Usually directed towards lazy or *inferior quality* players by *disgruntled* fans.
2. Being tricked by Barrack Obama.

Barren spell

A run in front of goal, which *yields* no return. Players tend to snatch at chances in an attempt to get the *monkey off their back*. Barren spells can be counted in games, hours or minutes. *"Can Grant Holt break himself out of this barren spell after nine and a half hours without a goal?"*

Basement dwellers

1. The *perennial* relegation candidates. They spend the season *flirting with the relegation zone*, or *rooted* to the *foot* of the table. Pundits, fans and journalists alike have *consigned them to the drop* early on in the season.
2. Men who still live with their parents, spending most of the day at home playing *World of Warcraft*.

Etymology: While it is certain that basement dweller is not a complimentary phrase, its origin cannot be pinpointed exactly; having said that, it is probably an American reference to the introverted, reclusive teenager who spends an excess amount of time in their basements hiding from the world.

Battering ram

A centre forward of *considerable clout*, for example 'The Beast' Adebayo Akinfenwa. See also old-fashioned *centre forward*. Many of these players can be found minus front teeth, plying their trade at unfashionable clubs and bulldozing their way through opposition defences on a weekly basis.

Etymology: A sizeable machine dating back to the Iron Age, this wheeled frame was used to break open various forms of fortification. Indeed, they can still be seen today, in hand-held form at dawn police raids.

Battle cry

A call issued by players or managers at the *business end of the season* in an attempt to *rally the troops*. *"Pulis issues battle cry ahead of crunch clash."*

Etymology: This form of display behaviour has been used by countless armies throughout the ages as a method of promoting unity and striking fear into the hearts of their opponents. Early references in Greek texts such as Homer's Iliad give evidence to its use across millennia; there is also widespread modern usage.

Beanpole

Almost exclusively applied to tall, gangling strikers who are able to provide an extra dimension; Peter Crouch is the epitome of such a player. Beanpoles have the ability to stick out a *telescopic leg* to divert the ball past the 'keeper.

Beans on toast

Cack-handed faux cockney-rhyming slang from everyone's favourite mis-pronouncing pundit-cum-wordsmith Paul Merson on Soccer Saturday. *"Oh no! Jeff! He's... he's hit the beans!"* Phrase has since been adopted by Matt Le Tissier. Phil Thompson prefers to say a player has *"hit the wine [bar]."*

Beckham territory

1. The range from which David Beckham scored the majority of his free kicks, approximately between 25 and 35 yards from goal. During his career, it was referred to as belonging to the man himself: *"Well Gary, this is very much David Beckham's territory, I think that much is clear."* However, following Beckham's retirement, the area has been annexed by other *dead ball specialists*, such as Andrea Pirlo, who has raised his flag on *Pirlo territory*.
2. David Beckham's house.

Beeline

In an attempt to run down the clock, players after often seen to be making a *beeline* for the corner flag. It is described as such because players go straight for it. This practice is frowned upon by the opposition but, as commentators say, it's nothing they wouldn't do themselves. *"It's all about keeping it in the corner now Clive."*

Etymology: A reference to the fact that bees are only able to fly in straight lines when searching for pollen and returning to the hive (and not across water, hence their use of bridges when navigating).

Behind closed doors
1. *Friendly*. Matches organised with the chief purpose of getting a key first team player back to full fitness, usually after a long lay-off.
2. Some sort of indiscretion may lead a nation's FA, UEFA, or FIFA to take action and order a side to play matches minus their home faithful roaring them on. Reasons include racist chanting, rioting, pitch invasions, or in the case of the Mexican league in 2009, because of a swine flu outbreak. In Brazil, it is called *portões fechados* or *closed gates*.
3. 1973 album by Charlie Rich.

Behind the sofa stuff
Horrendous showing of such desperate proportions that fans are barely able to watch; the footballing equivalent of a bloodbath. *"Let's get back to the game Charlie Nicholas is watching, and it's real behind the sofa stuff for the Sunderland fans at the Stadium of Light."*

Believing their own hype
A player or team who has *fallen foul* of others' opinions of their abilities. Usually means they will *fail to live up to expectations*. *"Diminutive star of yesteryear Freddy Adu could have been forgiven for believing his own hype at the age of 16, such was the clamour for his precocious talent."*

Benched
A player who loses his place in the team, perhaps due to a *poor run of form* or a lack of faith by the manager in the *big games*. Being benched suggests the player was once a first team regular; indeed many players react poorly to such a snub. Those who consistently find themselves as back-up would be termed *perennial bench warmers*. The opposite of *starting berth*.

Benchmark
Term often applied to those who have set the standard of success and is something to aspire to. Note this is always achievement and never failure. 30-goal a season men set benchmarks; goal starved ones do not. See also *yardstick*.

Bereft of confidence
A team who *cannot buy a win* are generally thought to be *bereft of confidence*. Usually caused by a series of knockbacks, such as conceding right at *the death* or going 27 matches without *tasting victory*.

Best piece of summer business
Usually not one of the *stellar* signings a club may make but possibly:
1. Nailing down the star performer to a long-term deal.

2. Ensuring the manager is not lured away to pastures new.
3. Welcoming back a key squad member who has spent many months on the sidelines.

Big boys

This is a term that is very much relative. Lower league teams will usually be hopeful of getting one of the *big boys* in a *money-spinning tie*, which will *boost the coffers*. Teams must always *earn the right* to be at the *top table*, no matter what competition they are in. *"Everyone attached to Celtic Football Club and Scottish football wants to see us compete with the big boys on the biggest European stage of them all."*

Big characters in the dressing room

The presence of which all clubs need, particularly in crisis. *"The big characters in the dressing room need to stand up and be counted if Cowdenbeath are to get out of the pickle they find themselves in."* Alternatively, clubs need the right characters in the dressing room to be successful; therefore no egos, *prima donnas* or *mercenaries*.

Big-time Charlies

When the big-time Charlies come to town, they arrive with all the pomp and ceremony you would expect. They are a squad of 16 Nivea boys, bedecked with Dre's Beats headphones, sleeve tattoos and fruity playing cards (for the bus). Much will be made of the fact that their bench will have cost more than the opposition's starting eleven.

Sir Alex Ferguson famously once called Paul Ince a *big time Charlie*, something he subsequently regretted, as he believed it left the Guv'nor with a tarnished reputation. Luckily for Fergie, Ince set the record straight with underwhelming spells as manager of Blackburn and Blackpool, the pinnacle of which was telling the fourth official Mark Pottage *"I'll knock you f****** out you c***."*

Birthday boy

When a player is celebrating his birthday, it is mandatory for the commentator to question whether he will be able to *deliver the perfect birthday present*. In case of defeat, it may very well be a *birthday to forget*. It is also common for players to give their manager *just what he wanted for his birthday*.

Birthday boy Yaya Toure kicked his toys out of the pram when Manchester City failed to sufficiently mark his birthday by only getting him a modestly size cake. His spokesperson, Dmitry Seluk said, *"They don't know money can't buy relationships"* before following that up with *"when it was Roberto Carlos's birthday, the president of Anzhi gave him a Bugatti."*

21

Bit-part role

A job of marginal importance to the overall team effort. Players are very often reduced to this role after previously being an important first team player. Indeed, it may become an even more desperate situation when they are consigned to train with the youths; as such, they are ordered to put out the cones for training, but not take part with the rest of the first team. *"Simone Pepe's anger with peripheral figure status at Juve prompted Chievo move."*

Etymology: Term for an actor who has a small role, which originated in the 1920s.

Blast

1. A forceful effort on goal, using extreme power just to *make sure*. It is quite often the case that this happens from *point-blank* range because no matter how hard a player hits it, he cannot miss. *"Vinny Samways blasts it home from all of two yards!"*
2. Furious riposte or barb from a player, manager or chairman towards any issue, which they feel, deserves their ire. *"Van Gaal blasts 'crazy' festive schedule."*

Bleeds black and white

A die-hard fan, so committed to the cause that the colour of their teams' home kit quite literally pumps through their bodies. Is a phrase particularly used by the Geordie nation. *"Love the Toon, win lose or draw. I bleed black and white me."* Emphasis is also placed on the word *bleed*. It is usually followed by one of three things:

1. Lifting of their top to reveal the club crest tattooed on the chest.
2. Loud chanting of *"TOON TOON black and white army!"*
3. Production of a picture of their bullmastiff *Shearer* wearing a Newcastle United top.

Fans of other clubs can also bleed their teams' colours; however, the phrase cannot be used for supporters of Crawley, Walsall or Kidderminster Harriers.

Blinder

Those who turn in a superb performance are commonly thought to have *played a blinder*. A performance of such magnitude they have *dazzled* the opposition.

Blockbuster

Comparisons of a superb goal to that of a big-budget Hollywood movie. A blockbuster is usually a strike scored from a considerable distance that leaves the 'keeper with absolutely no chance. See also *you don't save those.*

Clashes between *heavyweights* can also be described as such, as they are the type of game, which would produce record takings at the box office. *"Sevilla boss Unai Emery anticipates European blockbuster."*

Etymology: American description of bombs, which were capable of destroying entire blocks during World War Two.

Blooper reel

Video featuring cock-ups from across the *footballing landscape*. Something any professional footballer or manager really, *really* does not want to be a part of. *"Another one for the blooper reel there from Michael Duberry."* There are a number of different productions in existence, including *Nick Hancock's Football Nightmares, Danny Dyer's Funniest Football Foul-ups,* and *Emlyn Hughes' My Gran could do better* (only available on VHS).

Etymology: The term blooper originates from the phrase 'blue pencil' which would be used to edit out sensitive or unacceptable sections of wartime communications; a task undertaken by an individual known as the 'blue person.' It was popularised by American writer Kermit Schaefer in the 1950s who produced a record titled 'Pardon my Blooper: An Album of Radio and TV's most hilarious Boners.'

Blotted his copy book

Usually a goalkeeper, he does 95% of things right during a game only to be undone by a supreme howler, which ends up costing his side. May also refer to a manager who has had an ignominious end at a club, despite a stellar career. *"Hoddle's ill-conceived remarks when at the England helm really did blot his copy book."* Although this was probably more akin to spilling the entire inkwell on the book in question.

Blow hot and cold

A frustratingly inconsistent player. Those who *blow hot and cold exhibit* flashes of skill and possess many *game changing* attributes. However, it is just as likely they will go *missing* for extended periods or be *easily shackled* by the opposition. See Adriano, Finidi George, Royston Drenthe, etc.

Blow on their half time Bovrils

Whilst standing on the cold terraces, fans are known to purchase this popular meat extract drink in an effort to keep warm. *"That'll give the home faithful plenty to think about as they blow on their half time Bovrils."*

Blueprint
The formula for success pioneered by one manager and followed subsequently by others. For example, those who wish to follow an ethos of attractive, possession-based football would be a part of the *Wenger School*, while purveyors of a long ball game would be a pupil in Mr Allardyce's class.

Blu-tack hamstrings
A player who is prone to a pulled or torn hamstring. Usually seen when a player is in *full flight*, or *chasing down a loose ball*. There have been numerous TV images of Michael Owen *pulling up* after overstretching during his career (which were often accompanied by rather unkind cheers from the opposition fans).

It is something fairly easy to identify, as players generally hold their hamstring to indicate the injury; it is alone in this sense as players very rarely *hold a broken leg, or anterior cruciate ligament damage*. Commentators usually feel the need to state the obvious *"well that has to be a concern. He's pulled up with what looks like a hamstring injury."* One of the few injuries, which players signal immediately to the bench for.

Boardroom struggle
Alternatively described as a *battle* (with no end in sight), these grapplings in the boardroom may have a severely destabilising effect on a club. Reasons for such a struggle can be numerous, including a coup attempt, disagreement over sacking the gaffer, or a falling out over who had the stapler last.

Bogey team
A side, which for some inexplicable reason, always seem to have the *Indian sign* over a particular opposition. For example, QPR are consistently struck by the *curse of the City Ground*, where they have failed to win in 30 attempts since 1934.

Etymology: The literal term bogey was used by World War Two pilots to describe hostile aircraft in the vicinity. It has origins in the notion of a ghost or phantom type figure; the earliest form of usage was the term boggart, described as a 'specter that haunts a gloomy spot', first referenced in the 16th century.

Bolt from the blue
A strike that is often as unexpected as it is sublime. *"A bolt from the blue from Alvaro Recoba! Who knew he had THAT in his locker?!"*

Etymology: An idiom which can be traced back to the 19th century in English texts; intended to reference an event which is as surprising as a bolt of lightning from a clear blue sky. Thomas Carlyle said in his text The French Revolution, in 1837, 'arrestment, sudden really as a bolt out of the Blue, has hit strange victims.'

Boo boys

The disgruntled *fan base*. This section of support, which is always claimed to be a *minority* (whether true or not) must be dealt with. *"Ady Pennock backs Wright to silence the boo boys."* The boys may also turn into a *brigade*, depending on the level of discontent. A further escalation may see some fans organise a *protest* outside the stadium, the hiring of a plane to carry a banner above the ground during a match, or – in the case of Middlesbrough fans – an attempt to prosecute Jack Charlton under the *Trade Descriptions Act*.

Booked

1.   Receiving a *yellow card*. The player has his name taken by the referee. This may be for a *cynical* foul or *persistent offending*. When a player accumulates fouls, the referee will point to each area of the pitch where his previous indiscretions have taken place. It is customary for the commentator to remark, *"well he's had his name taken after more than one foul, and you can see the referee is reminding him of that."*
2.   *Ticket/seat*. When a player has hit a *rich vein of form* ahead of an international tournament, he can be said to have *booked his ticket* or *booked his seat* on the plane. Teams may also *book their tickets* or *place* in the next round of a cup competition.

Boot

1.   *Golden*. Accolade every striker wants.
2.   *The*. Something no manager wants.

Borrowed time

Time a manager must lend in order to try and coax a performance out of his bedraggled charges. This period may help him find a *lost* dressing room, but similarly pleas to the chairman for *"just five more minutes"* may fall on deaf ears.

Bosman

A player might move on a Bosman, get a Bosman, or have a Bosman free transfer. Whatever the parlance, it means he's moved for less than the cost of a half-time pie. Threats by a player to *"do a Bosman"* are also commonplace during contract renewal talks.

Etymology: Jean-Marc Bosman was a footballer for RFC Liege in Belgium. In 1990, his contract expired and he wanted to move to Dunkerque, however they refused to pay the transfer fee asked; in the meantime, his wages were cut and he was demoted to the reserves and was unable to leave. He obtained a European Court of Justice Ruling stating the free movement of workers must be allowed; and so the term 'on a Bosman' was born.

Bottle

Perhaps the best-known use is when a player *bottles it*, usually from six yards. Reasons for bottling a chance can be because a player has *crumbled under pressure*, or because they are in the *midst* of a crippling run of form. See *bereft of confidence*.

Bottle also carries positive connotations, *"If you could bottle this boy's talent, well you'd have a bestseller on your hands Jonathan."* Players also might possess a lot of bottle, leading from the front on the big occasions.

Etymology: Believed by some to derive from cockney rhyming slang 'bottle and glass', the term for 'arse'. It was thought that to lose one's bottle – or lose one's arse - was to no longer be in control of bodily functions. Of course, a simpler explanation for the phrase is the courage that drinking a bottle of alcohol seems to give an individual.

Bottom at Christmas

A favourite stat rolled out by the media during the festive period. They are of course now obliged to mention West Brom's Houdini-like escape in 2004, and Sunderland's surge of 2014. With Leicester's repeat trick a year later, Christmas 2015 will reveal whether this snippet is still in use, or whether it has been consigned to the history books, with the line 'no team has ever stayed up on 33 points' being the replacement.

Bouncing

1. Stadiums appear to do this after a particularly important goal goes in; alternatively it will be *rocking* (in more ramshackle affairs, this will literally be the case). Fans are no doubt in *raptures*. *"Stenhousemuir's late, late drama left Ochilview Park bouncing."*
2. Action of *the Poznan*.

Boutique player

The well-groomed version of a *Rolls Royce player*. Akin to a luxury version of a product, like a *Faberge Egg*, *Tesco Finest*, or *Ferrero Rocher*.

Box

1. *-to-box player.* A box-to-box player is one who has a *great engine*, and could *run all day* like a Duracell bunny.
2. *Of tricks.* The calling card of the tricky winger. *"Bolassie was a real box of tricks down the left flank as he gave Beevers a torrid time all afternoon."*
3. *The penalty area.*

Boxed in

The act of containment, whether it is a half, a third or obviously, a box. This may alternately be called penned in, pinned in or pegged back to a particular location. *"Boreham Wood kept on snapping at the heels of the Grimsby midfield, meaning they were boxed in for prolonged periods of the first half."*

Boyhood club

The club a player supported as a boy is of relevance when he either signs for them, or plays against them. The support for said club is rarely taken into adulthood. Robbie Keane once spoke of his joy at signing for *boyhood club* Liverpool, before expressing delight at signing for *boyhood club* Celtic around 18 months later. This led to much mirth and accusations that Keane was a *glory hunter*, or a *dirty turncoat*.

Bragging rights

The privilege of a team who have beaten their *fierce rivals*. They are usually cashed in *at work on Monday morning*. *"As the Canaries celebrate victory over Ipswich, they claimed the East Anglian bragging rights, and Barry's changed Martin's screensaver to a picture of Delia Smith."* Players very often come out and dedicate such wins *to the fans*.

Brains trust

Used often in irony as the camera pans across the bench showing glum-looking staff trying to figure out exactly how their side is trailing by four goals. *"There they are, the Brains trust. Another fine mess they have got themselves into here; work that one out lads."* The quintessential image is perhaps of Graham Taylor and co's *"what's going on here then?"* expressions whilst failing to qualify for the 1994 World Cup.

Etymology: Originally a BBC informational radio and TV service of the 1940s and 50s where a panel answered questions ranging from practical advice to moral dilemmas by a studio audience.

Brawl

Usually *mass* or multiple-man *(e.g. 14-man brawl)*, a fight which originates after a nasty challenge during the game. Escalating far beyond a simple contretemps, this can spark *ugly scenes* as all 22 players rush to get involved, with some acting as aggressors, while others play the role of peacemaker. Both benches will also become embroiled in the drama, *encroaching* onto the field of play to take an active part in proceedings. This without doubt will involve disciplinary action and a lengthy referee's report to discover just where blame will be apportioned.

Brazen foul

An obvious, intentional foul. A tackle of such *cynicism* it is impossible for the referee to ignore. Usually results in a *caution* or sometimes *straight red*. *"The Israel enforcer knew just what he was doing, and they will play a man down for the final 15 minutes."*

Break the bank

A very large transfer fee, which clubs will be reportedly willing to do in order to secure their intended targets. *"County to break the bank in order to secure Robins starlet."* Alternatively, managers can refuse to *break the bank* to sign someone, saying they will *not be held to ransom*.

Breathes new life

"Aitor Karanka called for the cavalry in the form of compatriot Kike - and boy did he breathe new life into 'Boro." Like Jesus raising Lazarus from the dead, a footballer asserts his divine authority regarding on-the-field matters by breathing new life into a situation. Alternatively, a flagging campaign might be revitalised by a *slew* of new signings. See also *effect*.

Brought in from the cold

A player *frozen out* only to be given a *second chance* by the gaffer. Those *bought in from the cold* are quickly warmed up and welcomed back into the first team fold. The alternative is being left to *rot* in the reserves, or loaned out, e.g. Nicklas Bendtner.

Etymology: The phrase was popularised by John Le Carré's 1963 novel The Spy Who Came in From the Cold.

Bumper

Usually a *deal* or *contract*. *"Ramires commits to Chelsea with bumper five-year deal."* Is occasionally a *crowd*, which occurs on key dates in the football calendar, such as the festive period, the opening day, or in the cup when the *big boys* roll into town.

Bung

A bribe. It is the sort of activity that takes place in the murky underbelly of football. Conducted through the exchange of brown paper bags at a motorway service station, e.g. Pease Pottage. Such scandals will *rock* the *footballing landscape*, causing much hand wringing and naval gazing from *the authorities*, with assurances that this will be *stamped out* because it has *no place in the game*.

Etymology: From the old English term pung which translates literally as a purse.

Buried

A straightforward opportunity, which is *gobbled up*. Players given this chance *do not need to be asked twice*. *"He's taken the ball down on the left hand side, and from that range he doesn't need to be asked twice... says thank you very much and buries it."*

Burst onto the scene

A previously unknown talent who comes from total *obscurity*. Catches fans, pundits and media unawares, as if they were wheeled onto the pitch in a large cake. Managers, however profess to have always known of their *precocious* talent. *"Well Adnan has been doing some amazing things in training all season, but we've been saving him until this point. We knew what he was capable of."*

Business end

1. The *end of season run-in*. The part of the campaign where players can obtain legendary status, and endless repeats of classic commentary such as *"Aguerooooooooooooo!"* are broadcast in the resulting years. It is thought to be the *business end* because this is when important issues are to be settled; everything from titles and cups to relegation and European qualification. There is no business end for those ensconced in mid-table obscurity.
2. The attacking portion of the pitch. *"Villa just haven't spent enough time at the business end of the pitch this season, evidenced by their meagre goals return."*
3. *Of the transfer window*. Seemingly, an ever-decreasing pocket of time, nowadays 95% of all deals seem to go through in the last 30-minutes of the window; the club secretary has no doubt printed off numerous special dispensation forms in readiness to send to the FA.

Buy back clause

A widely known phrase, but the execution of such a clause appears to be rare. It is not known how many *buy back clauses* have ever been activated, but it is relatively few. These stipulations are inserted into transfer deals by clubs who are worried the player they are selling may not actually be pony.

C

Cabinet

Where all clubs (except Rochdale) keep their trophies. Never are they kept on a shelf, on the mantelpiece or in a drawer, it is always the trophy *cabinet*.

Cagey encounter
A match, which *no team can afford to lose*, but equally a point may be no good to anyone. Either side is unwilling to commit too many men forward in fear of being exposed at the back; in other words, being *vulnerable* to the counter attack. First legs are traditionally tense too. *"A cagey encounter sets up a tense second leg after the Danish runners-up resisted their Ukrainian counterparts in a goalless draw."*

Call in the administrators
Whether, or not, some administration hotline exists, this is the phone call every chairman dreads making. Administrators are *called in* during dire financial times in an attempt to strip back the saleable assets of a club. Administrators are possibly men in brown overalls and flat caps who turn up at the ground in a rusty white Transit, and then proceed to load the chairman's mahogany desk into the back. They then hand over an envelope containing a *10-point deduction*, enforceable either immediately or at the start of the following season.

Called in on a Sunday morning
A severe form of punishment. Managers may call their players in for extra training due to the *thrashing* meted out the previous day. The news that they will be put through their paces is broken to the players as they are locked *in the dressing room* for a *post-match post-mortem*. Sunday morning sessions comprise much work, which mainly concentrates on getting *back to basics*. *Basics* include completing a beep test, running numerous laps of the training pitch, dribbling balls between cones and lying on the floor doing the *invisible pedalling* movement.

Called off
Matches are called off usually because of adverse weather conditions following a 9am pitch inspection (and possibly a secondary one at midday). However, it may be for other more obscure reasons - in London every so often, an unwelcome tube strike can bring the city to a halt, leading to matches being called off, or perhaps icy conditions outside the ground means a match is called off for safety reasons. It is worth noting that games are never *called on*, but instead given the *go ahead*.

Much consternation is caused when a club feels the postponement is unnecessary, perhaps even ludicrous, and the decision has a detrimental effect on their season. Everton's match versus Crystal Palace was scheduled when the Eagles were in a slump and Everton were riding high. However, the rescheduled match was played in somewhat of a role reversal, with Palace in the midst of their *hottest streak* of the season and they duly put the Toffees *to the sword* in their own backyard, putting a real spanner in the works for their Champions League push.

Referees also invoke the ire of sides when the match is called off mere minutes before kick-off; travelling fans are subsequently interviewed outside the ground by Sky, bemoaning the fact their 300-mile trip has been in vain, they have been up since 4.30am and didn't come to Wigan for its stunning vistas.

Calling card
Usually the high jinks of the Scarlet Pimpernel to taunt his enemies, *calling cards* have more ruthless connotations in football, such as the placing of stud marks on the ankle. They are left early on in proceedings and are intended to leave a lasting effect on the recipient. This can be verified from the treatment table as the physio furiously rubs away to prevent swelling. *"No one can deny Pepe's been a-knocking, because he's left his calling card on Casquero."*

Cameo
A short appearance in the latter stages of a game by one of the *stalwarts* of the side, perhaps returning from injury in a bid to *build up match fitness*. *"And what about Walcott? A brief cameo appearance, but it was game changing."* Cameo appearances can also highlight the struggles of a side: *"Cumming's effective cameo was further evidence of just how toothless Hibs had been up until his introduction."*

Cancelled Christmas party
Christmas parties are when players visit a local Italian, move on to a few bars, go to a strip joint and finally demolish a kebab. At some point during the night, this will be filmed and the contents put on the non-sport section of the *Daily Mail* website alongside a euphemistic headline about *'scoring'*. However, due to *that* run of five defeats in a row, managers may decide, *"there's nothing to celebrate."* They then cancel the shindig and consign the team to *Eastenders* on a Tuesday night, followed by cocoa and bed at 9.30pm. Accusations are then made by the press of the gaffer *stealing Christmas. See Harry Redknapp/QPR 2012/13.*

Capital punishment
A trip to London, which ends in defeat. The length of time a side has gone without experiencing victory is often referenced. *"Bobby Robson's men haven't won in London for 20 games, but will fancy their chances against a Charlton side who couldn't beat an egg."*

Capitulate
Shipping numerous goals in the space of a few second half minutes. From these moments on, the opposition are said to be on *easy street*, with the shell-shocked recipients embarking on a *damage limitation exercise* for the remainder of the game. *"It was a chastening experience Stan, an absolute capitulation."* Alternatively, a devastating

loss of form during the business end of the season leads to accusations that a lack of squad depth put paid to any ambitions a team might have had.

Captain fantastic

Favoured term of many for Steven Gerrard, both when he played for the *Three Lions* and Liverpool. Used whenever he scores or produces a *virtuoso* midfield performance. The term can also apply to any club captain in the match day programme.

Etymology: Captain Fantastic was a spoof superhero on the TV series 'Do Not Adjust Your Set' in the 1960s, played by David Jason; the wider programme featured a number of the future Monty Python cast including Michael Palin, Eric Idle and Terry Jones.

Card happy

A referee who doesn't mind *dishing out the cards like it's Christmas*. The standards are different from official to official however:

1. Some may deal a number of yellows and be seen to take a tough stance, thereby having a *firm control* of the game.
2. Others are accused of *wanting to be the centre of attention*, brandishing more cards than *Clintons*. *"Raging Inverness boss John Hughes blasted card-happy ref Andrew Dallas for wrecking a crucial top-six clash by flashing nine yellows and dismissing defender David Raven late on."*

Cardinal sin

There are a number of cardinal sins in football, but it is unclear as to whether they number seven. *Ball watching* is a particularly unforgivable act, however it is rivalled by the *telegraphed pass*. Also includes expecting to just turn up at a newly promoted side and win, and whether – as in David Cameron's case – you cannot remember if you support Aston Villa or West Ham United.

Etymology: In the Christian faith, the seven deadly sins were known as the cardinal sins: sloth, gluttony, lust, greed, wrath, envy and pride.

Carnival atmosphere

Bright, colourful scenes usually seen at stadiums in Latin America, or some of the more cultured European nations. End of season *carnival atmospheres* are popular too, when the pressure is lower or there is reason for celebration. Players also have the ability to bring the atmosphere with them; as with Juninho and Emerson who signed for Middlesbrough and brought Brazilian vitality to Teesside.

Carthorse

A useless lump.

Etymology: Of course, the true definition of carthorse is much more favourable. Strong, durable and with plenty of stamina for heavy work, the carthorse is an invaluable resource; much more so than the less-than-complimentary footballing equivalent.

Cash in on the rebound
A gift, after the goalkeeper fails to push the ball to safety, despite possible heroics. *"Great hands from Segers... but the ball is loose... the goal is gaping... Akinbiyi to cash in on the rebound! Marvellous!"*

Cast iron penalty
A *stonewaller*. Commonly asked of the offending party *"what was he thinking?"* There is no need for the benefit of a replay here, and commentary box stalwarts may decree it *"as clear a penalty as you're likely to see."* They are not always given, however, which leads to the manager *getting in the ear* of the – often blameless – fourth official to protest that his player clearly took the man, and not the ball. *"Quique Flores simply cannot believe his team haven't been awarded a penalty. Look at him! He's having a real go at the fourth official! That was a cast iron penalty."*

Etymology: Seen as the most durable of metals at one time, cast iron is actually rather brittle; however, this has not diminished its use in football. Many cast iron constructions collapsed in Britain, calling into question their suitability. As such, most were replaced by steel structures in the 19th century; although the phrase 'steel penalty' has not been subsequently adopted into football's lexicon.

Casualty
1. *Managerial.* It is a source of much speculation in the press over who will be the next *managerial casualty*; speculation abounds that the manager in question is on *borrowed time*. See also *sack race* and *trigger happy chairman*.
2. *Cup.* High-profile casualties also occur in cup competitions. *"Well on this FA Cup fourth round day, we've had our first high profile casualty, will Southampton be next?"*

Catalyst
The speciality of a player who brings *that little extra* to a side is the ability to be a catalyst. His *slaloming* runs and creative prowess produces a reaction in those around him, galvanising them to push on in pursuit of that all-important goal. *"Bertolacci comes with a €20m price tag and the expectation that he becomes the catalyst for glory at success-starved AC Milan."*

Catching practice
Low quality balls into the middle constitute this, for an erstwhile custodian who will clutch them to his chest *all day long*. *"The Derby corner is so poor, that's catching*

practice for Smithies as he takes it with ease." Can also be described as *meat and drink* or *bread and butter*. Dealing with a difficult cross may be described as a *great take*, although for some goalkeepers it is what is expected of him. *"You'd expect to see Neuer catching flies out there."*

Catwalk defender
A player at the back who is determined to put on a display for the assembled masses. Catwalk defenders possess attributes normally found in offensive players, such as *silky skills*, *swashbuckling* runs or *dead ball* specialism; however, it can be the case that they are all appearance and no substance, as Terry Venables once opined in his Sun column: *"Catwalk defender David looks like real... LUIZ-ER."*.

Caught cold
When a side catches the opposition defence cold, they may still be *in the dressing room* or have completely switched off. Game plans invariably go out of the window at this point. *"There must be something wrong with their warm up Clive."*

Etymology: Phrase popularised in sport by boxing. The meaning is similar to that of football – to be underprepared and subsequently going down in the early rounds; the one difference being in boxing there is probably much less chance of a comeback.

Caught it on the laces
Denotes a *fine strike*. Something he *couldn't have hit better if he tried*. The phrase may become obsolete with the introduction of laceless boots.

Caught napping
Players who are overtaken by sudden narcolepsy. It always seems to be defenders – or players performing defensive duties - who are *caught napping*, and not the midfield or strikers; the metaphorical short period of sleep, which occurs in the back line at the most inopportune of times. Images of Raheem Sterling waltzing through to score while Ryan Shawcross lies prone with teddy bear, *Nightol* and hot water bottle spring to mind.

Caught unawares
Very similar to being caught *totally off guard*. A surprise situation that departs from what a player might perceive as the norm, such as a *dodgy bounce*, a *bobbly pitch*, or by the defender *ghosting in* to score at the back post.

Cauldron
Usually a prefix to atmosphere, perhaps with the addition of *–like*, these are not for the faint hearted. Predominantly found in Balkan states where many teams fear to tread. Fans will make the atmosphere as *partisan* and *unwelcoming* as possible

in order to intimidate the opposition. A plethora of flares, smoke canisters and other pyrotechnics will contribute considerably to its creation. Galatasaray are particularly famed for having a *cauldron-like* atmosphere. As such, many other European opponents will declare they are *not looking forward to their visit*. In these situations, it is vital to get the early goal to silence the crowd. The nearest a side might come to this type of atmosphere in Britain is at Millwall, where away fans are led in through 'the cage'.

Censure
Players may find themselves in hot water with the FA for a number of incidents, including:
1. Swinging a flailing elbow into the face of an opponent.
2. Taking to social media to let off steam: *"Twitter outburst lands Ashley Cole in hot water with Football Association."*
3. Embarking on a Twitter rant about another club's manager.
4. Singing obscene chants on an open-top bus parade.

Chalked off
Disallowed goal. Players wheeling away celebrating unaware of the goal being disallowed is the source of much comedy for opposition supporters and neutrals. *Ironic cheers* are commonplace at this point, along with several unsavoury hand gestures. Gonzalo Higuain in the 2014 World Cup Final is a notable example. The new interpretation of the offside rule may increase these instances.

Champions elect
The title winners in waiting. Term applied to the runaway leaders of a division or the *stick on* favourites to win a cup such as the Champions League. Also described as *pretenders to the crown* and *heirs to the throne*. Those destined to go the other way out of a division are known as *relegation fodder*.

Channels
Exploiting the channels is an effective form of attack for a side that possesses either *mobile*, *pacy* wingers or perhaps a roving advanced midfielder who is in the *free role*. *"Almeria's success in the channels was the key to their victory."* Managers forever extol the virtues of getting the ball into these positions, as they are areas which will *hurt* the opposition – especially if the full backs are of questionable ability.

Charmed life
Goals lead charmed lives when they are *under siege* but for some inexplicable reason have not been breached. It is as though a magic spell has been cast before the game. Either that or Barry Fry has been urinating by the corner flags again.

Etymology: Originated as a line in Shakespeare's Macbeth 'Let fall thy blade on vulnerable crests; I bear a charmed life, which must not yield, To one of woman born.'

Chasing

1. *Pack.* Amassed group of teams behind the leaders or the side in *pole position.* Managers *throw down a challenge* to the chasing pack, or teams can alternatively *pull clear* of it.
2. *Shadows.* A painful watch. Insipid performance by a team who is half a yard slower than the opposition. *"We spent all afternoon chasing shadows. Their 'keeper was smoking cigars he had so little to do."* The length of time spent *chasing shadows* can be limited to one period of punishment. On the other hand, some players – particularly defenders – can be *chasing shadows all afternoon.*

Cheap seats

The opposite of the *posh seats*, these are to be found way *up in the Gods*. To emphasise its magnitude a crunching tackle, clash of heads or inadvertent ball in the spuds may be described as being heard all the way in the cheap seats too; known in the theatre as the *nosebleed seats*.

Chequebook

1. Despite the age of online banking and contactless cards, the preferred method of payment for all football chairmen is the chequebook, which will of course be *opened* – often at the behest of fans. In fact, in the football world it is the only form of payment deemed appropriate; fans would not demand that Mark Lawn gets out his credit card, insist that Maxim Demin goes down to his nearest Santander cash machine, or lobby Peter Swann to set up a standing order for the purchase of a new player.
2. *Chequebook manager.* The gaffer who on one hand proclaims to be a miracle worker, while on the other demands a sizeable *war chest* to achieve his aims. To his detractors, his transfer kitty talks a lot louder than his tactical acumen.

Choking

A team seemingly has the title in their hands, only a few more points are required from the final matches of the season until that long wait is over. Some bookies are so certain of the destination of the title that *all bets are off.* If it transpires that the said team does not finish the job off, accusations of choking will be made from far and wide. Players who fail to take a golden opportunity are also categorised as such, for example John Terry's penalty slip in the Champions League final. See also *bottle*.

Clanger

A huge mistake leading to a goal. Something that *99 times out of 100* a player would be expected to deal with. Almost exclusive to goalkeepers, clangers are mostly *dropped*. *"Bizarre goalkeeper clanger makes the difference on disappointing evening for Reggae Boyz."* Leads invariably to the individual in question *apologising in the changing rooms afterwards*; managers will *refuse to blame* them for the costly mistake however. See also *glaring error*.

Etymology: Not to do with the origin as such, but a clanger is also a large uncompromising pasty from Bedfordshire. The foodstuff of nutritionally-conscious former pro Neil 'Razor' Ruddock, perhaps.

Classic cup tie

Ingredients for a classic cup tie are as follows, where one or more may be present:
1. Open, attacking football.
2. A mudbath of a pitch where the conditions are without doubt a *leveller*.
3. A *giant killing*.
4. Plenty of spirit on both sides.
5. A full house with a cracking atmosphere.
6. A *come-from-behind* victory.

Of course, it could be argued that the classic cup ties of years to come will be reserve teams and half empty stadiums.

Classified football check

Full time results. Read famously for many years by the late James Alexander Gordon, and is now the responsibility of Charlotte Green. Often prefixed with *full*, as if the BBC weren't bothering with the result from the Sheffield United v Fleetwood clash. It is also unclear if there is an *unclassified football check*. Synonymous with the *pools panel*.

Clawed

1. Reducing the deficit. *"Spireites clawed a goal back through Ariyibi after good work from Lavery."*
2. Any side that *comes a cropper* against a team whose nickname is an animal with claws will in turn be *clawed* - or perhaps *mauled* such as the victims of Hull City.

Clean

1. *Pair of heels.* To describe those so quick the mud doesn't have time to stick. These heels are always *shown* to a floundering opponent who has all the acceleration and turning circle of an HGV.

2. *Sheet.* The most important stat for the defence to show *they really played their part.* Not the most important thing for a manager, which is the goals scored column, but it is a *nice little bonus. "Well the important thing is we won Geoff, but I'm also delighted with the clean sheet."* Some particularly demanding managers will be angry at their victorious side's inability to protect the clean sheet. In the US, this is known as a *shutout.*

Clear-the-air
These *talks* are required when there is some sort of *impasse* from within the club. Something has been triggered which causes friction, for example:
1. The differing opinions on what constitutes an unauthorised night out.
2. When England fail to beat one of the lesser nations in a major tournament.
3. An agreed weight the player must be when reporting back after the summer break.

Clever little ball
Pass of superior intelligence. Made by footballers who see things others don't, and who are attributed to having great *vision.* Footballers of this *mould* are not ones to spot the obvious. *"Clever little ball inside by David Silva, he's kept everyone guessing with that..."* Never is it a clever big ball, which is more akin to a *searching ball over the top.* Perhaps this owes itself to being more *route one,* i.e. the preserve of *kick and thump teams.*

Cleverly disguised pass
Tool favoured by the mercurial midfield playmaker who has the ability to produce a ball so well camouflaged it could have been an extra in *Apocalypse Now.*

Clinical finish
Shots *dispatched* into the back of the net with minimal fuss when *one-on-one*; doesn't require a second bite of the cherry. *"It was as clinical a finish as you'll see from anyone in League Two this season Clem."* A common type of score on a football video game after *pressing triangle.*

Cloud nine
A *victorious* team who are very pleased with an important win or trophy. A place of great joy revered by football fans and gravel-voiced Canadian soft-rocking denim enthusiast Bryan Adams.

Club mentality
1. *Big.* Those who possess this may exhibit the following:
   a) Hollywood celebrity fans.

b) Playing pre-season friendlies in Asia in front of 90,000 spectators.

c) Possession of their own *way*.

2. *Small*. Who have the following traits:

a) Signing over-the-hill players or unproven foreign talent.

b) A pre-season tour of Kent.

c) Constant profession to have *"the greatest fans in the world,"* based on purely arbitrary reasoning.

Club statement

Clubs never issue statements other than when the news is bad. They can be for a variety of reasons:

1. The most common club statement is announcing the sacking of a manager. Traditionally, the club will look to *place on record* their *thanks* to the departing man *for his efforts*, state their belief he *gave his all* in search of success, and *wish him luck* in the future.

2. To explain why it has chosen to ban a media publication from the ground — citing a spurious, pernicious and inaccurate article from the recent past. Possibly a charge sheet of perceived inaccuracies might be listed, depending on how irate the club in question is. Such items may include a) the anger at a flagrantly inaccurate article about a *training ground bust up*, b) an overly sensationalised account of a protest outside the ground or c) dissatisfaction about allegations of financial impropriety. A comical yet effective method of circumventing a ban is to draw cartoon pictures of the action for insertion into the next day's edition.

3. To express frustration at the actions of a player, saying that repeat behaviour will not be tolerated.

4. In order to deny constant speculation in the press over the future of one of their players or staff, saying that the only focus is on the next match.

Club versus country

The age-old debate, which never has, and probably never will have, a victor. Clubs get annoyed about players being played more than the *agreed 45*, while national team managers simply argue it is an honour to *pull on* the national jersey. Arguments escalate into talk of legal action against the country's FA when the player in question picks up an injury, causing him to miss a sizeable chunk of club fixtures. It is somewhat suspicious that while the entire squad are fit and ready for a World Cup (aside from the token metatarsal), a friendly versus Moldova sparks 14 withdrawals due to *"a knock"*.

Coaching badges

Necessary qualifications to allow one to manage a football team. Far from getting their mums to sew them onto their jumpers, Scouts-style, Roy Keane helpfully clarified in his autobiography *"there's no actual badge. It's an award."*

Cockney mafia

Five individuals who caused much ire among the *Geordie nation* in 2008. They were Mike Ashley, Dennis Wise, Derek Llambias, Joe Kinnear and Tony Jimenez. Somewhat of an inaccurate geographical slur as four of the five hailed from Buckinghamshire, Gibraltar, Dublin and Spain. Only Wise is a dyed-in-the-wool Londoner. Their main achievements included bringing in world-recognised talents such as Xisco, Ignacio Gonzales and relegation.

Collector's item

The rarest of goals from the unlikeliest of sources. *"Gary, there is more chance of Banksy drawing a mural on the wall of the dressing room than Tony Hibbert scoring but when he does, boy will that be a collector's item."*

Come and get me plea

Imploration by a *want-away* player who is desperate to *secure* a move to another club. The plea is usually issued before the start of a transfer window or at the end of the season. Examples of players who have issued pleas such as this in the past are Jackson Martinez and Bakary Sako. Sometimes pleas will be issued to a league as a whole, such as Bafetimbi Gomis in 2013 who made a *Premier League come and get me plea*.

Come back to haunt

Former players or managers who have, or who are looking, to *get one over* their former employers. Usually because they have a point to prove after an acrimonious split or sacking. *"Aloisi could come back to haunt Sky Blues."* Is very similar to *showing them what they're missing*. *"They'll be having nightmares for weeks about this one Martin."*

Come unstuck

Teams that have taken one risk too many. *"Blackpool's gung-ho style won many friends, but it's only a matter of time before the Seasiders come unstuck."* Managers may *come unstuck* after continuous *tinkering* with their starting XI in an ill-fated *squad rotation* policy.

Comeback Kings

The masters of a *turnaround*. Manchester United were synonymous with this under Sir Alex Ferguson, as they knew the game was played over 90 minutes. *How many times have we seen them do this Clive?"* See also *Never write them off.*

Comedy of errors

Numerous mistakes at the back committed with such regularity by a *hapless* defence to the extent they have become laughable. *"Slapstick defending by Andy Tod and Derek Stillie allowed Dundee United to take full advantage for the third."*

Etymology: Early Shakespeare play.

Coming in at pace

Marauding run from deep by a player, looking to attack the ball. Players can *come in at pace* to the tackle, potentially risking serious injury, or if the referee deems it worthy, *censure.*

Commentary box

Traditional home of the commentator. Because of the expansion of broadcasting, the *box* in many stadia has degenerated to little more than a chair and fold down table with little room for Bovril or a *half time pie*. Boxes do survive in lower levels of the football pyramid, such as at Holker Street, home of Barrow.

Commentator

Broadcaster who provides information and analysis about the game, which is taking place. Almost always begins by describing one team as kicking from *left to right*, and then the weather conditions followed by what the game means for either side. *"And we're underway here at Stadium MK, the home side kicking from left to right on a beautiful day in Hertfordshire. Of course they can move eighth with a win, while Wolves can put real pressure on the top of the table."* The subsequent 90 minutes drips with prosaisms, particularly from the ex-pro co-commentator.

Commentator's curse

Statement made which a matter of seconds later makes the commentator look rather foolish. *"Just after I said Mark Noble has looked composed and mature on the ball, he's promptly gone and got himself sent off."*

Commit to a challenge

A player who *throws himself* into a *full-blooded tackle*, putting everything into it without thought about the *potential consequences*. When the opposition player is *advancing*, if a player commits to the challenge and is *skinned*, then the resultant space may be exploited.

Competition winner

The only explanation for the unfathomable presence of a player or manager who quite simply does not cut the mustard is the fact he has won a competition to be there. *"John Carver had all the look of a competition winner during his tenure at Newcastle United."*

Complexion

Chiefly, a scoreline which has changed unexpectedly but also includes an injury or red card. *"Ross Wallace's strike gave the scoreline a very different and unexpected complexion."* A couple of late goals, turning a 2-1 into a 4-1 means the scoreline *doesn't tell the full story*. Additionally, a change in circumstances can mean future mundane fixtures will assume much greater importance. *"With Leyton Orient's failure to beat Shrewsbury and the bottom four all winning, their high noon clash with Colchester on Good Friday will take on a whole new complexion."*

Comprehensive

One sided victories or defeats. *"The win was comprehensive for Oxford, dominant in almost every area of the pitch."* Sides who record comprehensive victories are often a team of great ability who have allowed their class to *shine through* – though they may only see it as a routine win.

This type of result leaves an opposition manager pragmatic and accepting at the full time whistle. *"We just have to hold our hands up and accept they were better than us on the day."* Sometimes, the defeat will not elicit such a gracious response from the beaten gaffer. More likely is a period spent *locked in the dressing room* to receive the *hairdryer treatment* for at least 45 minutes after the game. *"Well, we were hoping to bring you Paul Tisdale, but we're hearing he is still in the dressing room with his players, so he's dodged the post-match media responsibilities for now I'm afraid."*

Concede

1. A goal.
2. Defeat.

It is an unwritten rule that seemingly the worst time to concede is just before half time. This is because it drastically alters the gaffer's team talk by putting a wholly different spin on things. It is worse even, than conceding *at the death*, when such goals make a draw *feel like a defeat*.

Concerned faces

Upon a bad injury to a player, there will be a number of concerned faces, which will extend to the pitch if it is a shocker. *"This looks like a bad one Motty, some concerned faces on the touchline, especially since they've just made their third and final substitution."*

Confetti
Referees who love to take centre stage in a game could be accused of *throwing their cards about with gay abandon.* *"Keith Stroud was dishing out the cards like they were hand grenades."*

Consolation
It actually transpires there is little consolation to be had in football. *"Franceschini strike scant consolation for insipid Torino."* Late strikes might provide a small amount of comfort to a team that has already succumbed to a defeat, or perhaps a drubbing; it isn't celebrated with much gusto, if at all – with the exception of Gibraltar reducing the arrears to seven in their 8 1 defeat against Poland.

Constant speculation
Managers quickly grow tired of being asked the same thing over and over again by the press. Having to put up with constant speculation about *protracted, drawn out negotiations* is enough to leave many reaching for the proverbial Prozac. Escalation of speculation and a reluctance of the selling club to do a deal may turn the situation into a *transfer saga.* Examples include Fabregas to Barcelona and Gareth Bale to Real Madrid.

Consulting the lawyers
"I can't comment on the issue, except to say the club is consulting the lawyers." Any borderline libellous press conference comment, transfer gazumping, Twitter accusation, tapping up scandal, (perceived) unjust sacking or explosive reveal-all, no-holds-barred autobiography revelations might leave the wronged party checking their legal standing.

Consummate ease
Action achieved without any problems at all. *"Graham Alexander dispatches his penalty with consummate ease; he really is deadly from 12 yards."*

When something is achieved so easily, the opposing player can be *made to look foolish.* A goalkeeper claims crosses with consummate ease, while a classy player will take things down in this fashion or beat a man as if he *isn't there.*

Contender
1. A peach of a strike. *"Yeboah's 30-yard howitzer will surely be a contender for goal of the season."* Previously voted for by Match of the Day viewers, voting irregularities stipulate the final decision must now rest with the esteemed

pundits on the sofa, in which case the award will go to the player with the lowest handicap. Conversely, howlers can also be contenders for miss of the season, or if particularly bad, century.

2. Title pretenders, where aspiring champions will be thought of as *in contention*.

Contingent

A collection of fans. *"The away contingent are making plenty of noise away to my right, and who would blame them after that stunning effort from Weimann."* Seems mainly to be the *away contingent* of *travelling fans* – home supporters are rarely called the *home contingent*.

Contract rebel

Hyperbolic term. Like he is spraying graffiti on the lockers, smoking behind the bike sheds wearing a leather jacket, or doing donuts on the pitch in a motorcycle. It is the *refusal* of a player to sign a new deal, often because the club and agent's valuation are some way apart. This fuels much speculation in the tabloids about said player's future. If a deal is announced, he will express relief at *penning* a new contract, as all he wanted to do was play for the club. For a price, obviously. See also *holding to ransom*.

Corridor of uncertainty

In football, it is the mythical area of the box that causes *confusion* and *disarray* amongst the opposition defence. Putting the ball into this area may *ask questions* which simply cannot be answered. It is often simply shortened to *corridor*. *"Swansea fizzed the ball into the corridor and Ayew did the rest."*

Etymology: Term borrowed from cricket. A bowler will aim just outside off stump in an attempt to make the batsman unsure of himself.

Couldn't hit a barn door

Less crude version of *couldn't hit a cow's arse with a banjo*, which is actually what commentators mean but cannot say. Essentially, it means the striker doesn't have his *shooting boots* on, or that he is Fernando Torres post-Liverpool.

Coup

Seen when a player of a certain calibre transfers to a club who would normally have no right to make the signing. Toni Kroos signing on the *dotted line* for Port Talbot Town would be a fitting example.

Coupon buster

The most unlikely of results that causes howls of derision nationwide as the betting community scrumple their slips in consternation and cancel their plans for a new plasma screen; with awkward conversations about where the kid's school shoes money is, possibly to follow. It is usually the red-hot 4/7 favourites losing to unfancied minnows, which leads to Jeff Stelling to do a double take in the Sky Sports studio.

Courage

This is a much-feted quality to possess, almost exclusively reserved for the *lionhearted* player. Is possibly most closely associated with the patriotic, old school British footballer. It is used as a compliment, especially if the player in question has *gone through the pain barrier* to aid his side. *"The bloodied image of Terry Butcher is the benchmark to any England international of lion-hearted courage."*

Cover at left back

Reserve players step up to provide this service should the first choice player be unavailable. They are the footballing equivalent of a supply teacher, i.e. they sort of know the subject, but the kids just don't quite respect them as much, and will throw paper aeroplanes at the first opportunity. It is very rare to offer *cover at right back,* for reasons that leave scholars baffled.

Covered every blade of grass

Players with *great engines* have the ability to *cover every blade of grass* on the pitch. Normally a midfielder who doesn't stop running all day long, producing an *all action* display *reminiscent* of the greats. *"What I really like about George Boyd is his boundless energy; he covers every blade of grass so will be a real asset to us."*

Coveted

An *in demand* player. Players of quality may attract *admiring glances* from other clubs. This will lead to much press speculation about their future, which his manager will have to *fend off.* Chasing clubs will use a variety of tactics in order to snare their man. To be *coveted* carries connotations of romance, with the manager and board wooing the target with candlelit dinners, flowers and lute playing; leaving the selling club suitably reimbursed to quickly attempt to replace him with 3-5 players who possess mere facets of the one that got away.

Coy

To be shy, evasive, and yet alluring about a potential transfer deal. Invites images of a bashful Mauricio Pochettino blushing in the Spurs press conference when asked about his Michy Batshuayi *interest.*

Cricket score

"You've got to fear for Wednesday now; this could be a cricket score." It does not mean the match might end up 134/5, nor does it suggest that rain may stop play and the result will rely on the Duckworth Lewis method. A cricket score is a *thumping*, a *beating* or a *thrashing* by at least six goals. If it was a boxing match, it would have been stopped in the third round.

Crisis

1. *Club.* An outfit, which lurches from one disaster to another; every season one team, will become the *perennial crisis club*. A club may be *in crisis* due to financial irregularities, be placed under a *transfer embargo*, or suffer simply because there are a number of *want-away* players who refuse to throw their weight behind the manager. Crackpot chairmen who don't understand the game can also throw a club into *turmoil*.

2. *Talks.* The sort which may lead bookies to suspend betting on the sack race markets. Crisis talks can be held for a number of reasons, including:
   a) A Christmas party punch up.
   b) 15 defeats in a row.
   c) Taking a call from a national tabloid to answer queries about why three players were caught in a sex-sting in Marbella.

Crisp half volley

Exhibiting superb technique, a crisp half volley is always a shot to which one thinks to oneself, *"I've caught that well."* In other words, it is the kind of shot that's *going in before you've hit it.* It is also the type of effort not solely reserved for the elite. The overweight man in his mid-forties might catch a *crisp half volley* down the 5-a-side shed or the AstroTurf pitches on a Thursday evening.

Critics

Critics are there to be answered to. Players might make a point of *not reading the newspapers*, but if they so happen to score a goal following heavy criticism in the press, they will no doubt make a show of their celebration; because of course the best way to *answer the critics* is to score. *"ROOOOONEYYYYY! Oh what a finish! He has taken some stick in the papers recently but he has really answered his critics there, a superb overhead kick! And look at that celebration, I think we all know who that is directed at!"*

Crock

Injury prone player who keeps the physio's hands full and the treatment table occupied. Term is also used in the press, indicating a long layoff. *"Shaw crocked after surgery on broken leg."*

Cross-cum-shot
Is it a cross? Is it a shot? Nobody knows.

Crossing the divide
A *defection*. A player will never be forgiven for defecting to their side's hated rivals; burning of club shirts and banners in the stands when the sides meet are commonplace. Sol Campbell has been forever referred to as *Judas* by Spurs fans for his defection across North London in the 90s, while Sunderland supporters will not forget Jack Colback's decision to swap Wearside for Tyneside. Retribution can often be swift and cutting, as Luis Figo can testify when he had a pig's head thrown at him after he left Barcelona for Real Madrid.

Crowd
1. *Pleaser.* A *fan favourite*. A *crowd pleaser* is a player who exhibits outrageous skill, entertaining the masses and producing the kind of trickery that results in *rapturous applause*. Their surname is one of the most common to be found on the back of a child's (or indeed an adult's) *replica strip*, leading to the club running out of the letter 'A.'
2. *Silencer.* A goal, which shuts the home faithful up. Players who silence the crowd may have been receiving dog's abuse prior to their strike. Such goals are celebrated with a cupped hand to the ear and finger to the lips in a *"ssshhhhhhhh"* gesture.
3. *Trouble.* The result of discontent among the fans, crowd trouble can manifest itself in various ways. Common forms are the lone pitch invader and scuffles among warring supporters. Less frequent (at least in the UK) is the setting off of flares and the use of seats as weapons.

Crowd are on the player's backs
"The crowd don't like what they're witnessing here, they're starting to get on the players' backs, and that can't be good for morale." The hallmark of the *boo boys*, this type of behaviour might cause divisions within the *fan base*. Some are very quick to *jump on* at *the earliest opportunity*, whereas others feel supporting *the lads* is the best way forward.

Crucial/crunch clash
Various instances in football take on this characteristic, none more so than crucial *title deciders* or *relegation six-pointers*. It is often said that a point gained could be crucial come the end of the season. Also described as a *do or die* affair.

Crucial third goal
At 2-0, the next goal is vital. 3-0 signals curtains for the trailing side, however if the deficit is halved it's very much *game on*. Phrase favoured by Jeff Stelling.

"Another goal down at the County ground, let's see who's got that crucial third goal... is it game on or game over Brian Beard?"

Cruel deflection
Cruel deflections are some of the worst things to happen in football. They are not anticipated by either side, but are enough to take *the ball out of the goalkeeper's grasp*. They are caused by a *trailing leg*, an *outstretched boot*, or maybe even a *thigh that just shouldn't have been there*. *"It's the deflection that's taken it past him, what a cruel blow that is."* Lesser sides which have battled hard will see this as a *cruel blow* after their sterling efforts.

Cul-de-sac
The place which no player wants to be *ushered* down as the destination is always *nowhere*.

Cultured left foot
Technically gifted players are often described as having a *cultured left foot*. Perhaps the left foot spent time soaking up the arts in the *Louvre* or the *Uffizi* maybe, before taking in the opera. Players who possess one of these have the ability to *spray* balls around *the park* with ease. They will also probably be a *dead ball specialist*, able to *wrap their foot around* it, and put one right on the *postage stamp* from 25 yards.

The cultured left foot is the *hallmark* of a foreign *maestro*, it being sculpted and refined in one of the great European schools of excellence, such as *Clairefontaine*. Only after many years of practice can it produce such *magic*, which draws gasps from the crowd. After the match, said player will probably retire to the nearest coffee establishment, to read John Paul Satre and smoke cafe crèmes.

It is *never* a *cultured right foot*. These are thought not to exist. A left foot opposed to right is possibly thought of as cultured because it is usually the weaker side. Therefore, anyone who is able to do *spellbinding* things with that peg should be *lauded* for it.

Cup fever
Football-related ailment contracted by reaching the latter stages of a cup competition. If cup fever is caught by a lower league team, it is usually because they are on a *fairytale* cup run. Symptoms of cup fever include increased sales in scarves, flags and badges. In addition, there will be pull-out supplements from the local newspaper, while local greasy spoons will have a *"Cup special"* on their menus, with the lucky holder of a match ticket entitled to a free coffee or *Toffee Crisp*. Memories of *giant killings* of the past will be discussed, and the goal scorer from the last time they reached this stage will be trotted out graciously opining,

"Now is the time to write a new chapter in this great club's history." The remedy for a cup fever is a hammering by the big boys and the sight of team scarves in the charity shop the following week.

Etymology: 1965 film starring Bernard Cribbins about a youth football team who enlist the help of Manchester United in their quest to win their local cup competition.

Cup final
1. The final game of a cup competition.
2. Big games at the business end of the season. *"We've got six cup finals now and we need to make sure we are up to the task."* The phrase has become somewhat overused, with every manager and his dog proclaiming that their matches are real *cup finals*. Such is the clamour to finish as high as possible to get the maximum prize fund, teams will proclaim to hit it hammer and tongs until the season's end, no matter how academic their situation is. There will be no donning of the beachwear or resting on the laurels, lest an earlier-than-expected return to training be enforced. At least that's the theory.

Currency
The currency of the United Kingdom is the pound sterling, in the currency of the United States it is the dollar, whereas in football the currency of entertaining attacking teams is finding the back of the net. *"Manchester City deal in goals... and business is booming!"*

Curtain raiser
The Charity Shield is seen as the traditional season opening *curtain raiser*. It is a match played at *pedestrian* pace, with most players not getting out of *second gear*. The team defeated will dismiss this game as nothing more than a glorified friendly, while the victors will view it as an important trophy for the *cabinet*.

Cushioned
Lightly padded pass, chest or header, often back to the man between the sticks. May also be a finish: *"Conor Newton delivered from the right and Ben Pringle was at the far post to send a lovely cushioned volley past Andy Lonergan."*

Custodian
Old-fashioned term for goalkeeper. The *custodian* is a reliable pair of hands, dealing admirably with anything which comes his way. He has responsibility for *minding the net*. In some rarer cases, the *custodian* can be a board member, responsible financially for the business as a whole.

Cut adrift

The fear of many a weak side is to lose touch with the rest of the division, and can only dream of being involved in a relegation *dogfight*. In the Premier League, being *cut off at Christmas* can mean only one thing: the club will be *plying its trade* in the Championship next term.

Cut a frustrated figure

Kicking and heading every ball, arguing with the fourth official and *encroachment from the technical area* are all sure-fire signs things are not going well for a manager. *"Look at Steve Evans on the touchline, screaming at his players. He's cutting such a frustrated figure, that sheeting rain just about sums up his mood right now as his team labour away."*

CV

Talked about with both positive and negative connotations. A trophy win is seen as a great addition to the CV, whereas a sacking or relegation would be seen as a *blot*. Questions are also asked by the press as to whether managers can *add* to it with further success. *"Will Gary Mills add another FA Trophy triumph to his CV?"*

Cynical

A type of *blatant* foul where the perpetrator is fully aware he is playing the *man and not the ball*. One step away from a *coward's challenge*, they are often committed with the intention of *breaking down* an attack; players with poor positional sense account for many of these tackles. Such fouls lead invariably to a caution, but this is simply seen as *taking one for the team*. *"Cynical foul by Vieira, but if he didn't do that, he could have been in."*

D

D, the

Colloquial name for the penalty arc. The reason for its existence is to ensure all players are 10 yards back from the ball when a penalty is being taken. Also referenced when taking a free kick if the ball *is just outside the D*.

D Day

The day of reckoning for clubs when their fate will be decided, when their fate is compared to a military operation which accrued tens of thousands of casualties. *"It's our D day Tony. I can assure you that no-one at Whaddon Road wants to be playing Conference football come 4.45."*

Etymology: Term originated in World War Two, from the D Day landings in Normandy.

Daisy cutter
The scourge of the jumping wall, particularly when getting it *up and over* from such a short distance is simply not an option; it skims the grass maintaining a constant height from boot to goal. If conditions are wet, it will likely pick up pace, even though this is a physical impossibility.

Etymology: Technically known as the BLU-82B/C-130 weapon system, the 'daisy cutter' bomb had the ability to flatten a densely forested area into a helicopter landing zone, and was mainly used in Vietnam – however there was further use in Iraq and Afghanistan in the 21st century.

Damage limitation exercise
Far from attempting to *reduce the arrears*, a *damage limitation exercise* is all about not conceding again, or if so, as few as possible against a team that has *run riot*. *"Well Clive, it's been a rout in this first half, if you offered them 3-0 at full time I'm sure they'd take that."* Is of particular concern to managers towards the end of the season when goal difference may have a say in their overall position. Also applies in advance to minnows up against footballing leviathans.

Damp squib
A game that won't last long in the memory. *"The whole affair was a damp squib from start to finish; super Sunday it was not."*

Etymology: A squib is a type of firework used in various forms, from military to pyrotechnic use. Of course if it was to become wet, it wouldn't explode – hence the phrase.

Danger zone
1. Undefined area of peril close to goal. The probability of conceding from this part of the pitch is much greater than from just outside the box. Balls in this area may produce *warning signs* that must be *heeded*.
2. The relegation places. *"Brackley will be looking to haul themselves clear of the danger zone with a victory over Marcus Bignot's Solihull outfit."*
3. 1986 hit for Kenny Loggins, and criminally underused montage for relegation candidates.

David versus Goliath
A game containing a significant mismatch. Manchester United versus Exeter City, Brazil against Montserrat, Juventus playing Pro Vercelli. The underdogs will be cheered on by all *neutrals*. Managers may feel – with all due respect to their opponents – that his heavily fancied side should prevail, but at the same time warning: *"We're taking no one lightly and nothing for granted at this stage."* These matchups do present pitfalls for either side. Giving too much respect could have

horrific consequences, while underestimating the *minnows* can cause huge embarrassment. This actually did come to pass when the Red Devils drew 0-0 at Old Trafford with the Grecians in 2005.

Dead
1. *Horse, flogging a.* Side trying to squeeze every last bit of football out a player long past his prime; someone looking for a final hurrah before hanging up his boots.
2. *Left for.* A player who goes past his opponent so easily he might as well be the fourth official.
3. *Leg.* An injury received by everyone from children in the playground to international standard footballers. Whilst a similar injury wears off within ten minutes for amateurs, this type of *knack* for the professional sportsman can leave him on the treatment table for a week or more.

Dead and buried
A situation offering no way back for a team, such as conceding that *killer* second goal in injury time. Not only does it put the *final nail in the coffin* but piles the earth on top, pats it down, carves an epitaph and pens an obituary.

Dead ball
1. *Line.* Disputes usually lead to the player and crowd pointing to the spot where the ball went out. Protestations post-match that it was *"clearly out"* may be made; so much so, that neither the referee nor the linesman saw it.
2. *Situation.* A circumstance that presents an opportunity to get in a strike on goal. They are only called *situations* when something might arise from them. I.e. a long free kick *slung* into the mixer, or a situation right on the edge of the area, otherwise known as a *presentable opportunity.*
3. *Specialist.* A player famed for their prowess at free kicks may be known as a *dead ball specialist.* Specialists include Roberto Carlos, although he is more by association rather than consistency following his strike in the 1997 Tournoi de France. Most other attempts found row Z...

Dead rubber
Meaningless end-of-season match, or in a group stage where both sides have their fate already decided.

Deadline day
Statistics suggest that since the inception of the *Transfer Window,* deals done on deadline day have jumped by 12,500%. Two thirds of these are alleged to be the doing of Sky Sports News. There was once some choice to be had, however it has

now become so saturated that a series of *panic buys* ensue on a frantic final day. *Deadline day* is something of a circus that delights and frustrates in equal measure. What's without doubt is that it is completely dominated by Jim White.

The lead up to the day features many adverts, to which his face adorns; the reporter will excitedly invite the viewer to *"Join Jim for the day that he has made his own. What would deadline day be without Jim White?"* On the day itself, at around 4pm, he arrives via helicopter like Scotland's Donald Trump, resplendent in the tie he will eventually donate to the National Football Museum. He removes his sunglasses, surveys his kingdom and begins the walk to the studio, all the while accompanied by a triumphant fanfare. From then on, reporters, carrying at least two phones appear breathless with accompanying graphics to explain the latest movements of Bury's third choice 'keeper. The 20 rent-a-crowds assume positions outside each top-flight stadium, ready to gyrate and pull faces behind a harangued looking reporter. Bianca Westwood appears to explain why the fax machine needs to be fired up, despite protestations that *"no one has used a fax machine since 1994 so why now?"* There's no need for the red info bar – it's all yellow breaking news. White then declares, *"Getting info here from the Proact stadium, Jacob Hazel has completed his loan move from Chesterfield to... FC United of Manchester."*

All the while agents are circling round the metaphorical carcass of a deadline day, already stripped to the bone, trying to eke out one last payday. And invariably all anyone ends up with is a washed up 35-year old centre half from the Greek second division.

Etymology: American newspaper terminology. The phrase possibly has its roots in the American Civil war and more specifically at the Andersonville prison camp; this was the line which prisoners were not allowed to cross, at risk of being shot dead; hence the term dead-line.

Deadlock
"Can either side break the deadlock?" asked John Murray in hope rather than expectation. When two clubs are tied, they remain in this state. 0-0 is the most common point, but it also applies at 1-1, 2-2, 3-3 and so forth. Always questioned whether it can be *broken*, but not restored. Transfer impasses also feature deadlock, usually due to a large disagreement over a player's suggested value.

Debunked the myth
Contradiction of a falsely held belief. Lampooning the idea of *defensive frailties* perhaps. Also used with heavy sarcasm. *"Craig Levein, debunking the myth you need strikers by setting up the Tartan Army in a 4-6-0 formation. You don't need to be a master-tactician to work out what he's playing for today Dougie."*

Deceptive

The term *deceptive* is an interesting concept within football. The physical impossibilities of having a *deceptive turn of pace* are obvious, but many players possess this, catching out unsuspecting opponents. Deception also extends to passing and shooting. *"Caspar Hughes' cleverly disguised pass released Matt Blinkhorn who finished emphatically."* Spin put on a shot may deceive the goalkeeper as the ball changes direction en route to goal, perhaps forcing an *unorthodox* save.

Deck

Idiom for pitch. Players who partake in the dark art of diving *hit the deck* with some relish, or possibly even like a *sack of spuds* as if there is a sniper in the crowd. *"He throws himself to the floor! Hits the deck like he's been shot! The little Spaniard's not fooling anyone there."* Fans of long ball teams may wish their side played a little more on here too.

Defence has gone missing

Opposition players allowed to waltz through unchallenged and score often benefit from the *defence* going *missing; may lead to "WANTED" posters being put up outside the ground.* One of many incidents, which can lead to *question marks, inquisitions* or *inquiries* (usually led by the goalkeeper).

Defence splitting pass

Killer ball, which prizes apart a defence at the seams, creating the classic *one-on-one* opportunity. The ability to do this is a key attribute of the *mercurial* playmaker in the side. *"The through ball from Jérémy Clément blew the Reims back line wide open."*

Defensive frailties

The hallmark of a *brittle back four* is to concede a number of cheap goals. These so-called *defensive frailties* can come back to haunt a side, especially in big games, when they are *unlocked* with ease. The phrase *wicker shield* is never far from the lips of commentators when a shaky defence rolls into town.

Deft chip

On the *chip scale*, this comes below *impudent*. Deft suggests *poise, craft* and a *perfect weighting*. Too high for the keeper's reach but not for the crossbar. It is a touch of real *finesse*.

Delicately poised

A game on a *knife-edge*. No one knows which way it is likely to go, with either side staying true to their attacking principles. *"With 20 minutes to go at the Cardiff City Stadium, this game is edge-of-your-seat stuff; both teams are going at* it *hammer and tongs to secure the points."*

Delves

The preserve of the referee. When the referee *delves for his pocket*, it means one thing; the offender is in *big trouble*.

Demands respect

An indignant and aloof manager can *demand respect* from fans, players and media alike, particularly if he has achieved many things as a player. No one has bothered to inform him that respect is earned, and that record on the CV reads three relegations, one gardening leave and an eight-match touchline ban.

The situation often arises when proper acknowledgment has not been given from certain quarters to the achievements of a team. The press do have a tendency to target managers who they perceive to be underqualified for the club they are in charge of (examples through the years include Avram Grant, Stuart Gray, Tim Sherwood, etc.) or have spent most their time as a number two or coach (Sammy Lee, Steve Clarke, Tony Adams).

Dent

Title hopes, survival chances, European aspirations and top four ambitions can all suffer such a setback.

Department

Varying positions, most commonly the front line. *"The Clarets are in need of serious reinforcement in the striking department following Ings departure."* When referring to part of the pitch, it is known as the *attacking area*.

Derby day

The day that stirs up a wide range of emotions in the football fan. Nerves, anxiety and nausea are staples of the derby day experience when one team goes head to head with their fiercest rivals. Victory leads to *derby day joy*, and the securing of *bragging rights*, whereas defeat brings *derby despair*.

Etymology: Originally the name of flat race founded in 1780 by the 12th Earl of Derby. This was subsequently known as the Derby, a term that filtered through to other sports; one of the first mentions of it in a footballing context was a 1914 edition of the Daily Express.

Derisory

Transfer offers considered *derisory* are branded as such and are not worth the paper they are printed on. Of course, the reason for submitting such a bid is obviously not in the hope it will be accepted, but an underhand ploy to try to turn the head of the target and turn him into a *want-away* player.

Desire

One of the staples of football. Showing desire can be equated with giving 110%. *"First and foremost the lad has to show he has the desire to pull on the blue and white shirt, and after that we will take it from there."* On the field of play, it denotes a greater will to win. *"Gallas showed real desire to get his head on the ball, knowing that a collision with the goal frame was a distinct possibility."*

Destiny

What is meant to be in football. *"It's my destiny to come here, and I hope we're going to achieve big things."* Perhaps the greatest motivation for any player, manager or chairman is to *fulfil* the ambition of a club. Teams may also have their *destiny in their own hands*, i.e. if they can win their remaining games then they will *secure* the title. Prior to big European nights, clubs are said to have a *date with destiny*. The fixture computer also reveals its sense of humour when it comes to this. *"It had to be destiny that Andre Gray would make his debut against his former club Bristol City."*

Did the rest

The finishing touches to a move from which a goal results, although the commentator will often dispense with any elaboration on the phrase. *"After great work through the middle by Lathrope, he slipped it in to Barnes-Homer, who did the rest."*

Didn't need to be asked twice

Opportunity taken at the first time of asking. When a player takes a chance at the first attempt, he's usually *emphatically* dispatching it. There's no messing around here, this one is going straight into the back of the net. It may of course be goalscorer in question has received an invite: *"Adam Moffat didn't need a second invitation to blast the ball home."*

Die-hard fans

The sort of supporters who would run through a brick wall for the club. Die-hards follow their club through thick and thin, home and away. They may have tattoos pledging their allegiance to the team, have doormats adorned with the club crest, and insist their newborn child is kitted out in one of the club's fine Babygro range. Ironically, the die-hards are usually the first to get on their side's back, standing up and shouting *"SHITE!"* at the winger who has just failed to control a pass, despite the fact they are 4-0 to the good.

Etymology: First used in the Battle of Albuera in 1811. The commanding officer of the British forces, Lieutenant-Colonel William Inglis of the 57th (West Middlesex) Regiment of Foot, sustained severe injuries; despite this he maintained his personal charge towards the French enemy, shouting "Die hard, 57th, die hard!" which subsequently became the nickname for the

Regiment. Of course, the term Die Hard achieved wider recognition via the action film series of the same name starring Bruce Willis as Detective John McClane.

Different

1. *Ball game.* Moments that transform the match sometimes have a meteoric effect; so much so that the players appear to have switched to playing rugby. A side, which has halved the deficit to one, may now be competing in such circumstances because they are *right back in with a shout.*
2. *Class. "I thought the lads were a different class today. They showed what they were all about."* Managers lavish this praise on their charges following a particularly impressive display. Whether they knew that this extra gear existed is often unclear, however what is certain is that a performance in this bracket will be used as the *benchmark* for any future matches.

Ding dong battle

A *blood and thunder* tie where *no quarter is given or asked.* Both teams will attempt to strike the *hammer blow. Ding dong* is either a *goal glut* such as a *seven-goal thriller,* or a series of *meaty challenges* flying in *left right and centre* throughout. One particular example is the alliteration-friendly *ding dong Devon derby,* between one of Torquay, Exeter and Plymouth. Guaranteed to arouse the attention of Helen Chamberlain.

Dink

A softly measured ball. Belongs to the *weighted chip* family of expressions. Almost always a *little* dink.

Dinner plans

Teams who start at a furious pace clearly have other places to be that evening, and as such need to wrap up the points *early doors. "Jonathan Obika and co. clearly had dinner plans because the Robins were three up inside the first 30 minutes."*

Director of Football

Perhaps through choice, but usually because of ability, managers *go upstairs* to become director of football. Taken literally of course, this means they direct the goings on, on the football pitch, and indeed many feel this is their remit (such as Joe Kinnear). In reality, this is far from being the case, with their sphere of influence perhaps stretching to deciding what colour the new carpets in the ticket office should be.

Those considered to be *dinosaurs* from a bygone era are prime candidates to fill this role. Sometimes it really doesn't sit well with a manager that a director of football is *up there calling the shots* and from this, a *power struggle* almost always results.

Disciplinarian

A *tough taskmaster*. It would be unwise to cross a manager of this mould. Very much of the old school, a disciplinarian takes a traditional attitude to getting the best out of his squad. This means training three times a day, running along the local beach and then up and down the sand dunes until someone is physically sick. Tactics are dismissed as *details*, its hard work that counts in his world. When things don't go right for a *disciplinarian*, sparks will fly, as John Sitton's former charges can attest to.

Dissent

Protestation to any match officials either verbally or through various actions, including:

1. Branding the referee or one of his decisions *"a complete joke"*.
2. On hearing the whistle, picking up the ball and throwing it as hard as possible at the floor.
3. Getting right in the face of the linesman on seeing him flag.

Any of the above will undoubtedly result in a *caution*.

Dive

Taking a dive is very likely to *invoke the fury* of fans. Sometimes referees will be *duped*, but if they don't fall for it – the triple pike will undoubtedly result in a yellow card and *"marks out of 10 from the judges Clive."* Players may gain an unwanted reputation for hitting the deck too easily, and, as such, are known to have a penchant for simulation.

Managers are all too happy to tell the assembled media that a fine will be dished out. *"The lad knows that's not what this club is about; he'll be getting fined for that."* It is a strange contrast that fines are never discussed after the commission of a *coward's tackle*, diving in with two feet. *"I haven't seen it back yet... I'll need to take another look"* being the usual party line.

Dividend

A reward for a punt taken that comes off. *"The switch to three up front has clearly paid dividends as Lincoln have turned this game on its head."* The successful implementation of a new tactic the team has been *working on all week*.

Divine intervention

No worldly interference can help a team in certain situations, meaning help from up on high is required, including:

1. When three goals down before halftime.

2. When cut adrift at the bottom of the league in March and in need of snookers. *"Seasiders praying for divine intervention."*

DNA
The self-replicating ethos found in the very genetics of a side. No matter what happens, it will be the case that they will play in this way. Stoke will be tough tackling and uncompromising, Arsenal will stroke it nicely around the turf and Wimbledon were always the aficionados of the long ball game (or *route-one*). A style that a team is synonymous with will be part of their *footballing DNA*. It would perhaps be nice if the in-the-know pundit expanded this one day to say that it was part of a team's *deoxyribonucleic acid*, which would certainly win *plaudits* from the science boffins.

Do our talking on the pitch
Talking a good game beforehand is all well and good but they are just words. Managers of substance like their players to do the talking on the pitch; the problem being, if that talking is a comprehensive defeat then what they are saying must be questioned. Often, players will say the time for excuses is over and it's now time to *"let our football do the talking."* Alternatively, players embroiled in pre-match mind games will focus on making sure this is the case. *"Hanlon laughed the jibes off and insists it doesn't matter what anyone says before kick-off – because the real talking will be done on the pitch."*

Doesn't go down for anything
The seemingly bulletproof midfield hard man who finds himself on the wrong end of a *reducer* and is clearly *crocked*. *"De Jong's down in a heap there, and this could spell bad news for Milan, because he doesn't go down for anything."*

Doomsday scenario
The use of hyperbole to explain whether the worst-case scenario has either been realised or dodged. *"Hewitt's 30-yard howitzer ensures Southport avoid a doomsday scenario."* Sometimes termed a *footballing Armageddon*.

Door
1. *Back door*: The lesser-known entrance to which a defence should be very wary that they do not leave open. Otherwise attackers may *steal in* and score, possibly because the defence was too pre-occupied with the main attacking threat, leaving his partner unmarked and *in acres of space*.
2. Managers are usually willing to leave the door open for a return by a former *fan favourite*. Similarly, they may leave it open for themselves to return to the club in the future, or they may *refuse* to *shut* the door in this circumstance.

Doubters
The subject of their criticism will always aim to *silence* this faction.

Down to the bare bones
When ravaged by an injury crisis, managers may have to rely on their ageing centre half who couldn't be trusted to tie his shoelaces and has all the pace of a milk float. Leads managers to ask journalists at the press conference *"Have any of you bought your boots?"* or *"Anybody of you lads fancy a game?"* prompting much laughter.

Draw
1. A tie game, stalemate, point apiece, etc. Particularly turgid affairs are known as *bore draws.*
2. *Specialists.* Those who excel in producing numerous *stalemates.* Would do well to remember that it is better to win one and lose one than draw two. Draw specialists can be found in the lower mid-table of the league and are often the proponents of turgid, play-it-safe football. Masters of the unadventurous, they win few friends.
3. *The defender.* The ploy of coaxing a defender out of his position to be able to maximise the space behind him. It is not, of course, the physical act of drawing the defender, as if Marouane Chamakh enjoys nothing more during an evening than to sit down with an easel, to some mood lighting and a little rouge, and sketch a superb likeness of Carl Jenkinson.

Dreaded metatarsal
An injury that seems to only *flare up* ahead of the World Cup or European Championships. First came to public awareness following David Beckham's injury scare before the 2002 tournament. It occurs around two to three months beforehand, leading to *extensive* newspaper *speculation* about said player facing a *race against time* to be fit. *"Rooney in dreaded metatarsal KO."* Pictures of injured foot will appear in the Sun, with Uri Geller professing to have the requisite healing powers to bring the player back to *full fitness.*

Dreaded vote of confidence
A statement of support, which in reality is anything but. Like kryptonite to Superman, the *dreaded vote of confidence* is considered anathema to any manager who receives it, but they will not profess to be concerned. *"I've been given a job to do and my focus is 100% on the players."*

Dream debut
A debut to remember, with speculation by the commentator that, *"he must have been dreaming of this last night!"* Often described as *the stuff dreams are made of.*

Dreamland

Wispy utopia, which players travel to on achieving success. Goal heroes are *in dreamland* after scoring a particularly crucial strike. Fans go to similar plains when their side triumphs over rivals, or secures an unexpected victory over loftier clubs. Players may also have a *dream debut*, endearing themselves immediately to the *home faithful*. For the neutrals, a *dream tie* might be Barcelona v Real Madrid in the Champions League semi-finals, which also incidentally may be the *dream scenario* for the other two teams in the competition.

Dressing room

The place where the most intimate politics of a football team take place. To be a fly on the wall in this particular room would no doubt throw up some surprises.

Generally, it is accepted that the goings-on in the dressing room remain very much private. There is *omerta* surrounding such talk, an unwritten code to maintain silence *beyond the four walls*. To divulge discussions would be seen as a gross betrayal of trust. Tales have escaped, such as the infamous football boot to the eye suffered by David Beckham at the hands of Sir Alex Ferguson, who also spectacularly broke *omerta* in his autobiography. While it also extends to the *training pitch*, what *goes on in the tunnel* is much more widely publicised. *Pizzagate* at Old Trafford was covered widely, the facts of which were laid bare for all to see by a gleeful press. See also *training ground bust up*.

Drilled

So named because the ball apparently has the penetration of a pneumatic tool. Usually put right into the *corridor of uncertainty*, this type of cross has real potential to cause *chaos* and *destruction* in the defence. It is hit hard, low and *at pace*. *"The drilled ball into the box caused the Bolton defence to go into meltdown."*

Drinks cabinet

Grandiose term for six water bottles bought on by the physio during a break in play. Not a wooden globe filled with *Taboo* and *Archers*. See also *isotonic sports drink*.

Drive to...

Fans and occasionally chairmen will become so exasperated with one of their *charges* that they will do anything to *offload* them. This includes driving them to any club that wants him. It is particularly the case when an offer seen as too good to refuse is received. *"Ji? £5m? For that I'll drive the lad to Augsburg."*

Freddie Shepherd (or *'the man who shot Bambi'*, aka fired Bobby Robson) famously offered (from the driver's seat of his Range Rover) to carry Michael Owen back to Liverpool for £9m. This, of course, would have represented quite a loss on a man signed for £16.8m a couple of years beforehand. See also *one-way ticket*.

Drop zone
The spiritual home of the *basement dwellers*.

Drought
A *barren spell* during which the goals *dry up*. Droughts are usually thought to start after no less than five games without scoring; however, they can be monumental in length. *"Vitaiola's free kick was San Marino's first away goal in fourteen years."* The long-term prognosis for a striker suffering a goal drought is not good. A spell spent *benched* and comparisons to a donkey are common. When droughts come to an end, the player is said to have *rediscovered his scoring touch*. *"The relief is palpable as Malonga ends goalscoring drought in style."*

Droves
Numbers in which fans will desert an under-performing, overpaid side. *"Tubb's fourth was the signal for Cobblers fans to exit in droves."*

Drubbing
A sound beating. Teams never look back on these results with pride, and lessons will undoubtedly be learned. *"Yoshida calls Everton defeat a huge wake-up call."*

Etymology: Thought to be from the Arabic term 'daraba,' meaning to beat.

Dubbed the next...
Anointment of expectation that a player will go on to *achieve greatness*. The phrase is widely thought of as a kiss of death for many a young pro, as they rarely go on to fulfil their promise. Comparisons are always with the true greats of the game. Nobody is ever *dubbed the next Eion Jess* or *Steve Stone*.

Many players in the past have been given this tag but have failed to live up to ambition. Jérémie Aliadière was once *dubbed* the next Thierry Henry, Freddy Adu was *dubbed* the next Pele, and Franco di Santo was *dubbed* the next Maradona.

Arguably now the phrase is becoming somewhat overused; players are now being *dubbed* as new versions of other players before they have fulfilled their own potential. They can also be described as their country's version of a famous talent for example, *'the Sudanese Suarez'* or *'Panamanian Pele'*.

Less glamorous clubs also like to anoint their star player with such an accolade. Bradley Johnson is known as the *Norfolk Pirlo* amongst the Norwich City fanbase. Alan Judge is well known as the *Irish Messi* owing to his propensity for long-range strikes and boundless energy all over the pitch. Meanwhile, in non-league circles, Lee Gregory could have potentially been known as the *Halifax Ronaldo* and Michael Gash was undoubtedly *Kidderminster's answer to Maradona.*

Etymology: In Old English 'dubbed' is to confer a knighthood upon a subject through striking him lightly with a sword.

Dubious goals panel

This panel decides who scored a goal when it is in doubt. The name is slightly misleading, as it suggests the goals to be reviewed are dubious in legitimacy (which of course the FA would rarely admit). The identities of those who sit on the panel are uncertain. However, it is thought that these people may be the very same ones who sit on the *pools panel*. Tuesdays and Thursdays may decide the destination of goal scorers while Monday and Wednesday might be the *pools panel* debate. Alternative schools of thought believe that the panel simply comprises of a few chaps, a Chinese and some strong European lager.

Dubious track record

Charlatan chairmen who have amazingly beaten the ever-stringent *fit-and-proper-persons test* often have *dubious track records*. Despite that fraud conviction in their native country, they are still deemed fit to run a multi-million pound business.

Many football chairmen have done strange and bizarre things over the years. Ken Bates once submitted an application to install electric fences around the pitch at Stamford Bridge as it *"worked on my farm."* Serial jailbird George Reynolds named the ground after himself at Darlington, which frankly only scratches the surface on his tenure at the Quakers.

Dummy

Illusory skill performed to try to deceive the opposition defender and in many ways, it is the pure art of deception. They are always available for purchase. *"Simpson was sold a superb dummy by the marauding Trippier."*

Duped the officials

Players often attempt to deceive the officials to gain an advantage over their opponents. Common ways to do this are through feigning injury, pretending the ball has stayed in play, and moving the ball behind the ref's back as he is *checking the yards* (although this has become harder with the introduction of invisible spray). Such behaviour will be remarked upon. *"He's got away with one there."*

Dwell

"He won't want to dwell on that, but it really was a glaring miss." It is never advisable for a player to *dwell* on the shot he's just blazed over the bar from close range. It's very probably because he didn't keep *his eye on the ball*, due to already *seeing his name in lights*. A team as a whole will never dwell on defeats – until it is revealed at the end of the season, it was that reverse which *turned* the campaign.

Dynamo
1. The energetic, vibrant box-to-box midfielder who provides zest and purpose to a side. Is based in the *engine room*.
2. Bradford-born magician.

Etymology: Initially taken from the German word dynamoelektrischemaschine, or its English variant dynamo electric machine.

E

Early
1. *Bath. "Early bath for Monkou, that's the tenth red card of his career, and possibly the most deserved."* Dubious privilege of the recipient of a *dismissal*, with the only positive being he will be able to enjoy it on his own; perhaps with Radox, Smooth FM and the latest Nicholas Sparks novel. The phrase is not really a replacement for *red card*, but a supplementary term. There is no such thing as *"that's the tenth early bath of his career."* It is always assumed the offender in question will choose to take a *bath* and not an *early shower*.
2. *Doors.* The preliminary action of a match, and never the time to concede. Another entrant in the *Ronglish* lexicon.
3. *Running.* Helps commentators assess how the match is shaping up. *"It was Maidstone who made all the early running, with the Met Police unable to handle the pacy forward line of Collin and Greenhalgh."*
4. *Season pacesetters.* The side that comes *flying out of the traps*. Usually only a *flash in the pan*, questions start to be asked about their *credentials* at Christmas, but *"if they are still up there in the New Year, who knows?"* It is the stage of the campaign where even those hotly tipped for a relegation scrap might find themselves up there at the top of the *embryonic* league table. Such sights lead rival supporters to pronounce said table is upside down.

Easy street
Situation of considerable security. A result, which has been *wrapped up* with *minimal fuss*. *"Easy street for the Rams."* See also *regulation victory*.

Etymology: From a 1902 book 'It's Up to You' in which the wealthy protagonist was said to walk down Easy Street. It is also the title of a 1917 Charlie Chaplin film.

Eaten too much turkey
"Well that was an insipid performance from Cardiff; clearly they must have eaten too much turkey yesterday." Boxing Day performances to forget are often attributed to the excessive consumption of turkey over the previous 24-hours. Teams may also serve up a *turkey* of a performance. The opposite of a *Christmas cracker*.

Etymology: Not etymology as such, however it is worth pointing out that although containing the natural sedative tryptophan, the quantities of turkey required to have the requisite effect would be large, and have to be consumed on an empty stomach. In short, you probably cannot eat too much turkey on Christmas day.

Echelons
The *upper echelons* of the Premier League are without doubt the place where everyone wants to be. Teams who are in *mid-table obscurity* will look to sign that *20-goal a season man* who has the ability to fire them up the table. The phrase is rarely used at the other end of the table, i.e. the lower echelons.

Etymology: *Old French word 'eschelon' meaning ladder; a step-like arrangement of troops. Echelon is also a highly secretive global spy programme, which came to prominence in the 1990s. Various centres around the world – which took the form of giant golf balls in remote areas – allowed almost every communication to be tracked. Neither the UK nor US admitted to its existence, but we knew...*

Effect
All teams crave a new signing or manager to have the desired *effect* upon their fortunes. It can take its form in goals, influence, victories, etc. Crystal Palace fans have particularly enjoyed the *Pulis effect* and *Pardew effect* in recent seasons; a mid-season *renaissance* when relegation was staring them in the face. Alternatively, a defeat is often said to make no difference. *"Terry says Charity Shield defeat will have no effect on champions Chelsea."* Meanwhile, the effect of playing Thursday nights in the Europa League may have a catastrophic impact on domestic form.

Elder statesman
Long-serving *stalwart* who has been at a club since the age of eight, and has been a *one-club man* save for a spell on loan at Rushden and Diamonds when he was 17.

The *elder statesman* will no doubt opine that, *"the place is unrecognisable from the position it was in when I first walked through the door"* and will almost certainly have cleaned the boots of a similar club legend who is now in his late-50s.

Electric

1. *Atmosphere.* A heightened atmosphere in anticipation, or because a player has *electrified* the stadium with a *charged* performance.
2. *Pace.* A *speed merchant* possesses this quality; he deals in pace and business is always good. Tight hamstrings are his kryptonite.

Embryonic table

"Well let's take a look at the embryonic Premier League table, for what it's worth." Standings in the first few weeks of a campaign are considered *embryonic*. Managers rarely give much attention to this before the *business end of the season* anyhow. Roberto Mancini was known to say, *"You win no prizes for being top in September"* and he was absolutely correct – you can't *win* the Premier League *but you can lose it.*

Emergency centre forward

Player, usually a lofty centre back who is sent forward by his manager as the *last throw of the dice* or to put a game *out of sight.* *"The second half was far from comfortable for Ajax until late in the game as de Boer deployed unlikely hero Mike van der Hoorn as an emergency centre forward."* Stuart Pearce once infamously believed David James would provide the goal threat his Manchester City side craved, by throwing him on outfield against Middlesbrough; his contribution totalled half a Cruyff turn, hacking down Doriva and an attempt at a 20-yard volley that only produced an air shot.

Emphatic

Emphatic being quite unequivocal, teams can experience *emphatic victories* and *defeats*, or the latest goal can *give the scoreline an emphatic look*, i.e. the *icing on the cake.* *"The emphatic nature of defeat will do little to improve Wayne Burnett's mood."* Victory also may be *more emphatic than the scoreline suggests*, in other words superiority hasn't been transformed into a glut of goals.

Encroachment

A big no-no for any manager. When standing in his technical area, match officials will take a very dim view of anyone who disregards the boundaries and encroaches onto the *field of play*, the manager is running the real risk of being *sent to the stands.* *"Jackett's absolutely livid with that challenge; he's encroached from his technical area to make his point but it could come at a cost."*

Some may be a little cannier about the practice than others; Roberto Martinez encroaches on a regular basis, perhaps getting away with it because of his debonair continental manner, casual machismo or that he celebrates like he is shaking invisible maracas. Also occurs during a penalty kick, when a defensive player enters the 18-yard box before the spot-kick has been taken.

Etymology: Common term in American Football where a defender makes contact with an opposition player before the snap. Refers to entry into an area previously unchartered or uncommon.

Ending ... years of hurt
Supporters are generally thought to have *endured* this period, in their long *hunt* for silverware. Commentators are guaranteed to mention the winning goal scorer was in nappies the last time his team won something, or perhaps that Dave Dee, Dozy, Beaky, Mick & Tich were at number 1 with *The Legend of Xanadu*.

End-to-end stuff
Swashbuckling football, both teams are *throwing caution to the wind* in an effort to get the all-important next goal. *"It's all-out-attack at Westfalenstadion as both teams look to secure the points in this knife-edge game."* Free-scoring sides that face each other can be expected to dispense with defending.

Engine room
Colloquial term for the midfield as a whole, or a midfielder with considerable energy, drive and determination. Technical, tough-tackling midfielders with an eye for a pass operate here, both breaking up opposition play and setting off moves of their own; *"Scott Brown looks completely at home in the engine room of this Scotland side; lion hearted and strong as an ox, he's a formidable opponent for any international-grade footballer."* The player who carries out his job with minimal fuss is known as the *quiet cog* in the engine room; an assured, calming presence.

Engineer
1. This gives the impression of industry, creation and forging together a *survival blueprint*. However, players may aim to *engineer a move away* from a club using the following methods:
   a) Sulking.
   b) Becoming embroiled in a training ground bust up.
   c) Getting their agent to leak carefully worded comments to the press about how nice the weather is in Malaga, and how awful it is in Smethwick.
2. *The.* Nickname for Manuel Pellegrini.

England expects

The phrase, which causes everyone else to hate England. Plays on the misguided notion that England deserve to win something because there is an expectation of victory (which probably isn't true, so in reality it is the press who are at fault). Men appear in public with it emblazoned on their t-shirts, drive round in their cars festooned with England flags, all the while pumping out their *England Expects: Football Anthems* on the CD player; this indicates a sea change in attitude from mid-May when said fan thought the cream of the crop didn't have a hope in hell of qualification, before the notion of having an outside chance was mooted and the belief began to morph into expectation. Meanwhile pints are snorted into in Glasgow as the *Three Lions* exit *early doors* once again.

Etymology: Originates from Admiral Lord Nelson's signal 'England expects every man will do his duty'.

English Messi

Almost always *affectionately* known as this, the name applies to the latest prodigious talent to be *snapped up* by one of the big clubs. Variants include *mini Messi* and *dubbed the next.*

Etymology: It is not known when the phrase first entered the press psyche; however what is certain is the phrase 'mini-Messi' was being used by 2008, when a German media outlet used the term to describe Levan Kenia, who went on to ply his trade at Karpaty Lviv, Fortuna Dusseldorf and Slavia Prague. It is also worth noting that Martin O'Neill compared Ashley Young to Lionel Messi when the two were at Aston Villa, although stopped short of adorning him with the above phrase.

Entrance fee

Admission money. The price of match tickets causes huge consternation among fans, particularly the visiting *contingent* who feel they have been ripped off, although it is still possible to hop over the fence at some lower league grounds, mercifully. The term is also used in relation to a goal of superior quality. *"The fine strike by Duguid was worth the entrance fee alone, sending the home faithful into raptures."*

-esque

The suffix *–esque* is attributed to a player who exhibits the skill borne at the foot of one of the greats of the game. *"Oh I say! Sublime turn by Stuart Beavon, it really was Cruyff-esque! Where did he get that from?"* The commentator may venture that the piece of trickery was not something he *learned on the streets of Reading.* There are many other *–esques*; Superb saves are *Buffon-eqsue*, great defending is *Beckenbauer-esque*, skill can be *Messi-esque* and an unerring finish may be *Ronaldo-esque in its quality.* See also *shades of.*

Etymology: From the Latin term -iscus, meaning resembling or in the style of.

European
1.   *Adventure.* A big old jolly that teams who don't usually qualify for Europe go on. Ever so slightly a patronising term, images of the Wigan squad squeezing into a fully loaded *Ford Transit* spring to mind.
2.   *Nights.* According to any ITV pundit, these are the best nights of the footballing calendar, and are given the prefix *famous*. The greatest of which are found at Anfield (as many of the Liverpool contingent in the commentary box can attest to).

Evasive action
This occurs in a few different instances:
1.   Action to prevent an own-goal. *"Sol Bamba had to take evasive action to prevent getting egg all over his face."*
2.   As an excuse for diving. *"It wasn't a dive. The lads gone to get out of the way of the 'keeper and taken evasive action."* Also known as *hurdling the challenge*.
3.   When a player follows through in the tackle on the touchline, forcing the linesman, fourth official or opposing manager to take such action to avoid injury.

Evergreen
A player whose career extends well into his 30s and beyond. The prime modern example is Ryan Giggs, but there have been many in the past including the late great Sir Stanley Matthews, and who could forget Dave Beasant occupying a place on the Stevenage bench at the grand old age of 52.

They are known to keep peak physical fitness, but as time passes, they lose their legs and move to a *cosy holding midfield role*. Interviews are given on a regular basis when they are asked what the secret is to their longevity, as if they are a super-centenarian who swears by three boiled eggs and a tot of whisky daily. *"If you had asked me at 17 whether I would still be playing at 40? Well, I'd have said you were mad but here I am, still enjoying my football and who knows? I may be back next season."*

Every right to go for it
A *50-50* challenge where the keeper usually comes off worse, and is possibly more *70-30*. *"Well the fans think he's been a bit naughty but he had every right to go for it, although Miklosko now has studs for teeth."*

Everyone's second club
Many teams lay claim to being every football fan's *second club*, but the criteria for this is somewhat arbitrary:

1. Because everybody loves the cheeky wit of the locals.
2. Their strips are nice.
3. They have endured a barren trophyless spell in recent times.

EXCLUSIVE!

Football stories during the transfer rumour mill which have scant exclusivity or basis in fact. *"Roo to become Mou's true Blue? EXCLUSIVE!"* More likely to have been dreamt up by Fleet Street's finest after seven-pints of Belhaven Best and a whisky chaser down the Balgonie Arms on a balmy Tuesday night during June's silly season.

Exhibition

"That is superb! Exhibition stuff from Armin Veh's men!" The assumption of course that anything fancy or intricate is *exhibition*, perhaps because the players in question are more relaxed as if they were playing in an *Africa United v Glenn Hoddle and Friends* charity match at Kingsmeadow. If it is used in the context that the play is of superior quality then the argument could be made that this so-called exhibition stuff should be on display *week-in week-out*.

Exiled

On rare occasions, players are warned to *stay away* from the training ground (although nothing is said about the stadium). When players are exiled, a serious infraction is likely to have taken place, such as:
1. Extra-curricular activities with the boss's daughter.
2. Clandestine hotel meetings with another club's director of football.
3. Producing highly offensive goal celebrations.

During a game, managers may be exiled to the stands following a *touchline altercation* or for protesting too energetically about a decision.

Expert analyst

Job title of ex-pros sitting on the *MOTD sofa*, the *ITV chair* or in the *Sky Sports Studio*. The role of an expert analyst can vary widely, from discussing the merits of a 4-5-1 formation to picking out the tightest trousers possible from *Moss Bros*, the forthcoming charity golf tournament in Marbella, and where to hide Chappers' car keys.

Expertly guided

A top class finish crafted on the training ground through many hours of hard work. *"Andy Johnson expertly guided the ball into the back of the net, past the 'keeper's despairing dive."*

Exponent

Football played as it is meant to be played; alternatively those who act as an advocate for a particular move, skill or quality. A player only ever seems to be an *exponent of the beautiful game*, their inordinate amount of talent meaning they are the toast of their fans. *"Ooooh I say, he's turned on a sixpence, what an exponent of the beautiful game Felipe Caicedo is. Football as pure as the driven snow."*

Extra man advantage

1. When a team goes down to 10 men, the opponents have the *extra man advantage*. It is a source of some embarrassment when this advantage isn't driven home. However, sometimes managers may disagree, or at least make excuses. *"Sometimes the hardest thing to do is play against 10 men Motty."*
2. Fans who believe that their team has been *given nothing all day long* off the referee. The common complaint therefore is that the opponents *have only got 12 men*.
3. Fans can also be the 12th man for a team, as many players have claimed in the past in order to fire them up.

Eye

1. To give a statement of transfer intent through admiring glances. *"Martin Canning eyes triple transfer swoop in raid on European markets."* Also refers to players who might *eye* a move to the Premier League. Additionally when thinking about league positioning, managers might *eye* a top half finish.
2. With a more important fixture coming up, the decision may be taken to rest some key players with *one eye on* the *crunch clash* to ensure they are fresh.
3. *For goal.* A deadly accurate player who knows exactly where the back of the net is.

Eyebrows

1. Method favoured by players in a penalty shootout to try to outfox the goalkeeper. *"What a cool finish by Alexander, he gave him the eyebrows there and sent him the wrong way."*
2. As in, *"he's given the little eyebrows."* A Ron Atkinson *Ronglish* special. To denote a flicked back header.

F

FA rap
1. Sanction handed down by the *authorities* after contravening rules, for example Mark Clattenburg's unauthorised attendance at an Ed Sheeran concert, apparently without taking his assistants with him.
2. Greg Dyke's impromptu performance of De la Soul's *"Me, myself and I"* at the FA's Christmas party at Nando's Leicester Square.

Fail to turn up
The side who are *nowhere to be seen*, providing an anonymous performance and usually a comprehensive defeat. They are jokingly assumed to still be on the team bus, or perhaps back in the dressing room. Derby days, cup finals and relegation six-pointers provoke the greatest level of ire. For away game *horror shows*, the club will refund the travelling fans their ticket prices.

Faintest of touches
Glancing touches which *make all the difference* – usually they are enough to divert the ball past the keeper. On occasion where the cross does elude the attacker, it is seen as an agonising moment. Paul Gascoigne's infamous failure to get the *faintest of touches* on a cross in the Euro '96 semi-final against Germany defined that England side as the *nearly men* of the tournament.

Fairytale
1. *Story.* Tale of the plucky *underdog* whose adventure has captivated the footballing world; a tale that could have come from the pen of Hans Christian Andersen himself.
2. *Moment.* Such instances nearly happen *"Almost a fairytale moment for Mark Marshall against his former employers Port Vale, Scott Minto has more..."*

Etymology: From French 'contes de feés', which was the name given by Madame Aulnoy for her short story collection.

Fall from grace
Much vaunted player or side suffering an unceremonious reversal of fortunes. The type of person who was once heralded as the *fulcrum* of a Premier League strike force, now finds himself plying his trade at Skelmersdale United in the Evo-Stik league.

It can also refer to one particular incident in a player's career, which has turned them into a pariah. Crude effigies are burned nationwide, whilst the player in question is booed at every ground he plays at the following season. The reaction to David Beckham's sending off at World Cup '98 is a notable example.

Etymology: From the New Testament, in which the apostle Paul writes in a letter to the Galatians: 'You who are trying to be justified by the law have been alienated from Christ; you have fallen away from grace.'

False nine
A Brendan Rogers special. It is a role which now features extensively in the *modern game* although it has been around for a number of years. A deep lying striker who possesses attributes reminiscent of a classic number 10, with added finishing ability.

False position
Clubs commonly find themselves in a *false position* at the beginning of a campaign. Being *in-form* doesn't mean a side will win the league; just ask David Pleat's *charges* at Sheffield Wednesday in the 90s, as they made a storming start to the 1996/97 season, winning their first four games. This landed Pleat the Manager of the Month *gong*, and sparked premature *title talk*; however, their challenge quickly fell by the wayside. Meanwhile Jose Mourinho's *little horse* routine, whilst having whiffs of gamesmanship also turned out to be correct as they won bugger all back in 2014.

Fan base
The bedrock of support for a side. The fan base is crucial to how a club is perceived. Larger fan bases (such as *one-club* cities) bring increased expectation but also a sense of entitlement from some sections of support.

Fancy
1. Used to describe some wondrous artistry. Fancy skills, perhaps.
2. A manager who expresses a desire or liking for a player may *fancy* them. It can be used both positively and negatively. Either they just do not *fancy* someone, who was perhaps a *staple* of the first team in the previous regime; on the other hand, they may *fancy* a player quite considerably, so much that they take him from club to club; it is a marriage made in heaven, such as Sam Allardyce and Kevin Nolan.

Fans are in superb voice
Fans are usually in this mood because they have been given something to shout about. Throughout the years many popular songs have been adopted by fans, perhaps to pay tribute to a revered player, poke fun at the opposition or to sing their own side's praises; for example *'We love our, Itsy Bitsy, Teeny Weeny, Baldy-*

headed Warren Feeney" sung by Notts County fans to the tune of *Yellow Polka Dot Bikini* by Timmy Mallet. The opposite of this would be accusations of a library-like atmosphere.

Fan favourite
Player in the side who, in the supporters' eyes, can do no wrong. In situations where the milk turns sour, said players become a *former fan favourite*.

Fans left purring
Usually caused by a stellar individual or team performance, although this may indeed be a prediction: *"I have no doubt that some of the performances we're going to see from Robbie Mustoe will leave the fans purring."*

Fate
1. Those who have been charged, or are about to be charged, by the FA for some indiscretion are said to be awaiting their *fate*. The fact that the FA has a conviction rate of close to 100% means that someone in this position shouldn't hold their breath. Of course, it can be an outcome across the whole season too; awaiting *relegation fate*, perhaps, i.e. a *date with destiny*.
2. Something that was meant to be. *Fate* may mean that a club's talisman scores the decisive goal in a key match. It was no doubt *written in the stars*.

Fax machine
The fax machine enters public consciousness every *deadline day*. As the media are at strains to point out, it is always *at the ready*; no doubt, clubs have given their respective bits of equipment a going over with Mr Sheen, stocked up with toner, and made sure the paper tray is full.

Fear factor
A staple of the pre-match mind games. A manager may use their side's reputation to press home an advantage as a form of *scare tactics*. A forward line *brimming with goals* may well induce such a factor in the opposition's psyche, while a more stout-hearted side could scoff at travelling to a ground once seen as a fortress. *"Arter says White Hart Lane holds no fear factor for daring Cherries."* In modern times, a fear factor bred by the possibility of failure, and the drive for instant success has led to chairmen becoming increasingly *trigger-happy*.

Feed
Balls can be fed into the penalty area by the *wide man*, and suggests the staple diet of a striker comprises of pinpoint crosses, cross-cum-shots and slide-rule passes.

Players with animals in their surnames are particularly susceptible to chants about feeding. Examples include *feed the Goat and he will score*, which the Maine Road faithful chanted about their hero Shaun Goater, and *feed the Yak and he will score* for beefy Nigerian hotshot Yakubu.

Fellow strugglers
Kindred spirits scratching around at the bottom of the table. There is a strange connection between fellow strugglers, bonded by the fact that all are questionable in squad depth, talent, and above all, whether *they are cut out for this division.*

Fergie time
Added on time in added on time; in other words the amount of time played until Manchester United score. Created at the behest of Sir Alex Ferguson, who felt that it just wasn't cricket to not have his side given ample opportunity to *complete a miraculous turnaround.* The phrase was initially coined after the Govan Godfather began bringing a stopwatch along to games and tapping his watch at the referee as an intimidation tactic. He would stand menacingly on the touchline, furiously chewing gum at a pneumatic rate, all the while turning an ever more dangerous shade of puce.

Feud
A staple favourite of the tabloid press. Over an extended period of time, managers are described as having a *running battle* with each other. Many feuds have *rumbled on* over the years, and in some cases they begin all over again; a seasonal one seems to be whether Jose Mourinho and Arsene Wenger will shake hands. See also *mind games.*

Fever pitch
1. *"What scenes! The crowd are in fever pitch!"* State of heightened excitement from the spectators because of what they are witnessing.
2. 1996 book by Nick Hornby, adapted into a hit film starring Colin Firth.

Filling ....'s shoes
It is an immeasurably difficult thing to fill another's shoes; however, this has to be done when a big presence leaves the club. The ultimate shoes to fill undoubtedly fell to David Moyes on replacing Sir Alex Ferguson at Manchester United, which of course didn't work out so well and he quickly became the *fall guy* as a result. Players may also struggle to replicate their predecessor's 25-goals from a vintage season, only *weighing in* with a measly single figure tally.

Final ball
The most important ball of all, which is so often *sadly lacking* and only mentioned when being criticised. *"Crawley's final ball has let them down all afternoon, which is why they are on the wrong end of a 2-0 scoreline."* Alternatively known as the *killer pass*.

Financial fair play obligations
Obscure requirements handed down by FIFA to ensure clubs don't spend, spend, spend to achieve success. Apparently is now obsolete, with many Premier League clubs splashing *mega bucks* on players bought for a fraction of the cost only a couple of years prior.

Financial irregularities
Hallmark of a club that has made bad financial decisions. The kind of business where even the goldfish have company cars and most of the money is squirreled away in an offshore bank account, probably in the Cayman Islands.

Financial oblivion
End game for the above side. Liquidation is likely to follow, before a *phoenix club* restarted by the fans appears in the ninth tier.

Fine margins
An event during the game that reminds everybody just how close football is. *"Those are the fine margins we're dealing with, we're talking centimetres"* it could be said, after Colchester come within a *whisker* of taking the lead before Sheffield United escape down the other end to strike a *hammer blow of their own*.

Fired a blank
A striker who hasn't bothered the goals column over the course of the afternoon, or indeed much during the whole season. Perhaps known as *goal shy*.

Fireworks
When it all really kicks off, probably in the aftermath of a nasty challenge. *"There's fireworks at the Bridge, Paul Merson..."*; *"Oh Jeff it's like Guy Fawkes night out there."*

First fixture to look for
"Ally McCoist says you boys are the first fixture he'll be looking for, what do you have to say to that?" Every team, regardless of league will have a fixture they look for first. Usually your local rivals, followed by one of the *big time Charlies*.

Fist
1. A common trait of the foreign goalkeeper – which is at least what commentators will have you believe – is to fist the ball away, or *elect* to

punch. He must make sure, however, that he gets good distance or there could be trouble.

2. Fist of it. A side beset by injuries, dressing room unrest or financial difficulties will nevertheless roll up their sleeves and have a go, because as their manager will say, *"we want to make a decent fist of it."*

Fit
Of course, in its most common sense, it denotes the physical condition of a footballer. I.e. are they at peak fitness, or did they report for pre-season training with the muscle tone of a service station chip?

It can also mean whether a person is a good *fit* for a club. This is often asked when looking at the leading candidates for a job. Whether someone's face fits depends quite a lot on their relationship with the club. They may have had a long love affair with the club in question, or their footballing ethos might also *fit* with the vision of the chairman. Roberto Martinez, for example, was a great fit for the vibrant, slick passing Swansea.

Fit-and-proper-persons test
Check to determine if the tycoon with a dubious track record should be allowed to complete a takeover. So far, nobody has ever failed this ever-so-stringent examination. It is thought the test involves being whisked down to FA HQ and asked if he prefers *"pie and chips or some of that foreign muck."*

Fitness test
Fitness tests are almost always *late*, to give the player with an injury *question mark* over them ample time to recover before a final decision is made. Despite the fact the test has been around for years, no one has ever divulged what one consists of. What, for example would a tight hamstring fitness test consist of? It is presumably different to a minor hernia; one might involve running short shuttles, and the other a quick cough-and-cup with the physio.

Fixture computer
Random generator that decides on the season's fixtures. Invokes a considerable amount of displeasure from club managers who think their side has been given the *short straw*. Leads to comments about a nightmare start or favourable beginning; *new boys* are invariably given a *baptism of fire* at one of the *title favourites*. When there are early season clashes between rivals, or if a player makes his debut against a former club, it is said the computer *has a sense of humour.*

Fixture pile-up
Such a *log jam* of matches will lead to complaints about the ridiculous schedule that one team has to contend with, while their opponents seemingly have it on *easy street*.

Champions League teams have a particular problem with the *pile up*. Playing on a Wednesday night in Russia before returning for a Saturday lunchtime title showdown at the home of their rivals leads to accusations of double standards and chronic fatigue.

Fizz
Onomatopoeic term. Usually applied to a cross that snaps, crackles and pops its way across the box.

Flag happy
The linesman who is always raising his flag is said to be *flag happy*, but could just as equally said to be *eagle eyed*. It is open to debate as to whether they are fussy or not. *"He was a bit quick to wave his flag there I think, Martin."* It should be noted that for an offside the flag is *raised*, for a foul it is *waved*, whilst a penalty award is simply described as *"the linesman's flagging"*. Equivalent of a *card happy* ref.

Flank
Colloquial term for the *wing*.

Flap
Half-hearted attempt by the man between the sticks to collect a cross, often with disastrous consequences. *"Maik Taylor came for the ball but he's merely flapped at it and it's ended up in the back of the net."*

Flash in the pan
Something which doesn't last; a period of form perhaps. It may also be over the season, and a player is therefore known as a *one-season-wonder*, such as Roque Santa Cruz's golden 2007/08 campaign. These players suffer from the most serious cases of *second season syndrome*.

Ideas and reforms surrounding the administration of the game may also be considered *flash in the pan*. For example, the 39th game proposal or, depending on how things turn out, the World Cup 2022 in Qatar.

Flashpoint
Moment within the game, which provides a defining or controversial moment. A *rash* challenge leading to a *mass brawl* is an excellent example. In an incident

involving two players, it is often the case that the referee must decide whether to send them both off, or issue yellow cards apiece. Either way, the commentator will always remark, *"The referee has a decision to make here."*

Etymology: The lowest temperature at which vapour can be ignited above a volatile combustible substance. To translate it to football, it would be the point at which tensions boil over.

Flat back four
The 1990s cabal of Winterburn, Adams, Bould, and Dixon are considered the archetypal flat back four. This type of formation can be expected to play an extremely effective offside trap. Never a flat back five, the four operate in tandem with each other to provide the team with a rock solid foundation. The *unadventurous* full back fits perfectly into this system.

Flatters to deceive
Player whose image does not correlate to their ability; i.e. the type of person who starts ten matches for his club all season yet consistently makes the England set up. Often someone with *no end product*, or alternatively *plays for himself*. He is the type of player who has all he needs to succeed in the modern game; the haircut, the sleeve tattoos, the oversized headphones and the garishly coloured soft top for the girlfriend.

Flirting with relegation
The team (and there is always one) who is making eyes at the *dreaded drop* all season. When relegation finally comes to pass, it's usually because over the course of 38 games, *they've just not been good enough.*

Flop
Someone who has been an *abject failure* or has failed to have the desired impact. Examples throughout the past are numerous, including Juan Sebastian Veron, Gazika Mendieta and Alberto Aquilani. The kind of player fans would *drive to the airport* themselves. Of particular disappointment are the *big money flops*, such as Alfonso Alves. Light-hearted *barbs* are made by opposition fans, asking if the buying club kept their receipt, or whether there is a returns policy in operation.

Fluffed his lines
The preserve of the mis-firing striker who fails to read the script. *"Once again, with the goal gaping, Altidore fluffed his lines and promptly exited stage right. There was no encore."*

Flurry
Chances in quick succession, with most if not all being *passed up.*

Fly on the wall in the dressing room

"Well wouldn't you just love to be a fly on the wall in the Chelsea dressing room right now? Mourinho must be livid with what he's seen so far, right Roy?" The proverbial fly on the wall is all seeing and all knowing. His favourite pastime is to listen in on half time bollockings being *dished out* by the manager. He will presumably also have to duck the *flying teacups* too.

Football folklore

Whoever happens to write their name into this particular book has clearly achieved something that *mere mortals* could only dream of. Moments can *go down in folklore* and will take their place in the *annals* of *footballing history*. *THAT night in Barcelona* being a prominent example. Eric Cantona's *impudent chip* and celebration that *drank in the adulation of the crowd* was another; there to be repeated again and again on *The Premiership Years*.

Football related activity

The beautiful game is only referred to as *football related activity* when some misdemeanour has been committed. Luis Suarez was banned from all *football related activity* for four months by FIFA following his bite on Giorgio Chiellini at the 2014 World Cup. Presumably, this meant he was banned from playing *Wembley singles*, and would be given severe *censure* if he took part in a game of *spot* on Anfield Road, or, upon his move to Barcelona, Las Ramblas.

Football traffic

Hated congestion created solely by the fact that the local team are playing at home. Is a particular problem for those who live near to the football stadium. The reason why Mrs Johnson can't reverse out her driveway at 3.30 is because high flying Alfreton are playing at home to resurgent Tamworth in a crunch clash.

Footballing brain

Type of grey matter possessed by only the most gifted of players who see things others don't. Often found in the heads of cultured playmakers, capable of reading a telegraphed pass with such skill that it might have been written on the side of an Egyptian tomb. *"George Best, often seen as the player with the ultimate footballing brain."* Footballing brains may not extend beyond the bounds of the pitch however.

Footballing dinosaur

A gaffer who doesn't understand the *modern game*. The kind of man who believes that football should be about 4-4-2, two points for a win, Leyton Orient are in fact Clapton Orient, Herbert Chapman was just a wisp of a lad in oversized shorts, and a gilet to be a kind of fish. These dinosaurs are the antithesis of a *pioneer of the modern game*, aka Brendan Rodgers and the *Brylcreem generation*.

Football[ing] lesson
"Brown's boys were given a real football lesson out there today. Second best in every department, that's for sure." These sort of chastening experiences are handed out by teams who on the day are technically, physically and tactically superior to their opponents. Such lessons often result in a *drubbing*, and conversely, matches to forget.

Footballing taboo
There are certain rules in football that everyone from the playground to the Premier League understands must not be broken, including:
1. Breaking the dressing room *omerta*.
2. *Crossing the divide* between rival clubs.
3. Managers criticising players in public.
4. *Tapping up* a player who belongs to another team.

... for a big man
It is often implied that *big men* are hopeless at most things. No matter what the price tag it is always a surprise when they produce something impressive. *"For a big man, Costa has some lovely close control, jinking away from three close tacklers to create space in the West Ham box, and his shot bends agonisingly wide after taking a deflection."* It is possible *for a big man* to show *good feet, good skill,* a *good first touch, good pace, good agility* and *great technique* and it is always worth pointing out. Big men such as Andy Carroll and Dion Dublin are also *great to have at the back* when defending a lead at the death. *("How invaluable are they?!")* They are old-fashioned, and straight out of the *blood and thunder* school of hard knocks. Perhaps the ultimate *big man* is Yaya Toure, whose performances generally resemble that of the precociously developed *big kid in the schoolyard.*

... for a small man
Small men are cut a much better deal than their counterparts, *the big man.* The only thing they are not expected to do is leap well, so it is of particular delight when a player showcases the attribute. *"For a small man, Aguero has got some height on his leap. How tall must Williamson be? All of six foot four and he's still beaten in the air."* Not something to be said to Gordon Strachan.

For all intents and purposes
Something that isn't quite a formality, but is sure to happen soon. A team perilously close to relegation may *for all intents and purposes* be down. The phrase is a favourite of Jeff Stelling from April onwards. It's *academic.*

For me...
The two words Andy Townsend begins or ends most of his sentences with. *"For me, Juve will have too much for them today Clive."; "For me it's a long road back for*

Galatasaray now Clive." Alternatively *"That's a yellow card, for me Clive.";* *"Really, Arsenal should be concentrating on their league campaign, that's their bread and butter for me Clive."*

Foray

Forays are usually rare and *into opposition territory.* By their very nature, it will usually be a defender who does this, and may indeed result in a *nosebleed.* *"Stephen McManus had to be given smelling salts because he'd ventured so far upfield."* Either that or a team as a whole who have struggled to get out of their own half *all afternoon.*

Force into reckoning

Someone who acquits himself so well in training or in a *cameo appearance* off the bench, he simply has to be in the manager's plans.

Forearm smash

The calling card of a coward. Quite often referees might not see this, leading to guaranteed *retrospective action.* However, when they are seen and not properly punished (i.e. only a yellow is *awarded*), there is often calls for a heavier punishment from the FA. E.g. Ben Thatcher's *horror challenge* on Pedro Mendes.

Foreign influx

Foreign players apparently are to blame for the following:
1. Inflated transfer fees.
2. Blocking development of British talent
3. Sky high wages.
4. An increase in diving.

The threat of the *foreign influx* is often feared by old school football men bought up in wartime Britain where half the boys on their street went on to play professional football. However, the blame for bringing in so many second-rate foreign players falls somewhat at the door of Premier League *basement dwellers.* In the hope of *plucking* a new hero from *obscurity,* they will often *go shopping* in the footballing backwaters of Europe only to come away with *the new* Bosko Balaban.

Foreign managers are also maligned as bed blockers. They are seen to halt the progress of British managers, particularly in the upper reaches of the football league, where many budding gaffers cut their teeth at the managerial game.

It also extends to the concourse, with many decrying *"all kinds of continental rubbish"* being served at grounds throughout the country (i.e. mushy peas, half pints and Dijon instead of English mustard). Gone are the days of *staying sharp and drinking Harp* during the interval with foreign brands taking preference.

Forgettable affair
These *drab* matches can last the entire match or for contained periods. *"The Sincil Bank crowd only came to life after the break with Bencherif bundling in at the far post, in what until that point had been a largely forgettable affair."*

Forgotten man
A player who has been left to *rot* in the reserves for what appears an eternity, and with seemingly no hope of redemption. On very rare occasions, they will *come in from the cold*, but this is unlikely. *"Forgotten man Tiago Ilori desperate for second shot at redemption."*

Forlorn
One of many types of figure a manager *cuts* on the touchline. Others include *frustrated, animated* and *edgy*, and of course *sick as a parrot*.

Form book goes out of the window
The proverbial *formbook* goes *out of the window*, without fail, every derby game. It matters not what has gone on in the recent fixtures the protagonists have been involved in, it's a *game of two halves* and *over the 90 minutes anything could happen*. Cynically it may be argued that this is a euphemism for *"we might get beaten today boys, so prepare yourself."*

Foul or abusive language
Seen often as a red card offence. Commonly mis-quoted phrase, and in actual fact there is no need for it to be both, just one or the other. The addition of *"you prick, ref"* would be rendered immaterial to the overall outcome therefore.

Fourth official indicates
For some reason the fourth official must always *indicate* the period of time that is added on. This, of course, is the *minimum* amount to be played at the end of *regulation time* in a half.

Fox in the box
Razor sharp striker, traditionally scores from no more than 18 yards; perhaps the best example in football today is Thomas Müller, who scores an abundance of scruffy – yet crucial – goals. No doubt is a talismanic presence.

Fray
Archaic term for squabble or fight, its relevance to football being:
1. The action, which players enter, often from the bench.
2. Fray Bentos, a football team based in Argentina who of course additionally lend their name to the nutritious tinned pie.

Freak
An incident which in the old days could have been whisked away by a travelling circus and paraded in front of crowds – charging half a shilling a look. The band of freaks include *goals*, own goals, *deflections* and *injuries*, such as Leroy Lita trapping a nerve while stretching in bed, Kasey Keller knocking his front teeth out when taking golf clubs from the boot of his car, or the unfortunate Kirk Broadfoot getting hospitalised by an exploding poached egg.

Freefall
A side on a terrible run of form are said to be *in* this, and will doubtless do anything to *arrest* the slide.

Frenetic pace
This type of tempo is found at the beginning of a game, because getting that early advantage is crucial. On the other hand, scoring early is potentially the *worst time to score*.

Frenzy
1. *Goal.* A number of goals scored in a period of play on the pitch. Also a popular betting coupon.
2. *Transfer.* These deals occur particularly on the last day of either transfer window when sides look to bolster their squads.

Fresh challenge
One of the principal reasons for players looking to move on is because they are seeking a *fresh challenge*. Such players have achieved all they can at the club and it may be best for both parties if they go elsewhere. Alternatively, their careers have seemingly *stalled*: *"Soldado feels career had stagnated at Spurs."*

Fresh legs
Immortal line uttered by commentators with 20 minutes to go: *"Time for a fresh pair of legs I think Clive."* These legs must be brought on when the side as a whole is flagging; they are there to replace, appropriately, the tired legs. Players coming into a team may provide fresh legs for a possible promotion or playoff push.

Fright
Opposition who are huge *underdogs* in a game but nevertheless have come close to beating their opponents can be said to have *given them* a *real fright*. *"Orient exit the cup but give the Dons a big fright."* If a side succeeds in upsetting the odds, they will give their opposition *nightmares*.

Front foot
The foot, which every side wants to be on. The opposite of the *back foot*.

Full blooded tackle
Crunching challenge, in which the perpetrator certainly doesn't hold back.

Full kit w***
Apt description of the person who should know better, parading around in his side's full kit, possibly with his own surname on the back. The type of person who still believes he can *make it* despite being 28 with dodgy knees and burgeoning type-2 diabetes.

Full marks
Full marks are awarded to the opposition for a *gallant effort*, yet no cigar. *"Full marks to the plucky Lichties who have come so close to a Tynecastle upset."*

Fully
To describe something literally. *"Juninho Pernambucano lines up the free kick, fully 40 yards out."* It is a term usually used to sex up the anticipation of a free kick, and reiterate the magnitude of the task at hand.

Fully functioning
A complete player who contributes to all phases of play. *"James Scowcroft really is a fully functioning centre forward. He's got real presence around the box, and we all know what he can do when he gets the ball at his feet too."*

Futile
Attempts to shut out a vastly superior opposition more often than not are futile. Applies also to attempts to apprehend an encroacher: *"The fluorescent clad stewards were unable to apprehend the spirited yet slippery pitch invader; all efforts were rendered futile, much, to the delight of the raucous crowd."*

G

Gaffe
A shambolic mistake, which leaves the perpetrator with egg on his face. They can fall into a few different categories: misses, goalkeeping howlers, refereeing errors and ill-judged comments to the media to name but a few.

Gaffer

The manager of the team. Also known as *boss*. Usually used colloquially by players. *"The gaffer has said all season we can get automatic, and the lads have really responded to that."*

Etymology: Gaffer is believed to be a 15ᵗʰ century variant of Godfather, i.e. the head. Also the head electrician in a film or TV production.

Gamble

Taking some sort of risk, which on one hand could provide an advantage but on the other may destabilise the balance of the side, such as:

1. Purchasing a striker who had banged them in on a regular basis before enduring a catastrophic loss of form, scoring a mere 12 goals across four seasons.
2. Bringing in a player with *baggage*. *"Alan Stubbs says Evo-Stik renegade Jamie Insall signing is a 'calculated gamble'."*

Formations too may be stretched in search of goals. *"Dickov has elected to roll the dice in search of goals, utilising an extra striker instead of his favoured four man midfield; he is taking a bit of a gamble… make no bones about it."*

Game over

The moment the opposition player grabs the killer goal and the fat lady is back at home with her slippers on. *"Jarvis' third goal for York meant it was game over for the Stags, but not before Hirst compounded their misery with a fourth."*

Game plan

Scrawled lines, arrows and crosses on a chalkboard – these are all the basis of a game plan. These instructions should be stuck to, but an early setback can lead to them *going out the window*. *"Well that's just what Paul Jewell's boys didn't want. You always set up to keep it tight in the first ten minutes, but they've gone and conceded virtually from kick off."* They can also be *torn up* and on rare occasions will have *gone awry*.

Game time

There are three reasons to want more of this:

1. To build fitness ahead of a new season or after a long-term injury.
2. When want-away players are sick of *warming the bench*. *"Podolski angling for exit door in order to secure more game time."*
3. To force themselves into international *reckoning*, particularly ahead of a major tournament. *"Michael O'Neill says Andrew Little needs more game time if he's going to establish himself as a permanent fixture in the Northern Ireland squad."*

Gamesmanship
Acts of dubious sporting behaviour, particularly during high stakes fixtures. The term is similar to *brinkmanship*. May include *mind games* and *jibes* aimed at the opposition camp, or some on-field rule bending. *"Diego Costa's cunning finds a way of winning games without cheating."*

Gardening leave
A long-winded dismissal. Managers who have become embroiled in some behind the scenes, not-for-public-consumption issue may be put here to try to sweep any unwanted headlines under the carpet. *"Phil Brown has spent so much time with his begonias on gardening leave he'll have an installation at the Chelsea Flower Show before long."*

Etymology: The Civil Service first adopted this term as a euphemism for suspension.

Garnered
Verb used to describe just how many (or few) points a team has accumulated. *"It's going to be interesting to see how the Rams set up for this clash, having gone through a tough run of fixtures in which they have garnered a single point since Boxing Day."*

-gate
Suffix adopted from the Watergate scandal, and used to describe various contentious incidents in football. E.g. *Pizzagate*, otherwise known as the *"battle of the buffet,"* and *spygate*, which involved the alleged leaking of teamsheets.

Etymology: The Watergate scandal in the 1970s was of course the first –gate from which the term took its name.

Gate receipts
Match proceeds. It is unlikely that receipts are produced in this manner anymore so is probably a bit of an anachronism; although some fans may wish they had kept theirs for a full refund.

German efficiency
Implied reference for a well-drilled, organised and ruthless side; from the same stereotyping school as crafty Argentinians, Dutch infighting and the belief that all African goalkeepers are eccentric. These teams get the job done, if not within the 90 minutes then most definitely on penalties. The phrase, of course, applies literally to the Germans too; commentators have a penchant for throwing it back in the faces of our Continental neighbours at an opportune moment, *"Wolfsburg were given a masterclass in German efficiency by Marek Hamsik and friends in their own backyard."*

Get out of jail
An extremely lucky player or team. *"Oh Morrison is a lucky boy. He's got out of jail with that one, because that was almost an own goal."* Getting out of jail can be achieved in a few ways:
1. By almost putting the ball through his own net, but some reason (not of his own creation) has prevented it from doing so.
2. By gaining redemption, perhaps by scoring the winner after committing a *cardinal sin* earlier in the game.
3. Not being sent off for something that really did warrant an *early bath*.
4. A side that has been battered for the best part of 90 minutes achieves a result, which does not reflect the overall pattern of play. Or a side, which was hot favourites to win comfortably, does so courtesy of a lucky strike.
5. Actually getting out of jail. Duncan Ferguson, Tony Adams, Joey Barton, etc. Eric Cantona escaped jail in another sense after his two-week sentence was commuted to community service following his kung-fu style kick at Selhurst Park in 1995. This, of course, was a response to Palace fan Matthew Simmons 'encouraging' the Frenchman off the pitch following his dismissal. *"There's the morning headline,"* remarked Clive Tyldesley immediately following the red card. If only he had waited another 30 seconds.

Get rid!
Exclamatory statement to demand a clearance; so synonymous that *"...of it!"* has been dispensed with. Note that while fans want players to *get rid* of the ball from the area, they expect their side, in turn, to *get out* of there.

Get the ball down
Playing football on the surface rather than in the sky is considered a good thing. *"Some of the stuff Gateshead play is fantastic, they get the ball down and knock it about really nicely. Not something you'd expect for a Conference side."*

Getting to grips with the pace of the game
The substitute who has just entered the fray may take a while to *get to grips with the pace of the game*. Unless they are an *impact player* or score with their first touch. *"One of the hardest things to do is get up to speed after you've just come on Gary."*

Ghost
1. *In.* Players will *ghost in unmarked*, with the defence failing to pick up their spirit-like presence. The back post is particularly susceptible to having players arrive in this manner. Those who *ghost in* on occasion may repeat their trick in the next matchup between the sides, and thus have *come back to haunt* the opposition.

2. *Ghosts laid to rest.* The settling of an old score, which extinguishes previous painful memories. Holland's 5-1 victory over Spain at the World Cup in 2014 avenged their defeat in the final four years previously. Also known as *exorcising their demons.*

Giant killers

The slayers of a relative *big boy.* The ground of a team in the lower *echelons* of the league pyramid may have forged a reputation for being a bit of a giant's graveyard. The team may have a giant killing history or form for causing an upset too, or if a particularly amusing journalist is writing the headlines – a *cupset.* Those on the wrong end of the result will promise to *"take a long hard look at ourselves."*

Gift

Usually a goal created almost entirely by the conceding team. Often called an *absolute gift.* The provider will probably have paid the extra £2.95 to get it gift-wrapped, complete with ribbon, little bell and carefully composed accompanying note. *"To Papiss, hope you enjoy, love Ron Vlaar xxx."*

Gilt-edged

Perhaps the most presentable of *chances,* which only a fool would *pass up.* *"As you could probably hear there has been a howler of a miss at the Hawthorns. What's happened Charlie Nicholas? 'Oh Jeff, the ball fell to van Wolfswinkel, and you're saying to yourself just slot it home Ricky! He had all the time in the world and he has spurned a glorious opportunity there Jeff. Gilt-edged.'"*

Etymology: Process of gilding something with fine gold leaf.

Gimme

A match, which is certain to go only one way. However, there are usually *no gimmes* in football, as any manager will tell you.

Ginger Mourinho

Name given to any manager, regardless of ability who has red hair. For example Gary Megson and Sean Dyche.

Give-and-go

Part of the *pass-and-move* style of football. *"It's been give-and-go by Wolves all afternoon. Lovely."*

Give the score line a one-sided look
Results, which do not accurately reflect the game. A narrow one goal lead which turns into 3-0 in the *blink of an eye*, e.g. Aston Villa 0-3 Arsenal in 2014/15 (although in reality this was a three minute *treble salvo*).

Given a stern examination
A real test of a side's mettle. Stern examinations include a *second half barrage*, numerous balls *pumped long* into the area, and having to defend a *succession of corners*. They are often expected ahead of a tough match.

Glamour tie
Taken at face value, glamour ties are tasty matchups between two heavyweights (getting the TV bosses salivating), or more commonly when cup minnows draw one of the big boys in a real *moneyspinner*. However, the phrase is often used with ill-disguised sarcastic undertones. *"Bromley v Chester is on BT Sport later… glamour tie."*

Glaring miss
A miss of such epic proportions that half the crowd will stare incredulously at the point where the ball should have hit the back of the net, while the *guilty* offender stands there with his hands on his head and mouth slightly gaping. *"I don't think anybody needs to tell him that was a glaring miss Gabby."* A photo of this moment would undoubtedly feature in a *spot the ball* competition.

Glimmer of hope
Reducing the arrears from three goals down to two is enough to provide this. However, if there are mere minutes left on the clock, a halving of the deficit will also give a similar effect. *"Andy Jacksons' late strike gave Brechin a glimmer of hope."*

Glittering career
A career in the game, which has been festooned with trophies, personal accolades and success. The mantelpiece at such a player's house is full to bursting with memorabilia of a wonderfully successful time. Players who have achieved such status in the game are invariably linked with top managerial posts upon retirement, or appointed to a football studio sofa to offer bland and banal comments to millions of viewers. The third option is a spot on *Celebrity Come Dine with Me*.

Glorious HD
The way most football fans see Chris Kamara's face these days. Predated, but outlasted, 3D.

Goal blitz

An *avalanche* of goals, which annihilates the opposition. *Blitzes* can mean scoring four or more goals in one 45-minute period. *"Morecambe blown apart by first half goal blitz."*

Etymology: From the German blitzkrieg, meaning 'lightning war'.

Goal city

Teams that have an *abundance of attacking riches* regularly visit this destination, with two tickets usually being issued. A side which has goals running through them like a stick of Brighton rock. *"It's goal city for Southend today Jamie." ; "I think it is Ian."*

Goal fest

Presumably short for goal festival, this is a real treat for the football fan. *Goal fests* are what the game is all about, and if found in the Premier League, reaffirms its status as the greatest in the world. They are a *great advert* for any level. *"It's raining goals here at Glanford Park."*

Goal machine

Player who loves to churn out the goals with such regularity he is akin to a factory production line. The goal machine has the *Midas touch* in front of goal and can often be seen *firing on all cylinders*.

Goal written all over it

Shot, which is heading straight for the top corner, but inexplicably doesn't find the back of the net. *"Andy Monkhouse's effort had goal written all over it before Javan Vidal's timely intervention."* Shots may also be *in as soon as he hit it*.

Goalscorer turned villain

The man who has written the headlines for all the right reasons either scores an *OG* or earns himself an *early bath*. May also be said to have gone from *hero to villain*. Will have undoubtedly had a *mixed afternoon*.

Gobbled up the chance

Goalscoring opportunity that is greedily accepted by the attacking player. They are *snaffled* from close range. *"The Gabon international gobbled up the chance with relish."*

Goes missing in the big games

Player who lays waste to lower opposition but lacks bottle against the crème de la crème. The first sign of those who *go missing in the big games* is when they are unceremoniously hauled off before the hour mark. The opposite of a *big-game player*.

Going for broke
It's do-or-die; the whole team is going for it. In this situation, sides will throw caution to the wind by going *all-out attack*. *"It doesn't matter if they go on to lose by three or four now Gary 'cos they have to throw the kitchen sink at this."*

Golden
1. Something or someone that is *admired, coveted* or *revered*. For example, Wayne Rooney is often called the *golden boy* of English football, despite *that* red against Portugal. A common headline in newspapers is to play on the phrase, e.g. *"GOALden boy fires Partick to victory."*
2. Players may also get a *golden chance* to score, or a *golden opportunity* to grab the points.

Gone down too easily
A player who could trip over a blade of grass; even the faintest of touches sends him rolling around the pitch like he has swallowed a wasp's nest. It is commonly held opinion that particularly talented players do not need to go to ground as their ability renders such an action unnecessary. It may be done when trying to *con* the referee and *buy a penalty*, à la Arjen Robben, or even more cynically when feigning a head-butt, something Kyle Lafferty amongst others famously did when playing for Rangers against Aberdeen.

It is also a very useful time-wasting tactic when trying to protect a lead, but those attempting to engage in this dark art should be warned – it carries the very real risk of being booked for *simulation*, along with shunning in football circles, and public admonishment from the manager.

Gone for the same ball
A challenge for the ball by two teammates without realising the other is going for it, resulting in a *clash of heads* (which can sometimes be *sickening*). *"Well Vennegoor of Hesselink and Marney have got their wires crossed there, went for the same ball and the former has taken a knock for his troubles."* The fact remains, however, that all 22 players are *going for the same ball*.

Gong
Those who have been nominated for monthly or end of season awards are said to be up for the player or manager of the month *gongs*. There is a perception the manager of the month gong carries some sort of jinx, as any good run of form is

certain to be brought to a shuddering halt. The unfortunate recipient is said to have been *struck by the manager of the month curse.*

Good engine
A player in possession of this is thought to have an *abundance of stamina.* They could quite literally *run all day* as if *powered* by a V12.

Good foul
An *illegal* challenge, which on the balance of interests has to be made; a seasoned pro with a wealth of experience and a high football IQ may take one for the team in certain situations. Perhaps committed on the halfway line when the opposition is looking for a late goal, a *cynical* yet necessary challenge is made. No doubt, the manager won't mind it one bit. *"Jon Guthrie's committed a good foul there, Barnsley were in otherwise."*

Good height for a goalkeeper
The level at which *regulation saves* are made, usually found between the shoulder and waist. It is the height at which a keeper will usually produce *one for the cameras*; i.e. an overly extravagant save from a speculative 20-yarder where a simple palm away would do. Sometimes, however, plaudits will still be handed out. *"Although his effort was at a good height for the goalkeeper, Cierzniak's save was still commendable."* Alternatively, a *tame* penalty may be at this level. *"He's given the 'keeper an opportunity to save it Martin."*

Good, honest pro
The opposite of a bad, dishonest amateur.

Got the footballing world at his feet
1. A prodigious talent. Only nightclubs, unscrupulous agents and a dodgy anterior cruciate will stop him now.
2. *Cristiano Ronaldo: The World at his Feet.* A film charting the Portuguese wizard's career, narrated by Benedict Cumberbatch.

Got the monkey off his back
To put an end to a problem, stat or issue. Consistent failures against an opponent who seem to have the *Indian sign* or some sort of *hoodoo* against them are of particular annoyance. Once the manager in question has put paid to this, he will have got the *monkey* off his *back*. The quintessential example is Stuart Pearce banishing his demons with his superbly dispatched penalty at Euro '96.

Etymology: First thought to have originated in ancient Egypt, the initial meaning of the phrase carried far more positive connotations; as a respected animal, the monkey was something to be welcomed.

Grandstand finish

Set up after one side comes back into the game from two or more goals down. *"Well that's given Bolton a lifeline, Dougie Freedman's side have set up a real Grandstand finish down at the Valley with five minutes left on the clock."* Longingly predicted on Soccer Saturday by Jeff Stelling, no matter what level of the football pyramid. *"Could we yet see a grandstand finish at Moss Lane?"*

Etymology: Taken from horse racing, where jockeys charge down the finishing straight neck and neck.

Grassroots

The bedrock of the game played by youths and the overweight. Only seems to feature in the news because of how much it is seemingly being neglected. Certain things happen in grassroots matches that will not be found in the professional game:
1. The unspoken rule of *kicker seeker*.
2. Touchline scuffles between parents.
3. The away team physio running the line after the linesman suffered a hamstring twang.

Great escape

Sides who produce a remarkable sequence of results to defy the odds and survive the drop have indeed pulled off the *great escape*. The theme tune is whistled extensively by the relegation-threatened fan base following unlikely goals, victories or runs of form.

Great feet

A step up from *good feet*, perhaps when a player shows remarkable skill as he *waltzes the ball into the net. "Fernando Boldrin displayed great feet to work an extra yard of space before thrashing it past Adrián from distance."* Ambidextrous footballers are often described as having this: *"He's got a fantastic engine, two great feet and a real footballing brain."*

Greatest

1. League in the world. AKA the Premier League.
2. Cup competition in the world. AKA the FA Cup.

As voted for by the media, ex-players-cum-pundits, and foreign talent during their first season on English soil. It is unclear what European counterparts think about this assertion. Perhaps Spain may feel the Copa del Rey knocks the socks off a half-filled Liberty Stadium for Swansea versus Fulham.

Ground out

Teams who have put in a *gritty* performance to win by the odd goal are said to have *ground out* the result. *"Quality was at a premium today but it's the three points that matter."*

Group of death

There will always be one at any major tournament. Conjecture beforehand is about what the possible group of death might be; particularly if one of the *big boys* has been placed in *pot two*.

Etymology: Originally used in the 1970 World Cup by Mexican journalists to describe the 'grupo de la muerte' of England, Brazil, Czechoslovakia and Romania.

Grudge match

Matches that aren't between two local rivals, but where there has been a bit of *needle* in the past. Such reasons for a grudge match can be:
1. Because Jose Mourinho is involved.
2. An opposing player had an affair with someone's wife.
3. There was a 22-man brawl in the previous fixture.

Gung-ho

Attacking with gusto while neglecting defensive duties, opinions on which will be mixed. *"Warburton has got off to a flying start at Ibrox, but Bees defender Harlee Dean has taken a dig at his gung-ho tactics."* See also *all-out attack*.

Etymology: From the Chinese symbols 'gōng' and 'hé', meaning 'work together.'

Gutsy defending

The sort of defensive shift where blood, sweat and tears are produced in order to prevent the opposition from scoring a goal. Gutsy defending implies bravery and valour, putting everything *on the line* to shut the opposition out. *"Although Yohan Cabaye caught the eye with his classy use of the ball, it was Palace's gutsy defending that was the most memorable aspect of their performance."*

H

Hacker's union
Old-fashioned term for a team of dirty bastards.

Had him in his back pocket
A defender who has his marker completely sussed. Quite often, this lasts *all night*. His opponent simply will not get a look in, having had doors continuously *slammed* in his face. *"Things that left-back Paddy Boyle keeps in his back pocket? His keys, his wallet, and Paul McMullan."*

Hairdryer treatment
Another Fergie-ism; to be blasted with hot-tempered air. The phrase was brought to light by Mark Hughes, when describing the *dressing down* players would receive from the Govan Godfather. The treatment is usually *dished out, turned on* or *received* after an *insipid* team performance or a *glaring individual error*. It is now in wider use, and most managers are now considered capable of producing it. *"Without a doubt the hairdryer treatment will be handed out to that lot in the dressing room. No shape, no discipline, but worst of all no desire. And if you exhibit that attitude in one of Alex McLeish's teams, you won't last long."*

Halcyon days
The glory days, looked back on wistfully by both fans and players. Banners will adorn the stadium reminding all and sundry of successes the team enjoyed, even though all they can hope for now is a run to the final of the Johnstone's Paint Trophy. Nottingham Forest's *halcyon days* contrast quite starkly with the current situation at the City Ground, where the *heady heights* of European glory seem a long way off. As do Leeds United's.

Etymology: Reference to the Greek Goddess Alcyone, who upon her death was reincarnated into a Halcyon bird. Her father Aeolus, God of Winds, calmed both winds and waves for a 14 day period either side of the shortest day of the year to allow his daughter (in reincarnate form) to lay her eggs safely. Any period of calm or prosperity has come to be known as such.

Half a yard
1. *Quicker in his head.* The type of player whose body isn't quite up to speed with his mind. The solution to this shortcoming of football's aged and infirm is to become *great readers* of the game, which is the hallmark of the *seasoned campaigner.*
2. The only amount of space the very best players need to exploit an opportunity. This type of distance is often *stolen.*

Half-hearted appeal

Penalty *shout* that no one really believes in. Fans will probably claim it much more vociferously than anyone on the pitch. The referee is never really interested, however, prompting anger from a few of the *die-hards*; he will either make the no penalty gesture with his arms, point to the spot where the ball was won, or simply remain unmoved.

Half the ground thought it was in

Optical illusion where many spectators are duped into thinking the ball has gone in. The realisation this isn't the case is met with *howls of derision* from opposing fans.

Hallowed turf

The sacred pitch of a football team, on which *dreams are made* (or *shattered*, of course). Wembley has the most famous *hallowed turf*, perhaps due to it being known as the home of football; however, it can apply to any ground at any level. *"The hallowed turf of Cressing Road has been graced by many a Braintree legend in years gone by."* It is a reminder that fans revere their heroes, no matter what level they are at, even if the star striker works part-time at *B & Q* during the week.

Hammer blow

A major setback for a side. It isn't just limited to injuries, however. Players may deliver *hammer blows* by scoring a decisive goal, or indeed managers are lavished with praise after his side delivers a *hammer blow* to another. *"Late strike a hammer blow to plucky Hornets."*

Hand of God

Of course, the infamous act by Diego Maradona at the 1986 World Cup will always be the original; however, any goal, which comes about as a result of a helping hand, may be described as such. Miroslav Klose infamously asked for his handball goal to be chalked off for Lazio against Napoli in 2012, becoming one of the great sporting gestures.

Handbags at ten paces

A bit of posturing and maybe a pre-dust up exchange of words; this is one of the staple stock phrases of the commentator. A favourite of (and possibly created by) Big Ron. Can also be called a handbag situation, a bit/a load of handbags, or just *handbags*.

Etymology: Some believe handbags originated from the threat by Margaret Thatcher to give some of her ministers 'a good handbagging' in the 1980s. Ten paces probably refers to the duelling with pistols at ten paces.

Handball claim
An *appeal for hands* in the box. It is one of the curious moments when both players and the crowd shout *"handball!"* and raise their arms in unison. Claims can range from *weak* to *strong*. A rejected *strong appeal* will lead to the referee being chased by the attacking side, with arms outstretched, looking indignant; this is known as *haranguing* (see below). If he does give the spot kick, the defending team will usually stand stock still, firmly gesturing to the floor with both hands, incredulous looks plastered across their faces.

Handily placed
A team, which has manoeuvred themselves into *contention*. *"Well if you look at the run that Southampton are on, they're really handily placed to make a late dash on the Europa league places. And what an achievement that would represent for everyone at St Mary's."*

Hands off warning
Common phrase in newspaper column inches, unwelcome advances by a club towards another's prize asset will be rebuffed with a *firm hands off warning*. *"Sassuolo slap hands off warning on Leicester City target Sime Vrsaljko."* The warnings will always be *issued* or *slapped*, along with quotes that the player in question is *going nowhere*.

Hang up his boots
Metaphor for retirement. Conjures sepia-tinged images of a club legend walking away from his trusty old boots after hanging them up one last time, before turning the dressing room light out. The image has become somewhat less romantic in recent years due to modern footballers wearing boots more befitting of a neon-lit Parisian brothel than a football pitch.

Hapless
A player (or indeed the whole section of a team, e.g. the defence) prone to mistakes, many of which are *unfortunate*. For example a ball might ricochet off the *hapless* defender's foot, loop up onto the backside of a teammate whose luck has deserted him, thereby diverting it unwittingly past the 'keeper into his own net.

Haranguing
Forcefully protesting against what is seen as a shocking decision by one of the officials. The classic example was Manchester United players chasing after Andy D'Urso, Benny Hill-style, following a contentious penalty award versus Middlesbrough in 2000.

Hard man
Players in this mould strike fear into the opposition. They have a high propensity to be fondly remembered by their club's faithful; their picture will adorn the walls

of the tunnel, fans will come to matches dressed like them and a local street in the area might bear their name. Embodying the very essence of commitment, hard men throw themselves into blood and thunder tackles, lead from the front and play on despite significant blood loss. So revered are they, that they have become the subject of football compilation tapes; see *Vinnie Jones' Football Hard Men*.

Hardest thing to do is score a goal

Scoring a goal is often said to be the most difficult thing to do in football. Often, the reason why a team gets relegated is because of a *lack of a proven goalscorer* to *stick it in the back of the net*. Of course *doing the hard part* is typically fashioning the opportunity, and not the act of scoring: *"Steven Schumacher did the hard part, and all Hitchcock had to do was stick it in the back of the net, but he's blazed wide."*

Hat

Old-fashioned but enduring term for a cup draw. *"Both sides had been limited to speculative shots when Chris Hussey nodded down to Kee, who controlled on his chest and lashed in from 18 yards to secure the Brewer's place in the third-round hat."*

Hatful

Universally, of *chances*. This measuring device can be *passed up, spurned, squandered* or conversely the opposition may be *presented with* them. Are normally *absolute*. *"Halifax will feel it is two points dropped as they squandered a hatful of chances."*

Having a tilt at next season's title

The perennial ambition of the *nearly men*. These teams will always look to have a *tilt* at the title, no matter how many *barren years* have been experienced. They still believe the dream is on despite being 15 points adrift at Christmas. By Easter, the club captain will insist the Champions League is still on and come the beginning of May it looks like they will have to make do with *Thursday nights on Channel 5*. Then the headlines about having a *tilt* at next season's title start all over again.

He is human after all

Phrase almost exclusively reserved for Lionel Messi. Most often used by Clive Tyldesley and followed imminently by questioning as to whether Messi could do it on *a cold Tuesday in Stoke*.

He looks like he wants the ground to swallow him up

The player who commits a horrendous error by scoring a particularly spectacular own goal lies prone on the turf in front of thousands of fans. All have witnessed the *howler*, and the expression on his face suggests he looks like *he wants the ground to swallow him up*. This is also true with penalty takers, of which there have been hundreds over the years including Baggio, Pearce, Gyan, Diana Ross, et al who failed on the *biggest stage of them all*.

Head tennis
Popular game of light relief played out in the middle of the park; the opposite of putting your foot on it. *"Prolonged bouts of head tennis in the quagmire here at the Memorial Ground. Who is going to take this game by the scruff of the neck?"* It should be noted that once in the box, the head tennis turns to *pinball*.

Headlines
Almost always *stolen* by a goal-hungry striker or the glitzy winger who has put in a match-winning performance. There is also the *headline treatment*, which is reserved for spectacular failure. Roy Hodgson received this after England's shambolic showing at the 2014 World Cup.

Heat seeker
A *missile*, which finds the back of the net with unerring accuracy. *"Gibson with a heat seeker from distance. My word he can get a hold of them!"*

Etymology: A weapons guidance system using infrared emissions to track a specific target. Missiles possessing this technology are known as 'heat-seekers'.

Helicopter Sunday
The 2005 event, which has become a by-phrase for high drama. *"It was a bit like Helicopter Sunday out there Gabby, we just didn't know which was it was going to swing."*

Etymology: The conclusion to the 2004/05 Scottish Premier League title race would only arguably be matched by Sergio Aguero's last-gasp winner for Manchester City v QPR seven years later. Going into the final day, the destination of the title was still not confirmed; Celtic were in the driving seat, needing to beat Motherwell to confirm their status as champions, while Rangers had to hope the Hoops would slip up and they beat Hibernian. As such, a helicopter was placed at a strategic location halfway between Motherwell and Edinburgh; a good job too as a quick-fire brace from Scott McDonald at the death broke Celtic hearts and handed the title to the blue half of Glasgow.

Hell
Periods of time spent at a football club that were less than fruitful are often described as *hell*. Newspaper headlines will suggest as much, particularly as an exclusive splashed on the back page. Such as *'Jack's injury Rod-Hell.'* Articles with such unsubtle *barbs* are accompanied by a shot of the player holding up a shirt with his new gaffer, and looking like a weight has been lifted from his shoulders.

Herculean effort

When a side finds themselves in the *mire*, it will require this level of exertion to get out of it.

Etymology: Taken from Greek mythology and the 12 labours of Hercules, in which he completed a dozen incredible tasks such as killing a man-eating lion and capturing Cerberus the three-headed hellhound of Hades. In modern times, overturning a three-goal deficit would possibly be considered the 13th labour.

Hero

1. *Penalty hero:* The main opportunity goalkeepers have to make themselves the star of the show. When a penalty is saved in regulation time, the man between the sticks doesn't have time to accept the adulation of his teammates; preferring instead to be super aggressive, pushing them off and bellowing as if in the middle of a warzone. This also applies to point-blank wondersaves when 'keepers will be more likely to bollock their defences than lap up the plaudits.

2. *Heroics.* A one-man performance or achievement by a manager. *"Carbone heroics keep Wednesday heads afloat."*

3. *Status.* Something to be attained through remarkable achievements on the pitch. *"And with that goal, Charlie Penny has sealed Wealdstone's promotion back to the Conference South. It's fair to say the lad has achieved hero status tonight."* On big occasions, it is also asked which player is willing to step up to the plate and *achieve hero status.*

4. *Time.* The late stage in a finely poised game when someone has their chance to write their name into folklore. Usually uttered when there is a last gasp corner, after which the ref will *blow up. "We're into hero time Martin."*

5. *Unlikely hero.* The much chastised player, all too often the target of the boo boys *silences the critics* by popping up with a dramatic winner in stoppage time. *"Demichelis the unlikely hero!"*

He's no...

If a player attempts a move that is either synonymous with another or does something that is normally beyond his range, he could be described as no [accomplished footballer's name]. So when Jon Parkin attempts a turn with all the grace of a midweek *Mecca Bingo* attendee, he may be described as *"no Cruyff".*

High, wide and not so handsome

A shot, which is blazed so far over, the offending player won't even wait *to see where it went.* He will probably be back in position before the ball is returned to the goalkeeper from *Row Z.* Usually accompanied by loud jeers from opposition fans.

Etymology: Originally, the phrase was high, wide and handsome. Originating in the USA, it is often used to describe how beautiful the rural parts of the country are.

Hijacked

Clubs who believe they have *sewn up* a deal to sign a player should be warned – the transfer could be nicked from under their noses, particularly on *deadline day*. Conjures up images of a balaclava-clad board of directors bursting into the selling club's stadium with a sawn-off shotgun screaming at the club secretary to *"hand over the damn paperwork!"*

Hint

Hinting things to the media surrounding a story is a staple of any player or manager's repertoire. It can be anything from dropping a *hint* that he will make alterations to his starting XI, to a star striker *hinting* that he'd love a move to a bigger club (although this, of course, can land him in *hot water*, as can unauthorised trips to another side's home ground or clandestine meetings in top London hotels).

Histrionics

Whether there will be any final day *histrionics* is the burning question for pundits and the media alike ahead of what could be a *scintillating* final day, most of which *couldn't be scripted*. Otherwise, this is an over-exaggerated on-field strop, possibly on being substituted, *crunched* or unfairly penalised.

Hit and hope

A shot or pass left very much to fate, such as the 45-yard *speculative effort* which is unlikely to cause the 'keeper too many problems. *"Chris Wondolowski's effort looks more like a hit and hope than anything else."* They are produced by the footballer who will have a go from *all angles*, or in the *dying seconds* when the attacking player must get a shot away before the referee calls time. Whatever the context, these players live by the mantra *you don't shoot you don't score*. Particularly attack-minded managers might employ a *shoot-on-sight* policy. Can also be in *hope* rather than *expectation*.

Hit in a sensitive area

Taking one in the *bread basket*. See also *unmentionables*.

Hit the self-destruct button

A team, which finds themselves in a mess entirely of their own making, can be said to have pressed this most devastating of devices. Instances include:
1. Comedy own goals. Some sides are more prone to this than others. Indeed some players seem to have their own personal issue self-destruct

button, such as Belgian ex-pro Stan van den Buys, who scored a hat-trick of own goals for Germinal Ekeren against Anderlecht in 1995/96.

2. Ending up with eight men after a series of rash challenges leads to a torrid afternoon and an FA fine; a team which has lost their discipline and without doubt, their *heads*.

Hit with a three-match ban

Upon reviewing the tapes, the FA may decide to *hit* a player with a three-match ban for an incident in the game, which went unnoticed by the referee. There are, of course, other length bans to be hit with; clubs too might be hit with a stadium ban for crowd trouble in a previous fixture. See also *retrospective action* and *behind closed doors*.

Hitman

Someone who knows exactly where the target is. The *in-demand hitman* will have admirers from many different corners, principally because *pulling the trigger* is his forte. *"Indian Super League beckons for Orient hitman Dagnall."*

Hold to ransom

A scenario arising in two situations:
1. Contract negotiations.
2. Transfer negotiations.

In these instances, clubs will refuse to be held as such; however, it is not always something in their control. A player who believes he is worth £100k per week or a club who is certain their reserve centre back is worth £10m are far more likely to be able to call the shots. On deadline day, the closer the clock ticks to midnight (or whenever the cut off is), the more power a player will wield.

Holding midfielder

Player in the centre of the park who dictates proceedings, holding the side together and providing a link between defence and attack. Jose Mourinho's early Chelsea sides were built around holding midfielder extraordinaire Claude Makélélé, who was the fulcrum of a wonderfully operating midfield *unit*.

Hollywood

1. *Pass*. The type of pass *pioneered* by Stevie G. Superficial spraying to the opposite flank that looks fantastic but achieves little except cricket ground applause from the crowd. The consequence of such a ball is that play is switched from one wing to the other only to see a considerably worse footballer in possession. I.e. Vladimir Smicer, Gregory Vignal etc.
2. *Save. One for the cameras* by the 'keeper who knows he's in the *shop window*.

Home

1. To denote a side playing on their own patch.
2. *Faithful.* Alternative name for the home crowd. *Faithful* obviously works on the premise that the crowd will stay loyal to their charges, however history dictates the moment their team *trails* the opposition, frustration will set in and the *boo boys* may very well announce their arrival. According to the manager, this is *"just a few idiots."*
3. The net. Can be combined with a plethora of adjectives, for example *rammed, prodded, guided, poked, smashed, belted* and *rifled.*
4. *Equally at.* The versatile *utility man* able to play in more than one position. The kind of player who would play in goal if he had to. *"Paul Dummett is equally at home on the left side compared to his central defensive berth."*

Honest

1. *Footballer.* Someone who is known for his fair play credentials and never looks to pull the wool over the official's eyes.
2. *Honest Men.* Nickname of Ayr United.
3. *Assessment.* Given by the manager at press conferences or interviews, something Ian Holloway is well known for: *"Most of our fans get behind us and are fantastic, but those who don't should shut the hell up or they can come round my house and I will fight them."*

Hoodoo

One side which has the *Indian sign* over another may describe their unexplained dominance as a *hoodoo.* This being some sort of magic art, which although normally the preserve of quackery or mythology, is most certainly possible to see it in the football world. This could explain how a team who are considered massive underdogs pull a rabbit out of the hat against their stellar opposition. Indeed, there are many types of *hoodoo* in the game; for example, for six straight years in the J. League, Ryoichi Maeda's first goal of the season was scored against a club who was subsequently relegated. Also known as *the hex.*

Etymology: Practiced throughout many southern States of America, the term originally means to conjure, often by unexplained means.

Horror

1. Show. A game to forget for a player or team. They are particularly common around Halloween, where *Halloween horror shows* strike with unerring regularity.
2. *Tackle.* A nasty, vicious challenge which may have real consequences for both parties; it will undoubtedly be *censured.* *"Boca Juniors and Racing Club 'friendly' marred by horror tackle."*

Hospital pass

The hospital pass, or ball, is a heavy weighted pass to a teammate, who undoubtedly will be put under pressure from an opponent immediately. It certainly does him no favours, leading to the commentary box assertion *"I'm not sure he'll thank him for that … bit of a hospital pass Clive."* It can also be an under-hit lackadaisical ball, which is *seized upon* by opposition strikers. In Denmark, the phrase is known as a *rigtig Jesper Olsen*, or a *real Jesper Olsen* as a tribute to the midfielder's square ball which provided Spain with their equaliser at Mexico '86.

Hot prospect

A possible *wonderkid* who is attracting *admiring glances* from afar. Carbon copy newspaper articles appear about the latest *in vogue* talent detailing the list of clubs that are *keeping tabs* on him. These always include, but are not limited to the top European sides desperate to stockpile talent.

Such interest is, of course, flattering, but a *hands off warning* is invariably issued, with the player's manager stating that his starlet is *"not ready"* to make the step up yet and *"they are much better off developing at this club for now."* National team managers may also be checking their lineage, with Greg Dyke furiously rifling through the archives to see if they had a grandparent born in Swanage.

Hot reception

A fiery welcome. Is usually *dished out* to those who have invoked the ire of the club, perhaps being an old *fan favourite* who has *gone to pastures new* (very possibly their local rivals) on a significantly improved deal. *"Sol Campbell making his return to White Hart Lane, will be guaranteed to receive a hot reception from the Spurs faithful."* See also *Judas*.

Hot seat

The manager's chair, which those taking their *badges* aspire to. It can also be something only a cool customer or possessor of a fiery temperament can occupy.

Hot streak

A hot streak is had by a player or team on a fine run of form whose backside (or collective backsides) is said to be glowing. *"AFC Hinckley's red-hot streak takes them to top in Midland League."* See also *purple patch*.

Hot water

Players land themselves in hot water with regularity. Reasons include:
1. *Taking to Twitter* to criticise a referee.
2. Flicking the *'Vs'* to the crowd.

3. Escaping immediate (but not retrospective) *censure* for an *off-the-ball* flailing arm.
4. Becoming embroiled in a totally unnecessary *off the ball* incident.

Hotly tipped
Phrase used in the media when nobody really knows what's going on. Players may be *hotly tipped* for summer action at the World Cup finals, or to make an impact on a brand new stage. *"Callum Wilson is being hotly tipped to make quite a splash for Bournemouth this season."*

Hotshot
The star striker, i.e. the first name on the team sheet.

Household name
A well-known name in the footballing world. *"Charlton's lack of household names might be their undoing; but that means they have the unpredictability factor. Will Reza Ghoochannejhad smash a hat trick or trip over his laces?"*

Howitzer
A shot so hard it could have been fired from this piece of heavy artillery. Named because such shots are powerful, direct and deadly. *"Hitzlsperger unleashed a howitzer which crashed into the net from fully 25 yards."*

Howler
1. A miss of such shocking proportions it causes the attacker to howl in anguish at his lack of ability from six yards out. *"What a howler from Jermaine Beckford! Dear me, he'll be having nightmares about that one tonight and probably for some time to come – and he won't be showing his face on the streets of Preston any time soon."*
2. A piece of goalkeeping so bad it causes a similar reaction to the above, except this time a goal does occur.

Hunt
1. *(Back) in the.* For *goals* perhaps; or the hunt for a title.
2. *Hunting.* Akin to being armed with tranquiliser darts and rifle, the rumour mill often sees managers hunting their targets. *"Neil hunting Finnbogason."*
3. *Glory hunter/seeker.* Someone who gives their allegiance to any team who is top of the table. This particular *barb* is commonly found in the playground; the kid who turns up wearing a Hartlepool United goalkeeper's jersey, only to reveal a Wycombe third kit underneath.

I

I can't wait to see what the pitch is like
The first thing any footballer worth their salt looks forward to ahead of a big game.

I don't read the newspapers anyway
Blatant lie by managers when the speculation about their future or team's performance is *rife*. *Someone* at the club must be reading the papers, because the publication that printed the story about a dressing room *mutiny* is now banned indefinitely.

I will love it if we beat them!
One of football's best-known quotes and perhaps the finest thing to ever come out of a manager's mouth in a post-match interview. Apparently Kevin Keegan kept *"real quiet"* about it.

I would rather he punched me in the face
There are many things that can be done to an opponent during a match. One such example (and perhaps the worst) is being spat at or on. Incidents usually cause uproar, and lead to quotes in the press later that week where the victim says *"I would rather he punched me in the face."* There are other equally unsavoury incidents, such as Edison Cavani's finger incident with Chile's Gonzalo Jara, and Luis Suarez's biting episodes.

I'm told they've been practicing penalties this week
In-the-know commentators trot out this line before any penalty shootout in either the World Cup or European Championships. *"Well I've been reliably informed England have been practicing spot kicks this week. A wise choice from Hodgson's boys."* Whether a team has been practising them during the week is usually the first question at the pre-match press conference.

Icon
1. The focal point of a team. The player who embodies everything about a club, and will no doubt go down in the annals of history as a true great. Reverence may be such that a statue could be commissioned and erected outside the ground, for example Derek Dooley at Bramall Lane.
2. Now defunct *wag mag* aimed at professional footballers and their wives. The brainchild of Jamie Redknapp and Tim Sherwood, it featured high-end products at barely believable prices. In circulation for a likewise barely believable seven years.

If anything, he hit that too well

One of the more bizarre comments made by pundits, mainly Andy Townsend. *"The ball sits up nicely for Pjanić, the connection is perfect but if anything he's hit that too well Clive."* It is unclear what this statement actually means or what value it has in commentary. Perhaps hitting a shot at 90% of its potential is the optimum level for a shot. I.e. the ones that will *ask real questions of the goalkeeper*.

If he did that on the street...

An incident which is considered so violent and/or outrageous, pundits back in the studio are often of the opinion that *if he did that on the street, he be going straight to jail.* Glen Hoddle, for example was of the opinion Luis Suarez would go straight to jail if he bit someone in public (note it is always on the street, not in the comfort of his own home). Obviously, if he did it in any other day job it would, no doubt, be frowned upon; taking a bite out of Karen from HR would send the office wild.

If you haven't played the game...

Opinions of the non-footballing fraternity are somewhat diluted by never having run out onto the turf and played a full 90 at professional level. This is commonly levelled at referees, whose decisions are lambasted because they have never played the game. *"There's a difference between the rulebook and practical application; and if you haven't played the game, you can't understand it."* This does not stop the local pint-swiller screaming peerless advice at the television.

Illustrious

1. *Career.* A career filled with trophies, big clubs and numerous personal awards.
2. *Opponents.* When the big boys come to town, it may be asked if the underdogs stand any chance of victory. *"With Crewe all set to welcome their illustrious opponents to Gresty Road, they'll have to be at their very best to get one over high flying Orient."*

Impeccably observed

If a minute's silence goes without a sound, then this is what they are.

Impotent attack

Forward play which lacks *bite*. A team that is clearly toothless in attack and will probably struggle to contribute more than 15 goals *to the cause* between them in a season.

In and around

A phrase, which makes a modicum of sense in certain applications: *"Altrincham's Simon Richman causes so many problems in and around the penalty area."* However, it makes little sense in others: *"The boy has great awareness of those in an around him Clive."*

In arrears

A goal deficit. As arrears are missed payments, it can be assumed any team in arrears has failed to *cash in* on their *goalscoring potential.*

In deep conversation with

"Steve Clarke is in deep conversation with Kevin Keen; it looks like the anonymous Orlando Sa is going to be replaced by Cox." Chats of this nature usually take place on the touchline. The content of these deep discussions is not always known, but it can be assumed it concerns the unfolding match, whether to employ the *livewire* substitute *in the hole*, or whether to deploy the much-feted Christmas tree formation.

In front of the TV cameras

"Join us at Portman Road on Tuesday night as Ipswich take on Neil Redfearn's Rotherham outfit in front of the TV cameras." With the blanket coverage that football receives, every game is now *in front of the cameras*; many National League teams even have their own YouTube channel, such as Chelmsford City's *Clarets TV.*

In the dark

A classic statement of ignorance by a manager. This could be a possible new signing, where the chairman runs the rule over recruitment, impending action over one of his player's actions in the previous game, or a bid which may come in from another club. *"Loui Fazakerley says he's in the dark over any Kieron St Amie bid."*

Inch perfect

A tackle or cross considered to be spot on. Although not as accurate as *centimetre perfect*, or indeed *millimetre perfect*, inches seem to be the choice measurement of perfection in football parlance. *"Katsouranis' inch perfect cross found Nikos Karelis who slammed home."*

Incumbent

The current occupier of the hot seat. Also refers to the previous manager of a club, and suggests a lack of permanence. *"Paul Cook, like the previous incumbent Andy Awford, faces an uphill task at Portsmouth."*

Indian sign
Teams who are considered another's bogey team have the *Indian sign* over them. See also *hoodoo*.

Etymology: Thought to have originated from the 'Indian blanket', which members of Indian tribes – particularly medicine men – would hold up in front of an uncaptured wild horse in order to hold their attention and exert control over it; the decorated blanket was said to be highly effective, and as such many Indians believed it had supernatural powers – hence the Indian sign we see in football today.

Indian summer
An enjoyable period of time later on in a players' career, long after he should have reached his *peak*. Teddy Sheringham enjoyed a very long *Indian summer* towards the end of his career, playing well into his forties.

Industrious
A footballer high on grit, determination and hard work, but low on skill, panache and verve. *"Quick, crafty and industrious, the ex-Bury man is as comfortable worrying goalkeepers as dropping deep and should prove the sort the Shoe Army take to."* Industrious footballers embody the spirit of many 90s old school players, such as Vinny Samways, Ian Crook and Chris Kiwomya.

Injury
1. *Plagued/prone.* A period of time not really measured in weeks or months, but generally to last half a season or longer. If the injury is something like a broken leg it probably wouldn't be described as a plague *per se*; of course, strictly speaking, the only types of injury plagues should be ones which are contagious. Other types of transmittable disease not related to injuries in football are known as *pandemics*, such as the dark art of diving.
2. *Time.* Always a *minimum* period of additional time, which the fourth official always *indicates*. Commentators will regularly predict the amount they think will see given. *"We should see at least four minutes here after that injury to Kyle Walker."* However, when the board goes up and it is less, the comment *"You can see what the crowd think of that!"* is often made. *"His watch obviously isn't Swiss, Martin."*

Inside
A few things are done *inside*:
1. *Jink.*
2. *Pass.*
3. *Cut.*
4. *Ghost.*

5. *Be a goal down inside five minutes.*

Instant control
Those who have good balance and a great first touch are adept at such a skill. *"Pahars' instant control and dainty pirouette takes the ball clear of Stimac."* This contrasts to the leaden-footed player whose second touch is always a tackle.

Intelligent footballer
Intelligent footballers possess a footballing brain, are rarely fazed, and *step up to the plate* in the *big games*.
They are likely to display the following attributes:
1. Instinct. Whether it is when a ball breaks free in the area – and as such is a *killer* instinct – or anticipating a dangerous ball into the box.
2. The ability to play blind passes even the crowd doesn't see.
3. Five or more GCSEs.

Intent
Sides who wish to make their intentions known early doors will either test the 'keeper in the first couple of minutes, play straight for the corner flag from kick-off, or get stuck in to tackles. On the other hand, players might be defended by their managers who will no doubt say they had no *intent* to cause injury with the *reducer* committed during the match.

Interim boss
Caretaker manager the chairman won't trust with the reins full-time, but who is seen as a stopgap before a proper replacement is found. The interim boss would love the gig on a full-time basis, and genuinely believes he's in with a shout; one token interview later and the club secretary is ringing him with the bad news. See also *competition winner*.

Inviting ball
Cross along the face of goal. *"Harte's inviting ball across the box was absolutely begging to be put in the back of the net."*

Ironic cheers
Heard in a number of situations, including when the referee awards a free kick in favour of the home side following a litany of decisions against them. *"The referee finally awarded Argyle a free kick, leading to ironic cheers from the Home Park faithful."*

Isotonic sports drinks
"The Costa Rica physio is dishing out the isotonic sports drinks during the break in play as conditions are sweltering here in Brazil." This is the BBC's term for extra fluids; of course on Sky it is simply *Lucozade*.

Etymology: A liquid solution, which has a similar salt and sugar concentration to blood.

It could have been double figures
Trouncing of such epic proportions that the result really could have been a cricket score; bizarrely goalkeepers are often credited with keeping the score down by producing a number of fine stops. On the sliding scale of defeats, the following is usually stated by commentators:
- 1-0: *"They were lucky they didn't turn their dominance into goals."*
- 2-0: *"The scoreline has flattered them here."*
- 3-0: *"It could have been five or six."*
- 4-0 or more: *"It could easily have been double figures."*

The last time a team scored double figures in the English leagues was 1987, as Manchester City trounced Huddersfield 10-1; however 2014/15 did see Hamilton batter Greenock Morton 10-2 in Scottish League One.

It's a massive club
Standard quote offered by a new signing at his first press conference. They will often declare, *"everybody knows this is a massive club"* and one of the big reasons for signing is because they want to *"help them get back where they belong"* and that they *"can't wait to run out in front of 50,000 screaming fans every week."* Exactly what they are screaming is left unsaid.

J

Jettisoned
To be cast out of the first team picture. *"Kevin van Veen has much work ahead of him after being jettisoned by Iron boss Mark Robins."*

Jibe
Insolent *taunt* by a manager or player in an attempt to get a *rise* out of the opposition. The recipients of such *zingers* will do one of two things:
1. *Refuse to respond* to such *jibes*, because they do not *dignify a response.*

2. Get drawn into a *war of words*. *"Alan Knill can say what he likes, but our football will do the talking. He likes to make his comments about other teams but I'm confident of a win. He'd do well to take a look at the league table."*

Jigsaw
Nickname of the mis-firing striker so called because he always *goes to pieces in the box*.

Jinking run
"He goes inside, and out... wonderful jinking run from David Eyres. This wide man really does know how to entertain." A *slaloming* run, which excites the crowd, perhaps bringing them to their feet in anticipation of a *superb solo effort*.

Jose Mourinho couldn't save this lot
A team possessing such a paucity of talent that even *the Special One* couldn't save them from certain relegation.

Jostling for position
This usually occurs when a *set play* is about to come into the area. Players size each other up, looking to *lose their marker*, or alternatively keep a *close eye* on their man. Jason McAteer once told a story of Neil Ruddock urinating himself from a corner whilst both sides jostled for position, perhaps gaining a crucial advantage and very probably *acres of space*.

Journeyman
"A torrid three-minute spell midway through the first half saw the home side surrender two goals, with poor defending totally exposing journeyman 'keeper Lutz Pfannenstiel." Journeymen who have fallen down through the leagues are quite often seen to have a number of clubs in one division, with each one attempting to *harness* the talent they exhibited in the *glory days*, usually without success. Trevor Benjamin for example had an impressive 30 clubs throughout his career, and the aforementioned Lutz Pfannenstiel is thought to be the only footballer who has played for a club in all six FIFA confederations. See also *mercenary*.

Judas
Name reserved for players who have committed the ultimate betrayal by moving to a club's hated rivals, usually to further their own career.

Jumped in with both feet
A poor challenge, which is sure to bring *censure* from the referee. Often seen as a leg breaker, a straight red card is a distinct possibility. *"The Kiwi's Ben Sigmund*

jumped in with both feet on UAE's Ali Mabkhout, leading to uproar from the bench." See also X-*rated challenge.*

Jupiter
The place where Lionel Messi is apparently from, such is his ability.

Just like watching Brazil
The silky passing movement of a side that can lead their fans to exclaim that it's just like watching Brazil. It matters not whether the team is Swansea City or Shepshed Dynamo.

K

Keep it tight
Space-limiting tactic used to establish a foothold in the match, before becoming more expansive in the following minutes. *"If Mark Yates' men want to get anything out of the game in East London today, it is imperative they keep it tight in the first ten."* It always seems to be the plucky, yet limited side that are looking to grind out a valuable point (or maybe even a *smash and grab raid*) who *keep it tight*; however no side should look to concede in the first 20 minutes.

Keeping tabs
Sides that show an interest in a player are said to be *keeping tabs* on him, especially if he is a *prospect*. In the same way, they might *earmark* him to monitor their progress before *launching* a bid. *"Wolves keeping tabs on Brighton schemer Jake Forster-Caskey."*

Keepy-ups
Or *keepie-uppies*; is the standard skill to be exhibited by a footballer of any level. From Wembley to the school playground, keepy-ups are the ultimate signal that this person knows how to play. If a spot in a Premier League starting XI doesn't beckon, a slot on the half time entertainment might.

It has also become something of a tradition for new Real Madrid signings to be paraded in front of tens of thousands of fans (if in the *Galactico* category) whilst doing numerous keepy-ups in order to provide confirmation of pedigree.

Keyboard warriors
Those who sit on Twitter all day riling professional footballers for no particular reason. Where most would not dare to utter some of the filth which they spout forth on the medium of the internet, they are able to do so in relative safety and

comfort from their bedroom at their parent's house. Unless your name is *Jimmyob88* and the person you have been targeting for months was footballer-turned-boxer Curtis Woodhouse. See also *backpedalling*.

Keystone Cops defending
Inference of an incompetent back line. *"Aaron Ramsey, though, still could not clear and when Jordan Henderson passed to Suárez, his shot deflected past Szczesny. The arrival of the Keystone Cops would have completed the scene."*

Etymology: Bungling policemen from silent film comedies of the early 20th century. There were various aspects of the production that draw parallels with such defending:
1. *A chase.*
2. *It would be filmed at low speed.*
3. *The policemen would never run in a straight line.*

This perhaps explains its use in football today.

Kicked
1. *Out.* Seen as a *cynical* act or a *petulant kick*. There is no attempt to play the ball by the offender in this situation. *Kicking out* can often be an *off-the-ball incident* (e.g. David Beckham versus Argentina), with a high probability of it leading to a red card. Unless of course it goes unnoticed by match officials in which case *retrospective action* may take place.
2. *Off.* A flashpoint often leads to a mass confrontation involving all 22 men on the pitch. See also *ugly scenes*.
3. *A ball.* Denotes the length of playing time a player has enjoyed (or not) under his manager. *"Alan Hutton did not kick a ball for Villa under Paul Lambert for the best part of two years."* Those who have been sidelined for some time may not have *kicked a ball in anger* all season.

Kicking and heading every ball
The ball, while very much imaginary, is *kicked and headed* by the more hyperactive of managers in the technical area. Also proffered by players who are sidelined. *"I'm gutted to be missing the game, but I'll be in the stands kicking and heading every ball, cheering the lads on."*

Kids
Alan Hansen is, of course, synonymous with the phrase *"you can't win anything with kids"* – after which Manchester United promptly did, back in the formative years of the Premier League. Managers may now toy with the idea of throwing the kids in when a game has little or nothing riding on it, to provide invaluable first team exposure.

Killer pass
Intricate build up play is usually completed by this type of *deadly precision*, or alternatively the absence of: *"Lack of killer pass proves fatal for Spireites."* The killer pass also comes in *instinct* and *goal* forms.

Kisses the badge
There are many reasons for players to kiss the badge:
1. To make a show of their love for the club. Frank Lampard was a prolific badge kisser at Chelsea, rarely passing up the opportunity to place his lips on the club crest. It is one of two gestures a player might make towards his shirt on scoring a goal; the other is pointing to his name on his back. Players do not gesture towards sponsors, as is sometimes the case in some other sports; you would not, for example, have seen Malcolm Shotton pointing towards the *Wang* computers logo emblazoned across his Oxford United shirt back in the 1980s.
2. To hit back against scorning press who have questioned their loyalty, ability or desire.
3. To wind up opposition fans. It was inferred in the press that AFC Wimbledon and MK Dons were banned from kissing the badge by the police ahead of their FA Cup clash in 2012.

Knack
1. The ability to be able to produce something time after time. Bad boy players on the other hand might have the *knack* of courting controversy.
2. An injury. *"Ronaldo knee knack spells trouble for Portugal."*

Knee-jerk
Similar to, but more immediate and unceremonious than, pressing the *panic button*. This response or reaction is universally warned against by managers in fear of becoming the next managerial *casualty*, imploring the club directors not to sack them in an attempt to erase the memories of the *horror show* just witnessed. *"Yes, we were poor, yes we shipped six, however, there shouldn't be a knee-jerk reaction to this. We'll be back in on Monday morning to put this right."*

Knock down price
A player who is available on the cheap. This could be for a number of reasons. The selling club may be *cash strapped*, or perhaps the player in question has breached club rules and they are looking to get rid. Alternatively, players in the final year of their contracts will be available at this fee, because their current club wouldn't want to lose them on a *Bosman*.

Knocking on the door

1. *Incessant pressure. "Colin Nish's men have been knocking on the door all game but cannot find a way past the stubborn Blue Toon defence."* Teams invariably do this throughout the match; sometimes a *breakthrough* is achieved, but on the other hand incessant knocking can still result in no answer. Or even worse, the door is *slammed in their face* by the no-nonsense defender, who then picks the attacker up and puts him *in his back pocket.*
2. *First team door.* Fringe players queue up to *knock* on this, particularly after impressive performances in the stiffs, pre-season or off the bench. Also known as *staking a claim for a first team place.*

KO

In football, it has two principal meanings:

1. Colloquial term used predominantly in newspaper headlines to denote injury *woe. "Posh rocked by striker KO."*
2. The *sucker punch* goal, late in the game, that can often lead to teams being *floored.* A *knock-out blow.*

L

Labelled

Although similar to *dubbed, labelled* may harbour more negative connotations. Players may be *labelled* a *disruptive influence on the dressing room,* by *leading a mutiny* against the *beleaguered boss.*

Labels are also there to be *shrugged off;* Kyle Lafferty, for example, was very keen to rid himself of his *playboy* label, saying, *"Now I'm back at Norwich I just want to rebuild my reputation and let my football do the talking. I like a bit of banter but basically I'm just a nice quiet lad really."*

Laboured

A *sluggish* performance, but that doesn't necessarily mean defeat is a formality. A team might *labour* to an FA Cup win over lower league opposition (i.e. they make *hard work* of it). *"Bristol City post laboured performance but squeeze past plucky Southend."* Teams may *labour* all season long, however when this is the case a team will be said to *languish* in the lower reaches of a division.

Lacklustre

Similar to laboured, but a performance of this description is even more *lifeless.* Lacklustre is perhaps the opposite of *lustre* – which suggests a glow or sheen – because this display has none. It is applied to *star-studded* line-ups in particular.

"Lacklustre Saints were undone as Mihran Manasyan's second-half strike secured Alashkert a deserved victory on their European debut." Managers will always *expect more* from a side in these circumstances.

Lads

Collective term for a football team, whether it is a Premier League *outfit* or the *basement dwellers* in the Cherry Red Records Division One. Suggests it is a status to be obtained: *"Sylvain has come in and fit into the dressing room really well; he's one of the lads already."* Also known as *the boys*, but never *the chaps*.

Landscape

1. Of world football. Something, which exists purely to be *rocked*, with sensational *mega deals* being one of the main causes that make the footballing seismometers twitch. Tremors extend worldwide, and are not confined to one particular area. *"Bale's record move to Real has the potential to rock the landscape of world football."*
2. The current standings, only commented on when the table has an *unfamiliar look*, which essentially does not involve Manchester City, Chelsea, Manchester United, Arsenal, Liverpool – and possibly Spurs. *"West Ham's surprise victory has changed the landscape at the top of the Premier League somewhat, catapulting them into second place."*

Landslide

1. Victory featuring an *avalanche* of goals for the winning team. Often the expected *landslide* fails to materialise.
2. 1975 single by Fleetwood Mac.

Lapse

Often in *concentration*, defences who exhibit this trait are often found asleep. *"Defensive lapses disappoint Wimborne boss Steve Cuss."* Managers may also display a lapse of judgement, such as deciding to sign the *bad boy* who came to the club with considerable baggage, no *desire*, and a *big time Charlie* attitude.

Last chance saloon

Last chance saloons are on offer to the following:
1. The team who have thrown *everything but the kitchen sink* at their opponents, and are one minute away from defeat – however they are in possession on the halfway line.
2. The player with a chequered past who will be given one more opportunity to prove his worth to the side. No doubt he will be snapped up by someone else should he be kicked out. *"Brendan Rodgers tells Mario Balotelli he is entering the last chance saloon at Liverpool."*

Etymology: Term for a bar in the USA located close to areas where alcohol was prohibited; this represented an opportunity for patrons to have a drink legally before entering territory where it was banned.

Last ditch defending

Defenders who put any part of their body in-between the ball and the goal could be said to be engaging in this. *"The heroic last ditch defending by Radosavljevic prevented Vale from bagging a second."* The ageing footballer whose *legs have gone* is a forerunner in this department, possibly because he very often finds himself five yards out of position.

Last gasp

The final recourse, which produces a decisive moment in the game. Last gasp instances occur right at the death, and produce *high drama* in *spades*. *"The strike by Claridge was as undeserved as it was last gasp."*

Last man

One of the few occasions when there can be *no complaints* is when a defender brings a player down *through on goal*, and as such is the *last man*. The direction of travel, presence of a *covering defender* and whether there was any contact all have a bearing on the level of protestation a side will make to the referee. The *last man debate* is a staple topic of discussion by the *true fans* in the pub whilst conducting the *post-match post-mortem*.

Late flag

Decision which will often *cruelly deny* the attacking player. Commentators will affirm the obvious that it was a *"late, very late flag from the lino, Clive."* It is particularly embarrassing for the blissfully unaware player who has *wheeled away* in delight, thinking he has scored that all-important goal, despite the clearly audible whistle from the referee. *Ironic cheers* may follow.

Late, late drama

Often used by radio commentators as a tease ahead of a live update: *"There's been some late, late drama over at the Globe Arena, let's get straight over there, Delyth Lloyd."* Drama comes in two forms: late, and late, late. The former is likely to come in the final five minutes of normal time, while the latter is to be found right at the death and will undoubtedly break hearts.

Laws of the game

Football rules handed down by FIFA. Actions on the pitch are seen as either within the laws of the game, or conversely outside. Actions considered outside the laws include *simulation*, stealing yards on a throw in and showing the referee a yellow card after he has dropped them. There is a certain degree of disconnect between the laws and the spirit of the game; spirit requires a higher moral standing than merely obeying the laws, such as Paolo Di Canio catching the ball versus Everton, whereas a strict interpretation would deem it a handball.

Leading from the front

A blood and thunder footballer taking his troops into battle. The actions of a man leading from the front include:

1. Fixing the roof of the tunnel with a mean glare before leading the team out; all the while absolutely refusing to look down the lens of the TV camera.
2. Producing multiple fist pumps.
3. At a corner, pointing to empty space and shouting.
4. Aggressively clapping a teammate on the back of the head as he boots another cross into row Z.

League ladder

In cup clashes, it is customary for the commentator to say how many places there are between two sides on the *league ladder*. *"Welcome to Brunton Park, home of Carlisle. Can they upset the odds against an Aston Villa side who are 61 places higher on the league ladder?"* There is an indeterminate minimum distance required before this is worthy of mention, although it can be assumed it would be at least one league's difference.

Leathered it

Alternative term for *put his foot through it*. *"Blundell leathered it past Miskelly who could merely stand there and admire."*

Left peg

The eminently more cultured sibling of the *right peg*.

Left to right

The direction of play as described by the commentator. *"And we're underway here at the Bescot Stadium, Walsall, kicking from left to right."* For those who don't know the geography of the ground and therefore the position of the media, it is arguably a rather redundant observation, yet this quaint old-fashioned addition to commentary remains. Other locations will be given by a commentator during a match; travelling supporters are often *"far away to our left"*, *"high up in the stands"* or possibly *"over in the corner."* The managers can be found *"down below us"* and the referee is usually *"in the middle".*

Leg breaker

1. A nasty looking challenge, so much so that the commentator always feels the need to point out that it could have caused serious damage; however, it rarely does. *"That's a real leg breaker on Grimandi, he's lucky to escape injury there Sam."* Tackles into standing legs cause particular outrage among pundits, leading to mutterings about a *coward's challenge*. Can also be thought of as a *potential* leg breaker.
2. A tackle that really does break a leg. Actual leg breakers are not pointed out, indeed television cameras might decline to show replays of the incident.

Legion

1. Away supporters are often described as the *travelling legion of fans*. Is an alternative to the *travelling army*. This is possibly because they are in *great numbers*.
2. The *foreign legion* applies to a team that has a number of foreign players in the dressing room. It may be narrowed down to a particular nationality; Newcastle, for example is well known for having a large *Francophone* contingent in their squad over recent years. Other clubs have been chastised for putting out a starting XI devoid of home nation players.

Etymology: The French Foreign Legion was created in 1831 for foreign nationals who were willing to serve in the French army, and has assisted in many conflicts since, including Rwanda, the first Gulf War and Afghanistan. Any soldier who is injured in battle serving in the foreign legion can apply for French citizenship under the doctrine of 'Français par le sang versé', or 'French by spilled blood'.

Let fly

Players often *let fly from distance*. Of course, it will always take something quite special to beat the 'keeper from there. However if a player *unleashes* a drive, you never know…

Level

The reference to a *level* reminds the player of the responsibilities that come with playing in a certain division: *"At this level it should be dead and buried,"* said Tim Sherwood after Aston Villa threw away a 2-0 lead against Leicester; as if this type of behaviour would be acceptable in the Central Taxis East of Scotland league. It may also relate to behaviour: *"He knows at this level of the game, that kind of carry on is not acceptable."* However, it may be referenced with positive connotations: *"At this level there are no easy games, this much we know."*

Level pegging
Back to *all square*.

Licence
1. To *roam*. Those who excel in this department must have the *engine* to be able to play the free role.
2. To get forward. A more positive variant of *roaming*. Implies direction and purpose, and a gameplan; it could also be down to the backing off of a defence: *"The Malta back line seem to be stuck in reverse and that's giving Hakan Şükür plenty of licence to get forward."*

Lick of paint away
A shot so close to being a goal that only the paint on the woodwork saves a side; if the Dulux matte wasn't there for all the world it would be 1-0. *"Jason Rockett came within a lick of paint to giving Scarborough the lead."*

Lightning pace
Incredible speed. So fast, in fact, that a player who possesses this will be away from his marker in a *flash*. *"The lightning pace of Salah was too much for the creaking Atalanta defence."* See also *pace to burn*.

Like for like
On substitution or injury, a player who has the exact same *game* as his team mate. Is also known as a *ready-made replacement*. Note that while interchangeable, these players can be criticised for being unable to play together in the same team.

Linchpin
The technically savvy midfield general through whom all good play is channelled, i.e. the fulcrum of the side. *"Michael Carrick ready to be England's midfield linchpin at Euro 2016."*

Link
1. Transfer speculation, which is particularly rife during the two windows and pre-season. Who is actually making the link is open to debate, however it's probably one of the ever-reliable *sources*.
2. *Up*. Inter-play between two or more players, credited to the team as a whole. *"Superb link up play from Cambridge United, the players seem to have that telepathic understanding. And you have to credit Richard Money for that."* Sometimes shortened to simply *link play*.

Listen to offers
Clubs that are willing to entertain transfer speculation over one of their players may very well be willing to *listen to offers*. It is the opposite of a *hands off warning*. Reasons for this include:
1. The need to comply with financial fair play regulations.
2. Or more often, the need to balance the books. Ailing clubs who must have a fire sale of their best assets will be able to do nothing to stop the vultures from circling.
3. The player in question is *want-away* and as such runs the risk of poisoning the dressing room.

Literally
Word used for emphasis to describe something, without being actually true; favoured by Jamie Redknapp. *"He's literally left Ben Haim for dead there."*

Little
Any diminutive player is commonly referred to as *little*. Can be used in a variety of ways, for example *little wizard, little magician,* or even when talking about a player's nationality. *"The little Spaniard has caused all sorts of problems this afternoon."* Note that the phrase 'little' is often the preserve of the more artisan nations such as Spain, France, Argentina or Italy. The same rules apply to *cultured* and *cultivated*, but not *no-nonsense*.

Little and large partnership
The traditional forward line. The *little and large partnership* is a superb combination for a number of styles of play. The *big man* can *take down long balls with ease,* providing *flick-ons* and bringing his erstwhile strike partner into the game. *Footballing dinosaurs* may prefer this combination in favour of the continental 4-4-1-1 formation. *"Quite possibly the best little and large strike partnership we have ever seen in the Premier League, Sunderland's deadly duo of Niall Quinn and Kevin Phillips were truly masters of their trade."*

Etymology: Phrase bought to wider popularity by the comedians Syd Little and Eddie Large, with their 1977 ITV programme 'The Little and Large Tellyshow' and the subsequent 'Little and Large show' which ran from 1978-1991 on BBC1.

Local boy comes good
The heart-warming good news story that fans up and down the country love to see is the local boy *banging them in* for his *hometown club*. Was also a phrase favoured by Jeff Stelling whenever Guylain Ndumbu-Nsungu scored for Sheffield Wednesday. Guylain was of course born in Kinshasa, which is apparently just outside Dungworth.

Locker
"What have the Silkmen got in their locker in order to get out of the predicament they find themselves in?" Lockers apparently contain abilities and attributes that provide solutions. When a player produces something unexpected, pundits may express surprise they had that particular skill *in their locker*, such as a *thumping header* from Kevin Thornton or superb acrobatics from *beanpole* striker Peter Crouch – which he has showcased to devastating effect.

Long awaited return to action
The return to the first team of the man *made of glass*. Usually one of many *returns to action*, such injury prone players usually break down in training again later on in the week after their *comeback match*. These long awaited returns can be combined to form a stat about how many appearances they have made over the previous couple of seasons: *"Two reserve games and a 30-minute run out in the Johnstone's Paint."*

Long hard look
The sort of consideration a referee will give to a possible penalty shout. If it is given, it may be said he, *"took ages to decide."* Slightly more analytical version of a *good long look*.

Long night
When a team goes two down in the opening ten minutes, particularly away from home, you could be in for a *long night* and *praying for the half time whistle* already. Less likely is *long afternoon*, but things still might look bleak. *"A quickfire Weston/Coaker double meant Stevenage were in for a long night."* Failing to pick up a win in their first 10 outings might mean a team is in for a *long season*.

Look away now
Advice given to fans of teams who have been thrashed during the classified football check. It is also a phrase uttered with ridiculously close proximity to the results prior to MOTD, when the viewer has done sterling work in avoiding the results for most of the afternoon. Hence, the chance to look away is a two-second window of opportunity. It is such an institution, the expression is often changed to, *"So if you don't want to know the results, you know what to do"* with *"look away now"* *left understood.*

Looking for a cup run to provide a welcome distraction
When a side is propping up the league, a good cup run might be the only crumb of comfort in what is otherwise a *season to forget*. On the other hand, cup runs may provide too much of a distraction, and league form might suffer as a result. Numerous examples pepper Premier League history, with Swansea being one of the most recent sides to suffer the pitfalls of a *gruelling* Europa League campaign.

Looking over their shoulders

"The latest in a catalogue of defeats means the Shrews will be looking over their shoulders." The nervous glances of the team who are *sliding* inexorably towards the *dreaded relegation trapdoor*. Looking over your shoulder is a real problem when you have *very little breathing space*, but it is still practised widely by those managers who are eight points clear with three to go. Can also be teams at the apex, whose season seems to have stagnated and one of the *chasing pack* is in red hot form.

Lost his…

1. *Head.* Occurrence, which stems from a rush of blood to the head. Manifests itself in a scything challenge, a head butt or a full-on scuffle. An *enforced early substitution* for his *own protection* is the best outcome a player can hope for.
2. *Legs.* Footballer lacking the ability to *cover every blade of grass* (like he once could) is known to have *lost his legs*. For *speed merchants* it is necessary to convert to a *holding midfielder* a la Dwight Yorke or Ryan Giggs, or it could be time to *hang up their boots*. Similar to being diagnosed with *losing a half a yard of pace* but with potentially more severe consequences.

Lost the dressing room

Managers who no longer have the backing of their squad are said to have *lost the dressing room*. Players are more likely to be listening to Kanye West's album *Yeezus*, texting their WAGs back at the pad or arranging delivery of their new Lamborghini than listening to his half time gee-up. It is the first of three events:

1. *The dressing room is lost.*
2. The *dreaded vote of confidence* is *issued.*
3. The *managerial axe* is *wielded.*

Lottery of penalties

Phrase which works on the assumption that penalties are in fact a lottery – unless you are the English national side, in which case defeat is almost 100% assured.

There are, actually, a number of constants when it comes to penalties. Germany conform to the stereotype of ruthless efficiency, while England will invariably suffer *penalty agony;* and of course, the commentator always knows if they have been *practised during the week*. In the aftermath of such events, experts will pore over the psychological aspects of penalty taking to see if there is a way to win. Sepp Blatter releases a statement saying they are looking at fairer alternatives to penalties, such as getting the most popular psychic animal of the day to pick the winner from two boxes.

Lowly

Term applied to a less accomplished side in a match or division. Certainly not intended as a compliment. *"Enrique's men demolish lowly Córdoba."* Sides who fail to see off weaker sides will have this term levelled at them as a form of criticism. *"It was coupon-busting time as Northern Ireland suffered the embarrassment of failing to beat lowly Liechtenstein on Wednesday."*

Lurk

Slightly disconcerting term for a player who is ready to *pounce* – probably *loitering with intent* in the *shadows*, unattended and unseen by the defender. *"The ball was missed by the whole defence and the lurking Mark Fish prodded home from six yards."* Playground parlance would label such players a *moocher*.

Luxury player

The kind of player who gives an aesthetically pleasing look to a team. Possesses *silky skills*, he is all too often the *catalyst* to the best moves of a match. There is a caveat however; while they are willing to take the glory, luxury players cannot be trusted to do some of the dirty work. To *track back*, make tackles and contribute to the defensive side of the game, and as such, he may be used *sparingly* from the bench.

M

Made him look like Beckenbauer

Balls consistently pumped long onto the head of the opposition centre back are a source of immense frustration to many fans. Because said balls are headed away with *consummate ease*, it is often complained that the defender in question bears a striking resemblance to *Die Mannschaft's* legendary centre back; when in actual fact, said player is more Boumsong than Beckenbauer.

Made of glass

Used to describe those players who are particularly injury prone. *"Is Wes Brown playing today? Nah mate, he's out. Made of glass that lad."* This player will strap ice packs to both knees post-match.

Maestro

Almost without exception, maestros hail from the midfield. *"Lampard and Villa must be drooling at the prospect of sharing a pitch with midfield maestro Pirlo."*

Etymology: Italian term meaning 'master'; usually refers to classical music or opera.

Magic

1. *Formula.* The existence of this is usually denied or hard to find, in sharp contrast to a *winning formula.* *"The boys are all brave footballers, and experience tells you that we are not too far away so I don't have to go looking for that magic formula."*

2. *Of the cup.* Reserved exclusively for the FA Cup. What exactly this magic is and why it elicits such a reaction in people remains unclear. The *romance* of the cup is also repeatedly referred to, harking back to the black and white days of 100,000 attendances at Wembley, admission prices of 7'6 and men in flat caps. Managers repeatedly refer to the magic of the cup in a way which implies they will not be *taking the opposition lightly*, before electing to give the academy graduate his debut up front. *Sponge.* The cure-all piece of equipment essential to any physio until circa 1997. The magic sponge had healing powers the like of which had not been seen before, bringing about a miraculous recovery in the stricken player. Replaced by magic spray, which was seen as far less effective than something which was on sale at Woolworths at two for 49p. *"Didier Drogba has hit the deck early doors. There doesn't look to be too much wrong with him, certainly nothing the magic sponge couldn't fix."*

Major silverware

Top clubs are judged by how much major silverware is collected. A Charity Shield here and an Intertoto Cup there will not suffice for the trophy-hungry, cash-laden *behemoths* of the football world. It's the FA Cup, Premier League or European competitions and nothing else for the *big boys*. Admittedly, Newport County would *lick their lips* at the prospect of a League Cup triumph.

Make up the numbers

Something which no club is *there to do.* *"Cod army boss refutes suggestions his charges are just there to make up the numbers."*

Makeshift

Usually a patched up defence with a left midfielder at left back, a defensive midfielder partnering the fourth choice centre half in the middle and someone at right back nobody has ever heard of. *Makeshift defences* are seen later on in a campaign when injuries have *ravaged* the first choice back line, although it may feature earlier on at the club which has failed to *bolster* their defence sufficiently in the preceding transfer window. As an aside it also breeds headlines about players being willing to *play anywhere* for the gaffer. Less commonly refers to an individual. *"Bikey is operating as a makeshift striker as Reading have one last throw of the dice."*

Making a real nuisance of himself
These include:
1. *Mazy dribbles.*
2. *Decoy runs.*
3. Getting into dangerous positions.
4. *Clattering* into opposition centre backs.

...and so on.

Man in black
The referee. Somewhat inaccurate now as many refereeing strips coming in a variety of fetching colours. The problem being *the man in fluorescent yellow* doesn't quite have the same ring about it.

Man on!
Collective cry from the crowd to warn of an opponent in close quarters. Is one of the few examples where supporters will talk en masse to a player. Others include *shoot, time!* and *get out!* (sometimes shortened to *out!*).

Manager of the month curse
Winning the manager of the month gong is a prestigious award for many. However, it is believed that this actually places a *curse* on the gaffer in question, causing him to lose his *Midas touch*, and go on a *barren* winless run. When the curse is beaten, it is often sneered at: *"So much for the manager of the month 'curse' as Ady Pennock's Forest Green continue their charge to the Football League."*

Managerial merry go round
Farcical situation, fuelled by rapacious media-hype, which sees managers switch clubs with alarming regularity. Once the *sack race* has been won, the merry go round swings into action with Glenn Hoddle, Alan Curbishley and Paul Jewell invariably seen looking on forlornly.

Mapping the route to
"What a performance by Tonbridge Angels, they're into round three... could they be mapping the route to Old Trafford, the Emirates or Stamford Bridge?" The privilege of a team who has so far enjoyed a *stellar year* in a cup competition. See also *setting their satnavs.*

Mar
Matches can be marred for two reasons:
1. Sendings off. *"Well, with York going down to 10 men in the first half, it really did spoil the game as a spectacle... completely changed the way they were set up and it's*

marred the match as a result." When red cards are seen as unnecessary it's usually thought the referee has *drawn attention to himself.*

2. Injuries. Injuries more commonly *mar* the match, particularly when they are the result of a *horror tackle. "You could see the Bradford boys were affected by the injury, it's no doubt marred their victory."* Such injuries can lead to a number of things:

   a) Both sides *signalling for the physio* straight away, with accompanying hand gestures.
   b) Players turning away and looking (in the commentator's words) *visibly upset.*
   c) In even rarer instances, oxygen is administered.
   d) Both sets of fans applauding the stricken player from the field.
   e) Eight or more minutes of injury time.

Marathon not a sprint

Cautionary words intended to bring focus to fans and players alike following a team's early season success. *"Well we've had a cracking win here at the Crabble Athletic ground, but this season is 42 games long, it's a marathon and not a sprint. Without doubt there are difficult times up ahead."*

Marauding left back

Full back who frequently *raids* opposition territory; however, he should be very careful indeed not to *leave the back door open. "Portugal's marauding left back Fabio Coentrao is clear proof of how the World Cup can catapult you to the big time thanks to a couple of great performances."* Players of this ilk perhaps wanted to be wingers, but lack the pace and finesse to succeed. Like cultured left feet, the right sided variant is less common.

Marching orders

Instructions given by the referee to a player who has been sent off. Marching orders are sometimes not taken well by the offending player, who may refuse to leave the field of play or have to be restrained by his teammates (or if really bad, sections of the bench).

Etymology: Military terminology where soldiers are given details of a march to be undertaken.

Mass exodus

A large-scale desertion of a club. *"The mass exodus from the Rossoneri means Mihajlovic will have to undertake a massive restructuring process."* Reasons for jumping ship are numerous. Financial constraints may necessitate the sale of prize assets, or perhaps the departure of a popular and respected manager will cause many of the squad left behind to get *itchy feet* (although the now ex-manager will no doubt return to poach some of the best players for his new team).

Etymology: From the Greek word 'exodos' meaning 'going out'. A central story in the history of Judaism, the book of Exodus describes the Israelites' departure from slavery in Egypt. The story also features in the books Leviticus, Deuteronomy and Numbers.

Maverick

Not one to do things by the book, a *maverick* looks to mix things up. He may produce an outrageous piece of skill that catches other players and the crowd *unawares*. There is always room within football for mavericks, but any suitors should be warned, they may be just as likely to announce their retirement on Twitter than score an outrageous 35-yard scissor volley. Mavericks include Zlatan Ibrahimovic, 1970s prankster Stan Bowles and, according to the title of his autobiography Terry Curran (*Regrets of a Football Maverick: The Terry Curran Autobiography*). Although the latter did start a full-scale riot after an on-the-pitch fight with Simon Stainrod once, so this may be justified.

Etymology: Samuel Augustus Maverick was an American rancher in the 19th century who allegedly gained a reputation for steadfastly refusing to brand his cattle; as such he was known as someone who was independently minded and would not conform to the norm. His surname became a by-word to describe any individual who goes against the grain in various situations.

Mazy run

A *spellbinding* dribble which leaves the defender in *knots*.

Meat and drink

Along with *bread and butter*, these are the basics which everyone expects a player to do well. *Meat and drink* is curiously applied to goalkeepers more than any other position. *"And Fabián Espíndola's shot goes straight down veteran US net-minder Busch's throat, that's just meat and drink for a stopper of his experience."*

Media conspiracy

Convenient excuse levelled at the fourth estate by the under-pressure manager. Often referred to as a *stir*, the media are blamed for a club's woes in a variety of circumstances:

1. Driving down squad morale by savaging team performances.
2. Constant speculation over the future of the manager.
3. Fabrication of stories surrounding allegedly unsettled players.

Mega

Informal adjective used to provide context to the magnitude of things, including:

1. *Mega deal.* A transfer deal of silly proportions, which could also be afforded the description *mind blowing*.
2. *Mega rich.* Usually reserved for the owners of clubs, particularly those who have recently completed a takeover, injecting many millions of pounds in the process (e.g. Paris St Germain). Although it can also apply to the long-established *behemoths* of the game too. Also called *mega bucks*.
3. *Mega offer.* A proposal tabled, presumably, by the *mega rich* owner; wages are usually talked of in *eye-watering* terms.

Melee
A confused, angry scuffle found either on the pitch or the touchline. *"The reducer from Ferguson and the resulting melee saw fists flying, and left referee Probert with some sorting out to do."*

Men against boys
1. A one sided affair.
2. Morpeth Town AFC v Morpeth Town U11s.

Mercenary
A *lone gun for hire* to the highest bidder. This type of player will have many clubs during a long and protracted career that may extend into his 40s. Doesn't really buy into the *way* of a club, is just after one last pay day, or in Gervinho's case a helicopter and private beach. Some of the later clubs in his career may read more like a *charge sheet*. A less than complimentary term for a *journeyman footballer*.

Etymology: Individual who takes part in an armed conflict and whose main motivation is money or other personal gain. According to the Geneva Convention, they do not have a right to be a combatant or a prisoner of war; however, on capture they are afforded the usual protections with regards to a fair trial and treatment.

Mercurial talent
Footballers who possess a *mercurial talent* have this attribute in spades, without doubt adding an *extra dimension* to the team. *"From leapfrogging players in a goalmouth scramble to sticking one in the top corner from 25 yards, Jimmy Bullard is the undoubtedly the ultimate mercurial talent."*

Etymology: Originating from the Roman God Mercury who among others was the patron of trickery.

Mere mortals
The masses who are just not blessed with the *prodigious talent* of the chosen few. Lionel Messi, for example does things that *mere mortals* can only dream of.

Suggests that whilst we are made of skin and bone, these footballers possess God-like abilities, which apparently is leaving three or more defenders *for dead*.

Messiah
The saviour of a football club, heralded by all for rescuing them. However, the term can be prematurely coined; Alan Shearer was anointed *the Messiah* in 2009 when given eight games to save the Magpies. It wasn't to be, and the Geordie Nation was consigned to the Championship.

Meteoric rise
The journey from *also ran* to *world beater* in an astonishingly short time. It is a paradox of sorts, as meteors fall to earth rather than rise. In footballing terms, a player might be turning out for Bedworth United one season, before being *snapped up* by Aston Villa the next. From meagre beginnings to *hero status*, there are many examples of these *rags to riches* stories such as Glenn Murray's meteoric rise from Workington Reds to Crystal Palace and then Bournemouth. See also *shelf stacker*.

Midfield general
A dog of war who *marshals the troops*. The midfield general has the meticulous *discipline* of a member of the armed forces, and may also be known as the *midfield enforcer*. Typical traits include:
1. Pulling shorts high up over the waist.
2. Belting out the national anthem while on international duty.
3. Producing spectacular *snot rockets*.

Examples include Roy Keane, Gennaro Gattuso and Sam Wedgbury.

Mid-season slump
The second of a season's *triumvirate* of events. Those *early-season pacesetters* will undoubtedly be purveyors of a confidence-sapping *mid-season slump*. The traditional period that follows this is the *Europa League push*.

Mile offside
The standard unit of distance a player might find themselves beyond the last defender; despite the fact that a standard pitch length is between 90 and 120 metres. *"Clive he's a mile offside; for a player of his ability he should know better than that."* Slightly more than *clear daylight* but less than a *country mile*.

Mind games
The psychological battle that rages between managers in an attempt to win the battle before it has been fought. Usually *employed*, the most common time for *mind*

games is ahead of a *crunch clash*. Clearly, managers believe that their *barbs*, aimed in a passive aggressive manner, can create a *climate of fear* in the opposition dressing room thus giving their team the advantage going into the game.

Casting doubt on their credentials is one way of playing mind games; saying a side is *not quite ready for a title charge*, lacks experience, or has found it *difficult on their travels* are others. Many managers are known for these tactics; Sir Alex Ferguson would psych his opposite number by informing the media they would be denied the traditional post-match glass of red, whilst Jose Mourinho's antics are possibly in a league of their own.

Minnows
The small fish struggling to stay afloat. Often described as *plucky*, they are usually *written off* before a match, with the chances of getting any sort of result rated as extremely unlikely. International minnows are the most common, such as San Marino, Andorra and Liechtenstein; however, they also feature in cup competitions.

Minority
The *"few idiots"* a manager says is responsible for a large majority of discontent in the stands. Also known as the *vocal minority*. Once fans are back onside, they are praised for showing their *true colours*.

Misfit
Player who fails to settle at a club (usually one of many throughout his career). It is often the case they are blessed with prodigious talent, but a lack of application means they are unable to harness it. *"Southampton misfit Osvaldo failed to adapt to 'physical' Premier League."* They are very likely to become the *journeymen* of tomorrow.

Mismatch
Something of a David and Goliath affair, it is one that you could put your house on going the way of the *big boys*. *"Bit of a mismatch out there today, but do you give Hemel Hempstead any chance against big-spending Ebsfleet?"* May also be an on-field *mismatch*, such as Cristiano Ronaldo versus pretty much any La Liga defender.

Modern day great
Working on the assumption that those who played in the olden days were usually the greats of the game. *"Mark Bresiano is a modern day great of Australian football. A true gentleman of the game. Quiet in nature, Bresc has always let his feet do the talking."* Modern day greats are few and far between, as it usually takes time to mature into one.

Modern era of football

A period of time which is hotly debated. For some it is the 90s onwards, however others believe it stretches back to anything after 1966. Grandads might have everyone else believe it was anything post-war. Essentially this era is subjective and probably comes down to whoever the person in question can remember from their childhood; that being Wilf Mannion, Ray Clemence or Eyal Berkovic.

Momentum

Momentum is a crucial thing in football. It can be *gained* through a series of positive results, and therefore taken into the next game. However, it may also be *handed* to the opposition through an error, giving them the all-important *impetus*. *"As the ding dong battle neared its conclusion, it was Conference new boys Guiseley who grabbed the momentum in search of the crucial winning goal."*

Money men

Traditionally, Sky.

Money spinner

A tie that produces a welcome boost to club *coffers*. The non-league side that has heroically battled its way to the FA Cup third round may be *salivating* at the *prospect* of a *money-spinning* tie with one of the Premier League's *big boys*.

Moneybags

Almost always applies to sides that have been the *subject* of a *billionaire takeover*. Often used when assessing an opponent's chances: *"Can Swansea get anything at the Etihad, home of moneybags Manchester City?"* Not generally applied to teams who have always been the *big spenders*, because presumably the tradition and history surrounding the club defines them as opposed to being seen as Johnny-come-latelys.

Morale

Mental state in reference to confidence, happiness or determination. Morale is a key component in any team, however it must be nurtured by embarking on a *run of results*. New signings may also boost the squad. *"You can see everyone has grown a couple of inches since Carlos arrived here."* On the other hand, losses which are heavy or unexpected can be described as *morale sapping defeats*.

Mountain to climb

1. A hefty first leg deficit may leave a side with a *mountain to climb* in the return fixture. That it is a mountain provides some indication of the sheer scale of the task facing the side in question, and the dusting off of crampons and down jackets is unlikely to have any effect. *"We've left*

ourselves with a mountain to climb next week. My advice to our fans is you don't need to book time off work for the semi-finals. " In true mixed metaphor form, managers refuse to throw in the towel when they have such a task on their hands.

2. Conceding two or more goals *early doors* creates a monumental task for a side that has been punished for their *sluggish start* and now find themselves *up against it.*

Mr

The player who has devoted many years of service (or indeed a *one club* player) is bestowed the prestigious title *Mr.* He is the sort of player who encompasses exactly what the club is about, because he knows their way and is the standard bearer for it. Keith Ryan is often described as *Mr Wycombe*, Steve Bull as *Mr Wolves*, and Alan Knight as *Mr Portsmouth*. Sol Campbell, without doubt is not *Mr Spurs*. Whether this phrase is transferred to other countries is not known; as such we will not know if Karl-Heinz Körbel is *Herr Eintracht Frankfurt*, neither if Claude Puel is *Monsieur Monaco.*

Much maligned

Term used about a player who is most certainly not the fans' favourite, i.e. a target of the *boo boys.* It causes uproar in the stands when said player is seen *stripping off* in readiness to come on, as there were *ironic cheers* when he was taken off last week.

The phrase can also be used when the player in question has done something positive (before it is qualified why he was *much maligned* in the first place). *"The ball fizzed across the area from the right before the much-maligned Trinidadian arrived at the back post for his first goal in almost 14 hours of football."*

Mudbath

A pitch which harks back to the good old days of caser footballs, rattles and manually operated scoreboards; mudbaths were commonly found in the 1950s but are now more the preserve of the lower leagues in May. These pitches are a great *leveller* in cup ties. Ramshackle grounds may also feature this: *"The changing rooms have a leak, the seats have splinters and the pitch is an absolute mudbath."*

Mullered

1. A shot *smashed* into the back of the net with *considerable force.* *"Straight back to St Andrews where the lead did not last long! What's happening Bryn Law? City straight back in it Jeff. Great work by Demarai Gray down the right flank, he drilled it across the face of goal, and there was Clayton Donaldson – who has been quiet until now – to muller it into the back of the net from six yards."*

2. An *uncompromising* tackle. For example Kevin Muscat was known on many an occasion to *muller* his opponent.

Murdered
The phrase is only used when a side didn't get the required result; for a manager to say his side *murdered* the other when they emerged victorious would of course be disrespectful – although it does happen.

Muted celebrations
More of an acknowledgment than anything else, they are seen when a player strikes against his former club; no doubt out of *respect* for his former employers. Includes looking at the floor, making apologetic hand gestures, and a refusal to let his teammates jump all over him. However, schools of thought now believe *making a point* of not celebrating is as bad as going *absolutely nuts*. A classic example is Frank Lampard's muted celebration on equalising for Manchester City against Chelsea in 2014, and the antithesis is Adebayor's full-pitch goad of Arsenal's travelling faithful for the Citizens in 2009.

My word
Phrase favoured by *sideways-passer* Ray Wilkins, who often utters it in surprise or pleasure. Students are known to partake in a drinking game where alcohol must be consumed every time he utters the phrase, apparently with numerous incidents of hospitalisation and stomach pumping. See also *young man*.

N

Nadir
The low point of a season or career. Teams are said to reach their *nadir* when it is thought that things can get no worse for them. *"Hammers humbling at hands of Forest sees them reach their nadir."* It is also the first name of Nadir Çiftçi, the surprisingly successful Turkish striker.

Naive
"The inability to close the game out at 2-1 was down to a bit of naivety on our part; we don't need to go chasing the third goal." Failure to transform a winning position into three points is one classic example of naivety in football; the other being reacting to provocation from a known wind-up merchant. *"He's got the reaction he wanted, and I'm afraid the lad has got to go."* Common retrospective advice from a pundit would be that *"there's no need for him to get involved"* because *"they are clearly trying to get one of the Arsenal lads sent off."*

Narrow angle

A *narrow* or *tight* angle is always described as such when a player fires in a shot from out wide. Shots never seem to come in from a *wide* angle, and very rarely from an *acute* angle (which only the geometrically gifted commentator might know, having remembered his 11+ maths lessons). Goalkeepers may also *narrow* the *angle* to try to reduce the chance of a goal.

Naysayers

Those who do not believe. The bloke down the pub who still thinks the hat trick hero is a *"shithouse"*.

Nearly men

The side within touching distance of success, who fall at the final hurdle. Certainly a tag to be *shed*. *"Benfica have been the nearly men of the Europa league in recent times, failing to win the trophy despite getting to the final in consecutive years."*

Nearly put through his own net

A close call, where a player almost scores an OG (the phrase isn't used that often when he actually does put the ball through his own net, although examples do exist). The term *through* is not based on the velocity or venom in the strike, as the ball doesn't go through the net in the literal sense. A dribbling, limp *scuff* has the same descriptor as an accidental three-yard howitzer that lands with the force of an atomic bomb – see Wayne Hatswell for Forest Green v Morecambe in the FA Cup third round in 2000.

Neutral

"Even more slapstick defending led to goal number eight of the day. A great game for the neutrals, but painful viewing for anyone with a vested interest; indeed, Lee Clark must have been tearing his hair out at what he was seeing." Neutrals are the luckiest of football fans, for it is they who are able to enjoy swashbuckling goal-fests in all their glory. For those who have a vested interest, it is certain to be nail-biting stuff. *"Both defences have had a day off today Gary."*

Never write them off

Certain sides should never be written off, and if an opposition does this, it is at their *peril*. Manchester United were perhaps the most dangerous side of all time to be written off; Fergie's boys had a fearsome reputation as *comeback Kings*, regularly snatching victory from the jaws of defeat, the most famous of all being their 1999 Champions League triumph.

Nibble

A foul to test the water with the referee. *"He's had a nibble at Mahrez there Martin, but the ref's let that one go; we're only in the first five after all. Second half and we might have been looking at a yellow."*

Niggle

Most commonly found in its adjective form of *niggly*, this encompasses two areas:

1. *Injury.* The hallmark of the *injury plagued.*
2. *Foul.* A scrappy war of attrition is likely to feature a plethora of *niggly fouls,* with play being broken up by a fussy ref at regular intervals. *"It's been one niggly foul after another Sam, no wonder Blackburn have struggled to find any sort of rhythm."*
3. An irritant. The type of footballer who consistently winds up the opposition by:
   a)   Throwing himself to the deck in a theatrical manner, with accompanying roll-overs.
   b)   Brandishing imaginary yellow cards.
   c)   Standing on the 'keeper's toes at a corner.

No end product

The most frustrating of players; one who gets the hard part right before getting the easy part very wrong. As Steve McClaren once said: *"One – you have to defend well. Two – you have to pass the ball well. Three – you have to have an end product."* Ron Atkinson would refer to this type of player as an *amusement arcade.*

No man's land

Area to which the goalkeeper strays after coming for and failing *to collect* a cross. *"Digby's been caught in no man's land, leaving the net totally unguarded."* Being caught here was a common trait of *eccentric French net minder* Fabian Barthez.

No nonsense

Different *no nonsense* traits exist for each position:

1. Goalkeeper: Will go through anyone to get the ball; even their own player. Likely to ignore the plaudits from teammates on saving a penalty.
2. Defender: Looks to clear the ball as far away from danger as possible. Will put his head on anything, at great personal risk.
3. Midfielder: Steams into challenges then quickly takes up their position for the resultant free kick. *"McManus doesn't even look back to check on his stricken opponent. It's no nonsense stuff, get the challenge in and get on with it."*
4. Striker: Lacks skill but possesses power in spades. Their strike-rate is usually the same as their yellow cards-per-game ratio – about one in five. Kevin Davies was perhaps the archetypal example of such a player.

No quarter given or asked

A *feisty* affair where both teams are going at it *full throttle*. Neither side will ask for the other to go easy, and nor would they be willing to oblige. The same applies to opponents *flying in* to the tackle. A favourite of Tony Gubba on International *Superstar Soccer '98* (along with *"Surely that's got to be a penalty!"*)

No right

"What a screamer from Pericard! The boy has no right to be scoring from there!" A goal plucked from such improbability that there is simply no entitlement on behalf of the scorer to even contemplate hitting the back of the net. Goalkeepers too have no right to save certain shots, particularly when clawing out a ball from right on the goal line at full-stretch, such as David Seaman versus Sheffield United in the FA Cup semi-final of 2003; a save which defies logic.

No split loyalties

"Let me tell you, I have the utmost respect for everyone up in Dingwall but once I cross that white line there'll be no split loyalties." Despite having a strong association in the past with an opponent, come the day of the game there will be no question about the allegiance of the player in question. It is similar to having *no time for sentiment,* when one may have the chance to hurt one's previous employers, especially when they are struggling. Should they score the player will decline to celebrate *out of respect.*

No stranger to controversy

Someone who finds himself making the *headlines* for all the wrong reasons. From insulting the club on social media to reacting furiously at being substituted, this hothead courts controversy on an almost weekly basis. Many footballers have amassed a lengthy *charge sheet* throughout the years, including such high profile names as Pepe, El-Hadji Diouf and Luis Suarez.

Nominal fee

A fee so small it is not worth reporting, for example two bottles of Teachers, a set of training bibs and a box set of At Home with the Braithwaites.

Nonsense players

Players who are better known for their off field shenanigans than what they do on the pitch. This type of player is prone to high profile antics that fill the tabloid press with glee. Gary Neville once – with some justification – described Mario Balotelli as a *nonsense player.* The sort of player who might be arrested more times than he scores in a season; no matter though, a succession of managers will profess themselves to be the one to finally tame them.

Not out of the woods
Managers will always believe their team to be in danger until they are mathematically certain of survival. As such, despite a wonderful run of 12 points from an available 15, the team will still be very much in the woods; essentially, they have found the path but the compass still isn't working and they don't have their orienteering badge yet.

Not talking about other team's players
Harry Redknapp during his managerial career, c.1983-2015. *"No he belongs to another club so I won't comment... but I'd love to make him part of the squad."*

Not that type of player
Someone who usually, most certainly, is *that type of player*. A comment trotted out post-match by the offender's manager in attempt to defend their 10 yard dash to execute a double-footed *coward's challenge* on a player they have a *bit of previous* with.

Notable absentee
The player everyone would have expected to start, but his omission is somewhat of a surprise as no injury was reported at the pre-match press conference. Perhaps the best example of a *notable absentee* is Ronaldo, and his failure to start the World Cup final in France '98.

Notch
1. Alternative to score. *"Danny Hylton bagged another to take his tally to 14 for the season, he's been notching left, right and centre for the Yellows."*
2. *Top-notch*. The cream of the crop. Players considered the best in the division could be heralded as a *top notch* player, whilst strikes of a similar ilk are also afforded this description.
3. Sporting Vereniging Notch, a football team in Suriname's top flight.

Nowhere to hide
Furtive statement made in the *gaffer's* post-match interview after an absolute *battering*. *"We have nowhere to hide... it's going to be a long week,"* said Gus Poyet after seeing his Sunderland side *mauled* 8-0 by Southampton. Managers will do one or more of the following:
1. Refuse to look at the lads until at least Tuesday.
2. Refuse to speak to them until at least Wednesday.
3. Close his living room curtains.

Numerical advantage
For some reason, when a team finds themselves a man to the good, *numerical* is often prefixed; either that or it is called an *extra-man advantage*. *"With the best part of*

half an hour to go, we shall see if the Southport boys can make their numerical advantage count. " This sort of benefit will often be transformed into all three points.

Nutmegged
Perhaps the easiest trick to pull off at any level, but arguably the most satisfying. It is mandatory for the player with the ball to shout out *"megs!"* or *"megged!"* as he is in the process of making his opponent look stupid. The term is not used in other countries but they do have their own variants. In The Ukraine, it is known as *p'yatdesyat kopiyok* meaning *50 cents*, as if this is what the player who has been nutmegged owes the other. In France it is called *petit pont* which translates as *little bridge*, and in Japan they call it *mata yuki*, which in English is *crotch punching*.

O

Obscurity
1. The murky underbelly of football concealed by the bright lights of the Premier League (although arguably is a relative term which differs from team to team). It is acceptable to say Charlie Austin was *plucked from non-league obscurity* at Poole Town by Swindon, but the higher up the football pyramid you go, Swindon themselves may be seen as obscure by, for example, Watford. Obscurity is different to the *wilderness*, which is a place to be *returned* from.
2. A side going nowhere. *"Darlington's season has tailed off, consigning them to mid-table obscurity for another year."*

Obviously, you know, I mean
Opening words to most post-match interviews with a footballer. It is more about stumbling vocabulary and run-of-the-mill stock phrases than anything else. *"Obviously, you know, I mean it was great to get the win today, it was nice to get on the score sheet but three points is the main thing."* The phrase is almost always delivered with a hand on the neck, a look away to their left and wincing expression as if they are looking up into the loft.

Off the ball incident
There are many kinds of *off the ball incidents* including head-butts, spitting, remonstrations with the opposition bench and furious reactions to crowd provocation. It is a moment when the linesman really can earn his corn by being that *extra pair of eyes*. If the incident is missed by the officials it may be referred to the TV panel for retrospective action (referee's match report pending). *"Moshni had been booked for an off-the-ball incident with Airdrie's Jim Lister before having to be restrained as the teams left the field at full time, when he earned a second yellow."*

Because these incidents aren't seen as part of the game itself, the sanctions may be much more severe. Clattering into the back of an opposition player is viewed in a much dimmer light if the play was right up the other end of the pitch, 100 yards away from the football.

Offers something different
To have an unusual style of play or a sought after physical attribute, although the 'something different' is left unspoken, and therefore understood: *"Izale offers something different to the team, but we all know he is a natural goalscorer and it provides us with strong competition up front."* *Lightning quick* players who can provide that *extra zip* in midfield, or those who are willing to *take on their man* time and time again also offer something different to the norm.

Offloaded
To clear the books, fringe players may be deemed *surplus to requirements*. Those who have been a marked disappointment are usually *shipped out* at the first opportunity, such as Cardiff City record purchase Andreas Cornelius who was *offloaded* in the January transfer window in 2014. Other reasons for offloading players are the need to *balance the books*, or comply with financial fair play obligations. Rarer occasions will see the ball offloaded during the match, which is possibly borrowed from the rugby term offload in the tackle.

Offside trap
Sneakily set by a defence who operate a *flat back four*. Some players are more susceptible than others, such as Filippo Inzaghi, who was apparently *born offside*. Commentators are often unwilling to make a decision as to whether he's *level* or *just off*, despite having the evidence before their very eyes. It is always a source of worry and/or hilarity when there is *clear daylight* and the pundit still can't decide, and as such give *benefit of the doubt* to the attacker. *"I'm not sure about that one Jonathan, but if there's no clear daylight you've got to say he's on."* If the striker does find a way past it, it will be considered *beaten* or *sprung*.

Old
1. *Adversary.* Seen when the greats clash; there is a very clear element of respect between the warring factions despite their differences, such as Sacchi/Capello, Keane/Vieira and Torquay/Exeter.
2. *Fashioned...* Any player considered to play the game the way it used to be. Seen somewhat as a *dying breed* because they *don't make them like that anymore*, and the modern game is struggling to incorporate their more direct style. Old fashioned players cover the following positions:
   a) *Centre forward.* The epitome of Englishness, a player who is beefy, good in the air and knows where the net is. There is no doubt his

manager will rate him as a *proper centre forward*. The phrase is seen by some as having slightly patronising connotations arguing that a player, such as Ricky Lambert, has *so much more to his game* than that.

b) *Winger*. Someone who mesmerises defences with his dribbling prowess. *"The Tractor Boy's Ryan Fraser produced skill reminiscent of the great Sir Stanley Matthews himself."*

c) *Centre half*. It's as if this breed of player was born 35 years old, immobile and made of granite. Is what the phrase *rock at the heart of defence* was created for. No doubt was barking instructions to his back four straight from the womb.

3. *Foe*. Similar to *old adversary*, *foes* carry a more sinister connotation. It is entirely possible there could have been a *touchline spat* between two opposing managers. Additionally, one may have made *inflammatory* comments about the other at a pre-match press conference, such as Arsene Wenger being labelled a *specialist in failure* by Jose Mourinho. *Post-match handshakes* may be foregone, causing a *media stir*.

4. *Guard*. Wielding considerable influence in the dressing room, they are the perfect mentors, role models and ambassadors for the club. On the negative side, *player power* can become an issue with such employees, who on occasion believe their opinions should be given more weight than perhaps they are entitled. A move to the coaching staff seems inevitable. The opposite of *young guns*.

5. *School footballer*. If British, these are stereotypically bald and overweight men who would burst into flames if they ever saw a tub of moisturiser in their immediate vicinity. They may also possess an industrious English name that would automatically rule them out of being an elite footballer these days; but this was never a problem for Steve Frogatt. If foreign they are identifiable by a couple of factors, including (i) being signed from abroad for a nominal fee yet slotted straight into the first team, and (ii) having a dodgy bowl haircut. This player is most likely to have appeared in Panini's Premier League sticker album at any time between 1992 and 2000.

Old head on young shoulders

Footballers who are capable of pulling things off that belie their tender years. Is always a technical or mental attribute which impresses: *"Christophe Berra has rightly been handed the armband at Tynecastle, although he's 21 he's got an old head on those young shoulders."*

Omens
Cryptic term regarding superstition in the same vein as *Indian sign* or *hoodoo*.
Omens carry an important weight to footballing matters. *"The omens are good for
Neil Harris' men having won five of their last six encounters in this fixture."* The term can
be a little more obscure; a commentator on a fact hunt may produce a murky
statistic to bring some level of gravitas to a game with little spice: *"Sunderland really
don't like Mondays, having failed to win under the floodlights for almost four years, so the
omens are not on their side."*

On a cold Tuesday in Stoke
Successor to the *cold Wednesday in Rochdale*. Prodigiously talented players might be
setting the continent alight, producing *scintillating football* on a weekly basis, however
there is one true acid test to determine whether they are able to cut the mustard
in the world's greatest league. *Would they be up for it on a cold Tuesday in Stoke?*

The battle-hardened may cope with temperatures that dip below two degrees, but
in the minds of some, Lionel Messi certainly couldn't. Many believe that the
familiar, comfortable surroundings of the Camp Nou would be too far away for
the Argentinian wizard, who would only have a post-match Hanley kebab to keep
him warm.

The phrase is now used almost entirely in jest, no-one, even the most humourless
of pundit, would fail to recognise this assessment has become a rather large
parody of itself.

On a collision course
Collision courses can be *set* for many reasons, including:
1. Casting *admiring glances* at an under contract player.
2. Contract *wrangles*.
3. International managers playing players for more than the agreed 45
   minutes, and an injury has resulted.
4. Cup draws which put a manager or player up against his former club as if
   it were destiny.
5. National governments who involve themselves in the nation's football
   administration, something expressly forbidden by FIFA.

On our day
Assertion by a manager that, *"On our day we can beat anyone."* So there will be no *fear
factor* from the less-fancied side. It is a contrast to the thoughts of a manager
when his team are playing an inferior team, such as in a cup competition when
they might say, *"We respect the opposition, they're a dangerous side and they have the players*

to hurt us." In essence, all managers believe they can beat the best and lose to the worst, because *that's football.*

On paper

The exercise of comparing two sides directly. Gives an indication as to which team has the stronger starting line-up. *"On paper, the Saddlers should win this at a canter, but we all know that football isn't played on paper and when it comes down to it, it's just eleven against eleven."*

On red alert

Rumours of an unsettled player will always put potential suitors on *red alert.* It is a phrase found in print rather than broadcast mediums. *"West Ham on red alert over Konoplyanka."*

On the cards

An outcome for a team or individual; however in football the phrase is often used to express surprise that something has happened: *"Superb comeback from AFC Wimbledon! Oh this most certainly was not on the cards at 4.15!"*

Etymology: Alludes to the possibility of an event happening based on what type of cards come up in a tarot reading; for example seeing death signals there is likely to be a great amount of change in the individual's life.

On the fringes

Mostly of the first team. The type of player who performs a *bit part role* and is just as likely to turn out for the *development squad* as the starting XI. It is seen as a positive for someone who has been in the youth set up (usually since the age of eight or nine), and might be on the verge of *breaking into* the first team; however it is not such a plus for a player who needs first team football at a particular stage of his career, especially if a major tournament is looming. Teams may also be *on the fringes* of the playoffs and as such are *in with a shout.*

On the plane

Every player in international *reckoning* wants to be *on the plane* when it comes to the major tournaments. The run up to such occasions leads to furious speculation in the press about whether someone has done enough to *book their ticket,* or perhaps to have *secured their seat. "Shelvey hoping club form will earn him plane ticket to France."* A late season surge of form may have fans up in arms at greasy spoon *brains trusts* across the nation to get him on the plane.

On the rocks

It tends to be relationships in soap operas that are *on the rocks*; however, in football there are a couple of situations to which the phrase applies in particular:

1. *Takeover deals.* Long and protracted discussions are likely to run aground for some reason or another. For example, a prospective owner may have trouble explaining to the FA why they were convicted of tax evasion in their own country. Or during due diligence, a huge hole may be discovered in a club's finances.

2. Transfer deals too can be *on the rocks*. However, they are more likely to hit the rocks. In a continuation of the nautical theme, these deals are said to be *scuppered*. Perhaps because of greedy agents or exorbitant wage demands.

One eye on

The justification for playing *the stiffs* in a cup tie is often because the gaffer has *one eye on* an important match the following week. Players may also be subbed early in the second half for the same reason. If it goes wrong, the decision can be tabloid fodder, however if the outcome is positive it's a masterstroke or clever use of squad rotation by a manager with the *Midas touch*.

One for the cameras

Over-egged *Hollywood save* from the 'keeper. Usually consists of an acrobatic dive across the goalmouth with three or four rolls added in for good measure. It is clearly for show with the express intention of putting himself in the *shop window*. *"Perhaps one for the cameras, but Gomes has to be alert to keep out Varney's drive after he ran at the Hornet's defence and lashed a shot towards goal."*

One of those

"It's one of those." One of what, Andy? Seemingly as innately known as it is esoteric.

One thing on his mind

The one-track, *tunnel-visioned* footballer who treads the line between clinical finishing *fan favourite* and *"a greedy bastard"* depending on strike rate and the ability to spot a teammate in space – who will no doubt be left howling as he elects to shoot. If a player knows that his run will end up in a goal, it implies supreme confidence: *"Bradley Goldberg had one thing on his mind as he ghosted past two defenders and arrowed a shot into the corner from 20 yards."*

One-club man
Someone who has devoted their entire career to one club. The legacy for this type of pro is to have their framed photos greeting you on arrival, possibly a function suite named after him, or if he's really lucky a stand.

One club men are revered at all levels. Ryan Giggs is perhaps the best-known example in the United Kingdom, *clocking up* almost 1,000 appearances in a Manchester United shirt (although this is arguably not so as he did play youth football for the blue half of the city). Many other one-club men have graced the English game throughout the years. John Askey probably never has to buy a pint in Macclesfield again, having amassed a whopping 698 appearances in a career that spanned 19 years (and two managerial stints on top of that). Colin Cowperthwaite played over 700 times for Barrow, and John Trollope over 800 for Swindon Town.

One-footed
The inability to use anything other than a player's strongest foot. It is a quirk that many of these players are left-footed; it is never expected that a right-footed player should intermittently use his weaker side. In actual fact, a right-footed player who commonly uses his left might be termed both-footed and praised as such; conversely a left footed player who never uses his right often comes in for criticism. *"Well Brian, if only James McClean had a right foot, we'd be putting him in the 'world beater' category."*

One-on-One
A straight shootout between the goalkeeper and the attacker. It is the quintessential *clear-cut* chance. Reference to this *situation* is used as justification for why a side didn't win, despite their best efforts. *"We created three one-on-one situations today, but Flinders was equal to everything our strikers threw at him."* Commentators will often opine: *"He usually buries those."*

One-two
Exchange of passes where a player receives the ball back from his teammate. Described quite often as a *nice little one two*. It is always a pleasant moment in the game when an unwitting one-two is played off the referee.

One-way ticket
The kind of air fare (usually) which is either bought by a player who is desperate for a route out of a club or by the fans on behalf of a player who is a) more trouble than he is worth (and no doubt will have to pay for the extra *baggage* allowance) or b) has failed to live up to his billing.

One-way traffic
Situation where one side is completely dominant. *"It's all one way traffic here at the Crown ground, with the Bees unable to get out of their own half."* There may be certain moments that change a game and from *there on in* it is *one-way traffic*; however sometimes it is just from the outset. A red card or a killer second goal is a good example.

Onion bag
Colloquial term for the net. Teams are often said to *billow* the back of it.

Opening
Openings in football can be a number of very different things:
1. *Day fixtures*. Perhaps the only time in a campaign when optimism sweeps the vast majority of the 92 football league clubs. For many, it is all downhill from this point.
2. *Ceremony*. Usually to a World Cup or European Championships. Are generally thought to be an unadulterated crap-fest, no more so than when Diana Ross managed to miss a gilt-edged chance from a mere six yards, destroying the goalposts in the process. A football first, no doubt.
3. A *chance*. *"For all Port Vale's dominance, it was the 49th minute before they fashioned an opening."*

Opportunity
There are many types of *opportunity* a player can have. It may be a *simple close range tap in, clear sight of goal or a golden* or *presentable opportunity*. Opportunism is a trait good strikers are known for; however it is usually because a chance has simply fallen into their lap – although they are still praised (in comparison to political opportunism which is always an accusation). *"Jack Muldoon showed great opportunism after the initial spill by the 'keeper."*

Orbit
The destination of wayward efforts which often come down with snow on top. *"Peter Fear put that one into orbit, the fans in row Z are more worried than the 'keeper."* References may also be made to a player's penalty sometimes weeks after he skied it in a top competition; *"it's still coming down Jeff."* In the United States this is known as a *moon shot*.

Orchestrator
The conductor of the team who is at the heart of *all that is good* about a side. A technically gifted player, he *pulls the strings* from the *engine room*, creating opportunities and generally dictating play. *"Hessenthaler was the orchestrator of wave after wave of Gillingham attacks."*

Out and out

The purest form of a position, mostly commonly a forward who earns the title because he does nothing but score goals. The phrase is often referenced to highlight deficiencies in a team, or squads of a certain calibre. *"What many of the basement boys lack is an out and out striker to pull them clear of the relegation mire; they all need that mystical 20-goal a season man."*

Out of his depth

The struggling *rookie* centre back who has had a torrid time all afternoon can be said to be clearly *out of his depth*. Fans might discuss how he is not *cut out* for this level, but may find his feet a little lower down the league ladder. Also applies to officials deemed inexperienced in handling a pressure cooker environment.

Out of sight

To describe a side who are totally dominant. However, it is a term often used during criticism of a side profligate in front of goal. *"The Owls have squandered a host of gilt-edged opportunities in the first half, and they really should be out of sight here."*

Outfit

Alternative name for a team. *"Can Conference outfit Boreham Wood cause a shock against their more illustrious opponents?"*

Outlay

A club may sanction a *sizeable* outlay on a player whom they think will really add something to the side. However, it can become embarrassing when it proves fruitless and the maths is done to find out how much they cost per match. Andy Carroll, for example, cost Liverpool a cool £795,000 per appearance. Calculations may also be on goals, which means Sergei Rebrov cost Spurs £1m per strike.

Outstretched

1. *Leg. Outstretched legs* can be utilised by crafty or cheating players to garner a free kick or claim a penalty. A famous exponent of this was Arsenal *Invincible* and hairband-bothering Alexandre Dumas enthusiast Robert Pires.
2. *Arm.* The betrayal of the *outstretched arm* often leads to a penalty kick. Sometimes players make outrageous attempts to conceal their transgression, none more famous than Steven Taylor's pretending-to-be-shot shenanigans for Newcastle against Aston Villa in 2005.

Over the moon

One of the early clichés, football brought this phrase into common usage, as Niall McGinn can illustrate: *"It was just an unbelievable feeling to score against Portugal, as well as it being my first international goal, so I am just over the moon."*

Overlap

Overlapping players excel when they are *blessed* with an *abundance of pace*, because there is a high chance they will leave any defender *trailing in their wake;* it would not be possible to get Gareth Barry or Seb Larsson to produce a particularly effective overlap (despite their other talents). It is a phrase used with increasingly regularity in isolation, such as *"Debuchy tried to cut out Rose's overlap"* where *run* is understood.

Overnight

Period of time when it is impossible for a side to turn into a bad team.

Own backyard

The home ground. Usually a place to be embarrassed or *found out* in. *"After the pasting Gateshead received in their own backyard in August, they will be looking to exact revenge on the Shrimpers."*

P

P45

Standard form that all professions are given on leaving a job, although much more seems to be made of it being given to *beleaguered* football managers. It has become a by-word for *sacked, fired, shown the door,* etc. West Ham against Spurs was branded the *P45 derby* in 2014 when both Sam Allardyce and Tim Sherwood were *neck and neck* in the *sack race.* A sending off and a 2-0 defeat later, Sherwood won it by a nose.

Pacesetters

Those teams leading an *embryonic* league table. Will therefore be the *early season pacesetters.*

It tends to be the eager yet limited sides which come *tearing out of the traps*, get a stitch half way round and allow those who are *seasoned title challengers* to stake their claim down the *home stretch.* Pacesetters are prime candidates for the *mid-season slump,* possibly because the heavyweights have tabled a £30m bid for their centre forward – an offer which they cannot refuse.

Pacy

Nippy, often *little*, player who adds a certain zest to the side. Such *pacy* players inject some much-needed urgency, especially in the last twenty minutes when time is running out. The term has also slightly evolved into *paciness*, which seems perhaps unique to football. *"The paciness of the Bloomfield Road turf meant the ball zipped around, causing problems for the less technically able in both sides."* Indeed, this term can also be a substitute for pacy: *"Danny Green's paciness was a constant thorn in the Daggers' side all afternoon."*

A player can also be described as having *pace to burn*, which could be *frightening*, *blistering* or *electric*; however there are those out there who have *deceptive* pace, possibly *for a big man*: *"Koller possessed remarkable pace for a player of his stature… and mobility."*

Pain barrier

The threshold to which a player is willing to *play through* in order to help his team. Players either promise to go through the barrier, or it emerges afterwards that they made such a sacrifice. *"Fredrik Ljungberg is expected to play through the pain barrier and take his place in Sweden's starting line-up when they meet England on Sunday."* It is of course relative, Bert Trautmann played on with a broken neck, while Shola Ameobi once came off with blisters.

Palmed away

On the sliding scale of goalkeeping clearances, *palmed away* does not feature highly, however it is one rung higher than a *flap*. Getting *two hands* to a shot, putting a *strong fist* on a cross, and *diverting it to safety* are all much more preferable choices. Palming a shot straight to the opposition is a distinct possibility, so is not advised. *"Enckeleman's attempt at a palm away from a Mateja Kezman drive only went as far as Gudjohnsen, who did the rest."*

Pandemonium

Common sight in the stands after a goal has been scored. Pandemonium is *absolute* or *complete*, provoking differing types of *scenes*.

Etymology: Pandæmonium is the name for the 'high capital of Satan and all his peers' in John Milton's 17th century epic poem Paradise Lost. It was reputed to have been built by the fallen angels in roughly one hour, yet far exceeded the size of earth. Pan is Latin for 'all' while 'dæmonium' roughly translates as 'evil spirit'.

Panenka

The ultimate *cheeky* penalty, chipped straight down the middle of the goal, *bamboozling* the 'keeper.

Etymology: Pioneered by Antonin Panenka during the 1976 European Championship final, when he produced an impudent chip in surely the finest display of nerves of steel ever seen. The penalty has been reproduced countless times since, not always successfully, as many on YouTube have discovered.

Panic

1. *Button.* Managers will always decline to press it with few, if any, ever admitting to doing so. *"Nigel Adkins is refusing to press the panic button in the transfer market despite the lack of new arrivals at Bramall Lane."* Reserved for difficult situations, it is unclear as to the benefits of pressing it.

2. *Buy.* Invariably is something that you can't polish, but you can roll in glitter. And pay £60k per week.

3. *Stations.* Anxious period, which applies in two main situations:

   a) The defence. The period of play will usually see them at *sixes and sevens* (or perhaps running around like headless chickens) when the opposition begin to ask *real* questions. Defences that are afflicted with this are considered to be flaky, leaky and prone to error. There is certainly no defensive rock *marshalling* them to victory (or indeed a *well-earned point*).

   b) A team or individual on a poor run of form will always deny that it is time for *panic stations* yet.

   Etymology: Another nautical phrase which has found its way into football; the order panic stations was given to a ship in distress.

Parade

End of season bus tour by a cup or league winning side. This tour may also be known as a *procession* or – if you are American – a *ticker tape parade*. It may also apply in matches with little riding on it: *"With the League One title safely in the bag, the final day stroll in the sunshine was a mere procession for Cotterill's Robins."*

Parked the bus

Putting *11 men behind the ball*. Managers with the express purpose of *grinding out a point* will attempt to *park the bus* in front of the goal and play a 4-6-0 formation. This can lead to accusations of *anti-football*. Teams can also park the bus having assumed that victory is secure although this can be a dangerous tactic that invites pressure.

Etymology: Perhaps one of the best-known recent editions to the language of football, Jose Mourinho said of Spurs after they drew 0-0 at Stamford Bridge in 2004, "As we say in Portugal, they brought the bus and they left the bus in front of the goal."

Part of the furniture

Club legends who have amassed many years of service are *part of the furniture* at a club. Upon retirement they will take their place alongside the *Lalique* table lamp in the chairman's office. See also *Mr.*

Parting shot

The jilted player, who has got more than a little to say for himself, might *lift the lid* on life at his previous club by *firing a parting shot*. *"My time there was pretty frustrating John, everybody knew the gaffer and me didn't see eye to eye. I either wasn't playing, or – when I was – it was out of position."* The jilted manager can also fire such shots; for example, Felix Magath at Fulham, who believed the English game had a lot to learn from the more advanced continent; the practice of applying cheese to injuries was perhaps more common at German clubs.

Etymology: The Parthian Empire ruled over parts of Persia in the 3rd century AD. Their horsemen and archers had a technique of confusing the enemy by appearing to flee whilst firing on them in order to lure them in and gain victory; it was seen as a highly effective and skilful tactic which became known as the 'Parthian shot'.

Partner in crime

The typical 'two up top' combination where the crime in question is goalscoring. The ideal partners in crime have a telepathic understanding with each other, one to provide the layoffs and the other to slam the ball into the back of the net. *"Nardiello and his partner in crime Lowe are the Bonnie and Clyde of League Two; they've been terrorising defences all season."* Can lead them to be on a big club's *most wanted* list.

Part-timers

Mildly patronising term to denote the status and ability of a side who are either playing a side way up the ladder or are achieving things far above their station. They are the most likely of sides to upset the apple cart. *"Can part-timers Blyth cause the ultimate shock after dispatching crisis club Hartlepool?"* During international games, the professions of the players are nearly always displayed on a graphic of their formation sheet. *"The San Marinese midfielder probably sold his teammates the boots they line up in tonight as he works in a sports shop."* A recent Faroe Islands squad included an electrician, a teacher and a road surfacer.

Passed up

Opportunities are most commonly *passed up*. If done so with regularity, the offending player may well gain a reputation as a *bottler*. Additionally, there are many famous examples of clubs that pass up the opportunity to sign players who go on to become world class; there is no better example than Jack Walker's response to the opportunity of signing Zinedine Zidane: *"We have Tim Sherwood."*

Peace talks
Acrimonious circumstances which are damaging to the club may require *such discussions* to make sure that things do not turn ugly. Implies that full on war has broken out in the dressing room, and it needs to be remedied through mediation. Players may have had a *bust up* with the manager, or there could be a *mutiny in the ranks* after a *winless run* leading to much *finger pointing*. Additionally the PFA will very often become involved when a player has told his manager that hell will freeze over before he plays under him again.

Pearler
A goal which would lead Andy Gray to exclaim, *"Oh you beauty!"*

Pecking order
The hierarchal system which decides whether a player starts a match or not. Those who are out of favour with the manager can be said to have *fallen down the pecking order*.

Etymology: It is initially believed this was a reference to dominance in the hen world, where pecking was one of the characteristics which asserted authority.

Pedestrian
The *pace* of pre-season friendlies, meaningless end of season fare, or drab matches which have *0-0 written all over them*. It can also denote a team's attitude towards a match. Those who adopt this stance will be frowned upon, but probably won't quite be afforded the label *anti-football*, despite their inability – or unwillingness – to get out of second gear.

Peel off the defender
The hallmark of a crafty striker. Escaping the attentions of the defender is critical when trying to establish an extra *yard or two* of space, which can make *all the difference*. Often happening at the back post, it leaves an unguarded net for the attacker to *gleefully gobble up* the chance.

Pelanty
Chris Waddle's version of a penalty. Mispronunciation is possibly rooted in some deep-seated traumatic episode.

Penalty heartache
Those who have failed in their test of nerve from 12 yards. Teams suffering penalty heartache exhibit the following symptoms:
1. Falling to their knees.
2. Crying.

3. Taking off shirt and draping it over the shoulder.
4. Participation in *Pizza Hut* adverts.

Penalty King

Someone who is lethal from 12 yards, such as Graham Alexander, Matt Le Tissier or Rickie Lambert. Teams are also penalty *Kings*; *the Germans*, for example, are known the world over for their efficiency and composure when it comes to the most pressured situation in all of football.

Penetrate

Also known as *inroads*, potent attacking forces with willing *runners* possess the ability to do this. As Alex Ferguson said in his autobiography, *"Ball retention is a religion at Man United. But possession without penetration is a waste of time."* Defences are most likely to be penetrated by a goal hungry *sharpshooter*. If they are penetrated too easily, various phrases such as *wicker shield* or *sieve-like* can be attached; whereas in contrast impenetrable, ironclad defences are likened to *Fort Knox* or termed *watertight*.

Peno

Faux-cockney, skinny-jeaned, Essex boy, Soccer AM-esque term for those who are too lazy to add *"alty".* An even more disappointing version is *peni*, as used by Paul Walsh.

Perennial

1. *Number two.* Assistant manager who never gets a look in at the *top job*. While great on the training ground with *the lads,* and able to provide a perfect link between them and the gaffer, their managerial skills often leave a lot to be desired, and his charges seem to have a hard time forgetting they cannot call him by his first name anymore, as *gaffer* is the preferred name, not *"Neil".* On the occasion when a number two is given the job, they are often gone in a matter of months. E.g. Chris Hutchings, Les Reed, Ricky Sbragia, Sammy Lee, Steve Clarke, etc.
2. *Relegation candidates.* The team who endure a never-ending battle with the drop. When perennial relegation candidates eventually slide out of the league, pundits pore over stats which show they have more often than not survived by the skin *of their teeth,* and question marks are raised over what exactly they contributed to the league anyway.
3. *Underachievers.* Teams who may never win anything, ever. In the past, these sides may have threatened a trophy haul but have come up short every time. Such clubs are said to have *long-suffering* fans.

Perfect
1. *Tonic.* The ultimate remedy to a *painful defeat*, and the prescription is three points.
2. *Workout.* Any pre-season friendly, no matter what the score is described as, since it's all about fitness rather than the result; as long as the players are put through their paces after a summer of *Jagermeisters*, strip clubs and *KFC Party Buckets*.

Peripheral figure
Someone who is on the fringes of the first team but is not considered a regular. Can react by either constantly knocking on the manager's door asking to start, or getting his head down in training and not complaining. *"Just how has Spurs' starlet Harry Kane gone from peripheral figure to England goalscorer?"*

Perma-crock
A player who is better acquainted with the treatment table than the field of play. Has the physio on speed dial and/or his BT call plan. Gets nervous every July when the squad numbers are dished out. Is a further escalation of *made of glass*.

Permutations
This phrase comes into use from early April onwards. Differing results throw up a range of possibilities, and sometimes the numbers are huge. Jeff Stelling enjoys discussing all the *potential permutations* on Soccer Saturday ahead of a crucial weekend in the English and Scottish Leagues. Later on that afternoon, he is very likely to use the phrase *"to all intents and purposes."*

Persistent fouling
Players who persistently foul run the real risk of being cautioned, in other words the hallmark of a walking booking. Referees seem to indicate that the caution is for *persistent fouling*, rather than one *cynical* challenge. Also known as the *totting up* process.

Phoenix club
Driving a club into *financial oblivion* is the hallmark of an eccentric local businessman or fly-by-night foreign tycoon. Clubs who are able to resurrect themselves from such a situation are known as a *phoenix club*, after the mythical bird. There have been many examples over the years, including Darlington 1883, Runcorn Linnets F.C. and AFC Wimbledon.

Picked his pocket
Situation in which a player has the ball *nicked* away so superbly, it could have come straight from the pages of *Oliver Twist*.

Piledriver

1. *Thunderbolt* from distance. *Piledrivers* cause the crowd to *go wild*. They are usually scored from open play, but can also be a dead ball situation, such as Jay Jay Okocha's *missile* versus Aston Villa back in 2003/04.
2. Professional wrestling move, of which there are many variants including the *Argentine Piledriver* and *Kryptonite Krunch*.

Etymology: A large piece of building industry equipment.

Pinball

Almost without exception *in the penalty area*. With one team desperately trying to clear their lines, and the other forcing it towards the net, a *goalmouth scramble* could ensue.

Pioneer of the (modern) game

Those who have played no small part in developing the modern game to include *false nines*, *possession-based play*, sports psychologists and the wearing of a gilet. Brendan Rodgers is very much at the forefront of this movement (where the gilet is substituted for a slim-fit *Topman* suit).

Pioneers have emerged in recent years with a progressive and easy-on-the-eye style of football, possibly of the high tempo *pass them to death* model. Before this, the modern game was very much limited to Terry Venables' *Christmas Tree* formation, and Harry Redknapp's direction to *"just fackin' ran abaaat a bit."*

Eric Cantona was a pioneer of the foreign influence on the English game. Before he turned up at Leeds United with his suitcase brimming with Arthur Rimbaud poetry, cigarillos, and allegorical seagull quotes the most exotic thing in football was Howard Wilkinson's Italian suede loafers from *Barratts*.

Pivotal

Decisive moment, when it could go either way for a side and on which their fate may hinge: *"We're going live to Jim Beglin now, and Jim, this is a game which could provide the pivotal moment in both Swansea and Spurs' season?"* It is definitely not the time to fluff your lines.

Plan

1. Strategy against the mercurial talent who must be stopped. *"Freedman has plans for Andre Gray."* Such plans may involve being kicked two feet in the air, having studs down the achilles or alternatively being shackled by two markers.

2. When rock-bottom and without a prayer, this is a good time for managers to plan for life in the division below.

Platitudes
A trite, meaningless statement. While they mean either very little or the blindingly obvious, platitudes are a favourite method of speaking for many a *football man*. Selected examples include:
1. *"We'll take each game as it comes"* - Sammy Lee.
2. *"We must make sure we take the positives from defeat"* - Martin O'Neill.
3. *"We need to get nasty"* – Richard Dunne.
4. *"Failure is not an option"* - every *under-pressure* manager at *crunch time*, because failure is of course *unthinkable*.

Plaudits
Those attracting praise for their work on the pitch *receive, earn* or *take the plaudits* for a *superlative* display. The *plaudits* can also be taken from the crowd who are giving a player all the *éclat* he deserves. *"Van Vossen is lapping up the adulation out there."*

Etymology: From the Latin term plaudere; to applaud.

Play acting
Player who adds one too many rolls to a triple pike, leading to the usually correct assumption that he is putting on a bit of *amateur dramatics. "He'll be running around like nothing has happened in five minutes Gary."*

Play all night and not score
When bemoaning their side's impotency in front of goal, managers may exclaim they could have *played all night and not scored*. Slight variation is *we could have played until next week and not scored* which suggests a more chronic *goal drought*.

Play down the significance of
"Coleman keen to play down significance of crunch Euro qualifier." Arguably managers do this for the very reason that the forthcoming match in question is crucial, not wanting to burden their side with extra expectation. On the other hand, some managers *delight* in *ramping up the rhetoric*, applying more heat to what is already a *pressure cooker* situation.

Playboy antics
Also known as *lifestyle*, defines the behaviour of young footballers who are known more for their off the field activities than what they do on the pitch. Pioneered by George Best and carried into the modern era by the *Spice Boy* generation of the

early nineties when players no longer lived three doors down, choosing instead to migrate to gated Cheshire communes, such was the amount of money flooding the game. Playboy antics include but are not limited to:

1. Waving an air pistol out of a car window.
2. Using £20 notes as toilet paper.
3. Appearing in a Magaluf sex tape.
4. Fathering a child out of wedlock with a celebrity.

When the behaviour comes to light, comments are made from the manager about said player getting his head down in training, turning over a new leaf, growing as both a person and professional, and of course making sure he lets his football do the talking from now on. That is until he moves on for an *undisclosed fee*.

Played it square
Playing it square is seen as a safe method of play, and the hallmark of a crab, such as Michael Carrick or Scott Parker. Other shapes include playing in *triangles* and a *diamond formation*. Slightly more tenuous is *running round in circles*.

Played the man
And not the ball; a hack. *"Paulo Rink got some of the ball but he also played the man, which you obviously can't do."* Alternatively a player may go through the man in order to get to the ball, or even *get a bit of both*.

Player power
There may be players in the dressing room who attempt to wield their influence, possibly in an attempt to cause a *dressing room revolt* and undermine their manager's authority. This so-called *player power* is never tolerated, if identified, because *"no one individual is bigger than this club."*

Some players, who are *part of the furniture* or who have a wealth of experience in the game might have their input welcomed. This is particularly the case when they become part of the backroom staff during their *twilight years*, see Lee McCulloch at Kilmarnock.

Playing between the lines
What this actually means is a source of some confusion for many. The lines could mean those found on the pitch, or indeed it may mean playing between the lines considered to be the lines in a formation. An attacking midfielder may *play well between the lines* because he is adept at linking up the midfield and attack.

Playing the right way
Another innately known ideology unique to individual perceptions. Although some may align themselves with a certain style such as getting it down and playing it, as opposed to *lumping it* over the top, there is a general consensus over the right way to play football. *"We'll go out there and do as we always do. Play football in the right way, and hopefully that will get a result for Barnsley Football Club."* Managers who revert to any means to get the desired result might not agree with this philosophy, such as those who *park the proverbial bus*.

Playoff push
The end-of-season *run* for one of the four prized playoff places. There's always one team who conjures up a dazzling string of results to pinch a last day final spot. The Premier League equivalent is the *Europa League push* (although this is seen as something of a *poisoned chalice*).

Poacher
A *fox in the box*. Opportunistic striker who rarely *passes up* an opportunity.

Pocket of fans
Such fans are usually *up in the Gods* and have undertaken a 400-mile round trip on a cold Tuesday evening, despite the match being on TV. They always get a mention from broadcasters, and if they are on the end of a heavy beating, the club may subsidise any future away games or, in exceptional circumstances, provide a refund; it's their way of *"giving something back."*

Point blank
In football, there exists a *range* in which chances are considered *point blank*; usually within the six yard area or if the goalkeeper is extremely close to the striker. They are *clear cut* opportunities and as such are typically considered to be *gilt-edged* in quality. Goalkeepers may also pull off a *point blank save*.

Etymology: Ballistics term to describe a bullet which does not deviate in trajectory from the barrel of a firearm to target.

Points out of a possible
A yardstick measurement of emphasising just how poor (or sometimes good) a team has been over a period of games is to work out how many points they have taken in this time. *"Wigan's winless run stretched to seven, taking just two points out of a possible 21."*

Points the finger
Accusatory in tone and explicit in intent, *pointing the finger* has long been a tradition in the game. It may be done in public, when managers *point fingers* at their players for serving up a *shocker* of a performance, or in the confines of the dressing room, once the *inquest* has begun. *"I'm not going to stand here and point any fingers but some of our defending was diabolical today."* Of course, players may very well be *singled out*, although this is fairly rare.

Poisoned chalice
The apparently attractive managerial position that in essence turns out to be a huge error. There are two types of poisoned chalice gigs:
1.   Working underneath a *charlatan* owner who is hell bent on influencing team selection, and *trigger happy* to boot. No doubt the P45 will be in the post in a matter of months, along with a copy of the Radio Times (daytime TV sections highlighted).
2.   The England job.

Etymology: Another phrase which has some of its early origins in Shakespeare's Macbeth; 'to plague the inventor: this even-handed justice commends the ingredients of our poison'd chalice to our own lips.'

Polarising
1.   *Figure.* A man loved and hated in equal measure. Fans of his club might refuse to hear a bad word about the man, whilst he is despised by opposing teams. Obvious examples are Robbie Savage, Craig Bellamy and Joey Barton. *"You love to hate him, but would love to have him. Somewhat of a polarising figure isn't he Jon?"*
2.   A situation which splits the fans into two distinct camps. I.e. the attempt by Assem Allam to change Hull City's name to Hull Tigers.

Pole-axed
1.   Unsubtle tackle more at home on the rugby field than the football pitch.
2.   Headline whenever England is beaten by Poland.

Pools panel
1.   Betting pool played exclusively by men in their 50s, 60s and 70s, writing out their bets with a Stanley knife sharpened HB pencil while keeping one eye on the 14:20 at Uttoxeter.
2.   Panel created to predict the scores of games which were postponed, had a late kick off, or had been shifted to a Sunday or Monday evening. Formed in 1963 after cold weather wiped out three weeks of football, it consists of three men: Ex-England internationals Gordon Banks and

Roger Hunt and Scotland counterpart Tony Green. Rumour has it that Mark Lawrenson will be invited due to his unerring accuracy in *Lawro's predictions*.

Poor man's
The knock-off version of the real deal. Clubs may have high hopes for the striker signed for a record fee, only for the milk to turn sour as they realise he is more *Boogers* than *Bergkamp*. David Bentley was described by many as a *poor man's* David Beckham, briefly threatening to become an England regular before suffering a terminal decline and retirement by the age of 29.

Porous defence
A back line with more holes in it than Edam cheese.

Posh seats
The seats in a football ground that come with padding. Occupied by the England manager (when in attendance), managers who have been banished to the stands, the chairman's kids and the *prawn sandwich brigade*.

Postage stamp
The spot which no goalkeeper in the world can reach, due to its size. Shots which are supremely accurate are put *right on the postage stamp*.

Post-match
After the game. Many things take place post-match:
1. *Analysis.* Experts and ex-pros dissect the action from the match. Pearls of wisdom will undoubtedly be offered, as well as horrendous shirts, knee slapping and clubhouse banter.
2. *Press conference/interview.* Where managers make an appearance to answer the questions of the assembled press or one-on-one for the TV cameras. The result will make a big difference as to the tone and tolerance displayed:

   Rob Palmer: *"You've made your name as a wheeler and dealer… there's not been much wheeling and dealing…"*
   Harry Redknapp: *"No, I'm not a wheeler and dealer, f*** off."* [walks off]
   Rob Palmer: *"Oh Harry, I didn't mean it like that."*
   Harry Redknapp: [off camera] *"Why've I got a name as a dealer, don't say that. I'm a f****** football manager."*
   Redknapp's Spurs had just lost to Wigan.

On odd occasions, the post-match interview will be ducked by the gaffer and his assistant will be put into the firing line instead.

3. *Handshake*. The most scrutinised action of all between the two managers as it is seen as a mark of mutual respect. Jose Mourinho has acquired a reputation for offering his hand before a match has concluded, safe in the knowledge the result is *sewn up*, however the gesture is not always accepted, as Roy Keane made clear whilst Aston Villa assistant manager. Arsene Wenger is notorious for shunning the post-match handshake, having perceived some slight on him or his side by the opposite number. The following season it will always be noted that last time around there were no *pleasantries* between the two. It implies the *post-match red* wasn't shared either.

4. *Post-mortem*. Where managers pick through the bones of a bad day at the office.

5. *Reaction*. Getting the thoughts of some of the leading lights of the football punditry world, including Lee Dixon, Jamie Carragher and Clarke Carlisle.

Potential world beater
Youngster equipped with all the necessary attributes to play right at the very top. They could equally (and as easily) become the *forgotten man* who once promised so much on *Championship Manager*, Freddy Adu, who is now on his 13th club, Michael Johnson – once seen as the future of the Manchester City midfield, and Cherno Samba – who announced his retirement in July 2015 following much early promise.

Pot-shot
Speculative effort usually taken from distance. Players who have poor decision-making abilities or frequently see their *name in lights* are prone to excessive pot-shots. Distinguished examples include Darron Gibson, Djibril Cisse and Hatem Ben Arfa.

Pounce
Like a coiled spring, a player ready and waiting to take *full* advantage will *pounce* on an opportunity, often from a half-clearance, a spilled cross or another goalkeeping error. *"Schwarzer's flap only went as far as Cole who pounced from ten yards."*

Powder-puff
Usually tackle of little or no substance which has no chance of stopping a player in his *tracks*. Indeed, blowing fairy dust at the player in question might have more of an effect. *"The pace, skill and trickery of James Rodriguez was easily enough to go by*

Kolodziejczak's powder-puff challenge." Also refers to performances and shots. *"What the lads put on show out there today was real powder-puff stuff."*

Prawn sandwich brigade
Apparently the foodstuff of choice for the emotionally detached *fan* so despised by Roy Keane. They are consumed in the corporate boxes or by those who don't usually bother to take their places in the *posh seats* until at least five minutes of the second half have *elapsed*; indeed they may not do so at all, as ogling the attractive waitress and/or watching iPhone videos of the previous day's fun on the lash at the races take precedence. In subsequent years, it has become a phrase to refer to all Manchester United fans: *"When the teams emerged at the interval, it appeared that the prawn sandwich brigade would become the latest set of top-flight supporters to get Bramall Lane's Greasy Chip Butty experience."*

Etymology: The phrase was attributed to Roy Keane following the Red Devils' match versus Dynamo Kiev in 2000. 'Away from home our fans are fantastic, I'd call them the hardcore fans. But at home they have a few drinks and probably the prawn sandwiches, and they don't realise what's going on out on the pitch.' In fact, it was the media who coined the term prawn sandwich brigade, though the seeds were sown by Keane.

Praying for the half time whistle
For teams experiencing a chastening first half experience, the referee's *whistle* cannot come quickly enough; only divine intervention is able to save them. This can be for two reasons; either a *shellacking* has taken place, or conversely the side has survived a *bombardment* and desperately need to get inside and regroup. *"Glenn Pennyfather must have been praying for the half-time whistle to try and lift his Chelmsford side, but the Essex team's woes continued to grow before the break."*

Precedent
Of which there generally exists two types:
1. *Dangerous*. This can encompass many things: lenient bans, criticism of referees, over-inflated transfer fees and changes to the offside rule to name a few.
2. *Early*. *"Matt Messias sets the early precedent in this match, dishing out two yellows in the opening stages."*

Precision finish
A goal placed right where the 'keeper can't reach it. *"On a night when players charged about like their hair was on fire, the precision of Abel Balbo's finish was a contradiction."* The term is reserved for instruments of supreme quality such as a Swiss watch, a Mach3 Turbo, or former Charlton hero Clive Mendonca's right *peg*.

Predator
1. The *fox in the box* of a side that rarely passes up an opportunity to get his name on the scoresheet, often with a certain distance referenced: *"There is no doubt that the Dagger's Jamie Cureton is a real predator from 12 yards."* Strikers of this ilk may, alternatively, be described as *deadly*. Most aspiring young footballers harbour ambitions of being a predator on the pitch, plundering goals aplenty week in and week out for their school team; that is until they tank a gilt-edged chance into Gary's mam's face on the touchline and the dream dies.
2. Brand of football boots which arguably had their heyday in the 90s, before the option of multi-coloured styles became commonplace.

Predictable results
A player tries something they clearly lack the ability for. *"Paul McShane attempts an audacious 35 yard volley; with predictable results."*

Pre-match huddle
Gathering together of a side right before kick-off in a show of unity and/or to discuss final tactics.

Etymology: The pre-match huddle was invented in 1892 by Paul D. Hubbard of Gallaudet University. The reason behind its creation was due to the University being an establishment exclusively for the deaf or hard of hearing, and its teams were comprised entirely as such. As a result, their hand gestures stipulating certain tactics could be easily read by the opposition, with the huddle a way to remedy this.

Premier League thoroughbred
Someone who knows the top flight like the back of his hand. Possessing speed, agility and prowess, this type of player was born to play in the greatest league in the world. Reared in the stables of yore, he won't be seeing out his days on the farm; he'll be coaching the youth team in his old stallion ways, i.e. *Sir Les.*

Premium
1. *Fare.* The real top quality stuff, such as a 4-4 draw between Colchester United and Bradford City in the *Johnstone's Paint*. A barnstormer of a match, which is no doubt a *great watch* for the neutral.
2. At the other end of the scale, in drab games, chances will be at a *premium*. I.e. it would be more interesting watching paint dry than tuning into this turgid *snooze fest*.

Problem

1. *"Callum McManaman's wing wizardry caused Forest problems all day long down the right flank."* Similar to *asking real questions* of.
2. Players who are injured and look unable to continue. *"Muniesa has gone down, and he looks like he has a problem."* The ensuing injury crisis causes *selection problems* in turn for the gaffer.
3. *Position.* The weak link of a team; numerous transfer windows have failed to correct the *issue* with the opposition exposing it time and time again. *"Right-back has been a bit of a problem position for the Buddies over the last few years. They've tried a number of players in this department in that time, with little consistency."*

Prodigal son

In a footballing sense, the prodigal son – like in the Bible – returns to his home after a big money move elsewhere. Examples include Stewart Downing's return to Middlesbrough after a number of years away, and Dirk Kuyt, who went back to Feyenoord.

Etymology: Taken from the story Return of the Prodigal Son in the Gospel of Luke; the difference being he was probably not on 60k a week.

Professional foul

A deliberate foul that is worthy of a sending off. This type of challenge is not considered as bad as *serious foul play*, but is reserved for more cynical breaches of the rules such as *denial of an obvious goalscoring opportunity* (i.e. *last man*). *"Manuel Pascali's professional foul on Stefan Scepovic, earned the Kilmarnock captain a red card from the referee Willie Collum."* A contradiction of sorts as the foul is anything but professional.

Project

Projects are the privilege of managers who enjoy an *enviable reputation* within the game. Clive Tyldesley may refer to *"Project Guardiola"* as he takes on his next challenge. *The Mourinho Project* is another popular plan, as the *Special One* looks to continue his legacy at Stamford Bridge. Managers lower down the league or with less than stellar reputations are not bestowed the distinction of having a project. There is no *Project Allardyce*, for example.

Promotion hopefuls

Those desperate to be *in the mix* come the end of the season.

Proper football man

Someone who has *bags* of experience in *the game*. Usually a manager seen by many as a *footballing dinosaur*, but who commands great respect from within *football circles*, despite a sometimes dubious track record. He often finds favour with tabloid journalists or Mark Clemmit.

Examples include Harry Redknapp, Iain Dowie, Phil Brown, Joe Kinnear, Glen Hoddle, George Graham, Howard Wilkinson, Ray Wilkins, Russell Slade, etc.

Proponent of the beautiful game

A player whose ability is *worth the entrance fee alone*. There have been many proponents throughout the years, including Cristiano Ronaldo, Alfredo di Stefano, and Alf Common. It could be argued that Ali Dia, Eric Djemba-Djemba and Lee Dong-Gook were proponents of something quite different.

Proven

Adjective only applied to the established front man; i.e. someone who was *born to score goals* and has done it on a regular basis throughout his career. *"On the stroke of half time it was Le Fondre who finished like the proven striker he is."*

Pull

1. *The strings*. Usually from midfield, this player is the creative *heartbeat* of the side, making things *tick* all afternoon.
2. *Up trees*. To give the maximum effort in order to succeed. However, in footballing terminology, it is used more often with negative connotations. *"Vlad Chiriches has been a massive disappointment this season, let's just say he hasn't exactly been pulling up any trees for Spurs."*
3. *The trigger*. The literal act of having a dig, or alternatively used to highlight hesitancy when a shot might be on. *"The ball fell to Daish who had a clear sight of goal, but the defender failed to pull the trigger and put the Iron to the sword."*

Punt

1. Usually a long aimless ball to no one in particular, perhaps because the punter simply wants to *get rid*. Is very much of the *hit and hope* school and most certainly will not please the paying public. If the exponent of this plays in a top 4 side this is more generously considered a long, *searching* ball over the top.
2. *Toe*. Unorthodox attempt on goal, and an alternative to *toe poke*.

Purist

Those who want to see football played the right way. *Route one* simply does not exist in the football purists' world. Certain things are described as *not one for the purists*, such as a turgid stalemate battled out on a *quagmire* of a pitch. Or anything one of Alex McLeish's teams serve up. *"Keith Alexander's direct style does not win the Imps many admirers among football purists. But it is hard to argue against the effectiveness of a system that has taken Lincoln into the play-offs for three successive seasons."*

Purple patch
Run of exquisite goal scoring form. *"Oh look at Tevez, such confidence! This boy is really going through a real purple patch, blazed the ball home with aplomb!"*

Etymology: A variant of purple passage, an ornate piece of writing, for example, "If football is a religion then Wembley is its Pantheon. Fanatical worshippers abundant, craving for victory, glory, pride. Its altar the hallowed turf, where prayers are answered and divine intervention is sought."

Put his body on the line
Players willing to do anything to prevent the opposition from getting a sight of goal. Often done for the *cause*, it is a guaranteed way to win the hearts of fans. Is an alternative for *playing through the pain barrier*. *"Battered and bruised striker Charlie Wyke putting his body on the line for Pools."*

Put the tie to bed
A decisive strike always *puts the tie to bed*, tucked right underneath the covers with the night light on, if required. *"Leading 3-1 from the first leg, Greig McDonald's men quickly set about putting the tie to bed early on with early goals from David McClune and White."*

Put their domestic differences aside
Two rivals in club football must always put these aside when turning out for the national team. This is particularly difficult for fierce rivals, and might lead to a multitude of *football lad banter* on the training pitch, particularly if one team has prevailed over the other. *"As I nutmegged Wayne, I reminded him of the score last Saturday."*

Put through his paces
A stern examination. *"Gary, I've got to say it was a superb match-up between Gayle and Tomkins, who was really put through his paces today."* However, this does not mean they were in the opponent's *back pocket*. It also has fitness connotations, such as during pre-season when players will be *put through their paces* on the training pitch in preparation for the new campaign.

Put to the sword
In footballing terms, this is to hand out a *merciless* defeat. *"Morris stunner puts Yeovil to the sword."*

Put your foot through it
A shot of considerable force; one to sting the palms of the 'keeper at least. *"He has absolutely smashed that Jeff, jinks inside the defender and puts his foot through it for 1-0. Worldie."*

Put your money on him to score
A *golden* opportunity that looks for all the world like it will be a goal. The phrase is exclaimed usually when he fails to do so, leaving the crowd *scratching their heads*. Is a variant of *I would have put my house on him to score*.

Puts pen to paper
Signing a new deal for a club or, alternatively, signing on the dotted line for a new club. Before the ink is even dry said player will make comments *like "this is a big club"* and he has *"come here to win things"* all the while reserving praise for the passionate fans, *"I've played here a few times before and I was really impressed."*

Q

Quandary
A difficult situation. Quandaries include the prospect of winning a game which helps your fierce local rivals, or what to do with an unsettled player who has *slapped down* a transfer request. Selection quandaries also exist: *"If Lennon succeeds in finding a solution to his full-back quandary, it would release Vela to operate further upfield where he enjoys it best."*

Quash
Stories must be quashed in order to quell speculation. This is because the media-driven *rumour mill* is required to be in constant operation. In instances where it goes into *overdrive*, a *half-hearted rebuttal* may be offered by the manager in question. *"Nando is part of our club, so do I want him here on February 1st? Yes if he's still with us, great."*

Rumours of a dressing room rift can be *quashed*, players can *quash rumours* they are angling for a move, or chairmen can even *quash speculation* they are looking for a quick sale of the club.

Question

1. Phrase used as a negative barb. This is particularly to challenge the credentials of a side, causing a flurry of tabloid activity. *"Pellegrini questions van Gaal's title aspirations."*

2. Asking questions is an important feature of any striker's ability, making a goalie or defender sweat like he is in the *Mastermind* chair. *"It's important that the Cumbrians ask plenty of questions of the Argyle 'keeper today as his shot stopping ability is suspect to say the least."*

Question marks

These will be asked of the back line in times of suspect defending, no matter what the quality of the goal. *"It was a good finish by Sam Winnall, but there remained question marks over the defence as to just why he was allowed into that position."* Question marks will also be raised over temperament, work ethic, disciplinary record or extracurricular activities of a player.

Queueing up

Teams that load the box may be lucky enough to have a number of players who are waiting to stick it away. Of course, if forming a queue to score were literally the case, the home nations would excel; whereas the Germans would be terrible at it.

Quick fire double

Two goals scored in quick succession. The *quick fire double* can often result in the game being *turned on its head.*

Quota

It is believed football teams only have a certain number of goals in them; this so-called *goals quota* is referenced on a weekend which sees a *goal glut*, with them *raining down* left, right and centre across the country on a Saturday afternoon, causing steam to emit from the *vidiprinter*. This is invariably followed by a warning from Jeff Stelling that teams should be careful not to use up their *quota*, because it is a finite source. It can also apply to a player who rarely finds the back of the net, yet does so in quick succession: *"After seven goals in his previous 252 appearances, Danny Butterfield's six-minute hat-trick surely saw him fill his goals quota for the season."*

R

Rack

1. *On the.* Referencing a form of medieval torture to highlight pressure. *"The Valiants had their visitors on the rack at times and created all the chances in an ill-tempered affair that saw eight yellow cards."*
2. *Up.* Goals, wins, trophies, clean sheets, plaudits, cricket score, the cards etc.

Radar

Transfer windows are the optimum time for any club's radar to swing into action. *"[player] is on [club's] radar"* is perhaps one of the most common headlines to be seen during this time, yet is probably a creation of the rumour-mongering press in an attempt to fill column inches.

Raft of withdrawals

A common occurrence during *international week*. A player who isn't bothered about his side's friendly match takes the decision that his groin is playing up, and should withdraw as a *precautionary measure*, leaving the manager with a *selection headache. "Feeney was summoned by boss Sanchez following a raft of withdrawals for the trip to Azerbaijan, but had to refuse the offer to travel to Baku."* Clearly, the lure of a *May the Best House Win* marathon is preferable to braving the sub-zero temperatures and *hotbed* atmosphere of Zagreb. The fury of many an international boss is invoked when said player plays a *full ninety* the following Saturday.

Raid

Adjective used in headline often awarded *EXCLUSIVE!* status. *"Megson plotting raid on his former club: EXCLUSIVE!"* It is very common for managers to *return* and raid their old club, inviting images of them in the trophy room with a stocking over their heads at 2am.

Raise his/their game

This phenomenon occurs for two reasons; the *big boys* are in town, and he's the kind of footballer who likes to put himself in the *shop window. "The lad played a blinder against United but couldn't keep the Bees in the Cup."*

Alternatively, managers may inform one of their charges they must *raise their game* if they want to stay in the first team. This particularly applies to putting the *hard yards* in on the training pitch, and bringing their *'A' game* to the table; however, it can also be self-inflicted pressure.

Rally the troops

Building up to a *crunch clash*, one of the senior members of a team may *rally the troops* in an attempt to make sure *the lads* are up for the fight. Phrases such as *"stand up and be counted"*, *"payback for last time"*, and *"let's do this for the fans, they're the ones who pay our wages"* are used. Similar to issuing a *rallying cry*. *"Dundee FC in crisis: Matt Lockwood tries to rally the troops."*

Ran their socks off

A gargantuan effort by a player or collective XI raises the very real risk of socks being *run off*. Presumably this means the boots have been run off too (although when a boot is lost, the player in question is commended for keeping going, as he selflessly risks damp toes for the cause). In these circumstances, managers will certainly not be able to *fault the lads for effort*, regardless of the outcome, because they left it all out there. *"They came and did what all lower league teams are supposed to do against glamourous opposition. They ran their socks off, took their chances and kept the back door shut."*

Raptures

Otherwise known as *pandemonium, scenes*, etc. *"The visitors made no impact in the second half and were drinking at the last-chance saloon when a hopeful overhead kick in the box landed on the right boot of danger man Er Rafik, who volleyed past Ashley Morris to send the travelling party into raptures."* In football terms, to be *in raptures* suggests that the faith has been kept and is now paying *dividends*, whereas the non-believers who ducked out of the stadium early with their team almost assured of defeat are left on earth to die – or less severely avoid the rush.

Rapturous receptions are also *given* by fans to players, perhaps when they are paraded for the first time in front of their adoring public, doing multiple keepy-ups in their new team strip; or if you are Gareth Bale, just the 11.

Etymology: Refers to the biblical idea that all true believers will ascend to heaven at the end of the world.

Rare foray

Sorties reserved almost exclusively for the opposition territory, and are always *rare*. This occurs in two main situations:
1. Defensive-minded full backs encouraged to *get forward* are very much prone to having their run tagged as such; particularly when acting as the *overlap*, the winger has been taken out of action and they are all alone down the wing with it *all to do*. This does not apply to *marauding* (or *buccaneering*) full backs, e.g. Marcelo, Zabaleta, Dani Alves, etc.

2. A team as a whole may have a *rare foray* forward. *"United's stand-in goalkeeper Stuart Taylor was alerted to the odd danger – Igor Vetokele deflecting a drive onto the base of the post in a rare foray forward – but the game really was with Leeds."* The opposite of being *camped* in *opposition territory.*

3. The transfer market. *"Wenger hints at rare foray into the striking section of the transfer market."*

Rash

1. *Challenge.* A tackle of poor quality, in a hot-headed moment by the offender who goes steaming in. *"A rash challenge from Batty, rubber stamping his reputation with a reducer on Butt."*

2. *Decision.* The goalkeeper, *charging* out of his area in an attempt to try and beat the attacker to the ball is guilty of this for one of two reasons: either his opponent will beat him to it and score, or they are alternatively bought down and a red card is produced for the denial of an *obvious goalscoring opportunity.* *"Wapenaar's charge off his line was a rash decision; he left the net completely unguarded and Dalmat fired home."*

Rasper

Onomatopoeic term denoting a shot from distance, which maintains a near constant elevation from boot to net. *"The rasper from Kljestans found the upper 90."*

Rattled

1. *The woodwork.* Commentators may advise *"the crossbar is still shaking"* long after the ball has ricocheted away to safety. Such comments are accompanied by a close up of the unlucky player in question, agony etched all over his face. Some believe there is a degree of pride in *rattling* the woodwork. The bar does tend to be struck in a more violent manner than any other area of the goal frame, for a ball may *smash, crash, thud* or *thunder* off it.

2. Teams, individuals or back lines can be *rattled* by something completely unforeseen. *"Oldham look really rattled by the Crewe attack here, they just haven't anticipated quite how tough a proposition they would be."* Experienced defenders may have expected a walk in the park; however they have found themselves shot to bits by the *lightning pace* of the youthful opposition forward line, and are consequently two down in ten minutes with a *mountain to climb.*

Raw talent

Ability which is yet to be realised or harnessed; a rough diamond. *"Ravel Morrison is such a raw talent right now, but if he's nurtured in the right way, England could have a player on their hands.*" Raw talent still has question marks over whether they will realise their potential, for the following reasons:

1.   Can they deal with fame?
2.   Can they keep out the nightclubs?
3.   Are they willing to get their head down in training, giving it *110%*?
4.   Will they surround themselves with the right people? I.e. is it best their Dad is their agent?
5.   Can they handle a *mega bucks* transfer and life in a big city?

Neither Wayne Rooney nor David Beckham was prescribed the tag *raw talent*, perhaps because they were very much of *international class* or the *finished article* from a young age.

Read the riot act
Any reading of this act by the manager means the recipients are in serious trouble. Off the field activities, such as newspaper scandals are leading reasons why the gaffer will dust off his copy of the Riot Act. It can also be used for footballing reasons, such as a disinterested, *out of sorts* display. *"After that first half performance, there's going to be recriminations in the dressing room. Danny Bergara will be reading the Riot Act to his boys during the interval, make no bones about that."*

Etymology: Originally, the Riot Act gave local authorities the ability to declare any gathering of 12 or more people unlawful. If the Riot Act was indeed read to the starting XI it would have no jurisdiction over this rag-tag band of miscreants (unless the substitutes were included in the dressing down if course).

Readying another sub
At least the second *throw of the dice* by the manager. Cameras pan to the bench showing the player getting *stripped and ready*. Meanwhile the assistant furiously scribbles notes, as the manager puts his arm round the player about to enter the *fray*, making the universal *four-fingered* hand gesture, while pointing to it with his free hand from above; the fourth official then checks his studs and makes sure his jewellery is either removed or taped up. Commentators will reflect on previous appearances off the bench by the player, particularly if they have scored from four in the last six.

Real
1.   *Fans.* Represents the true fans of a football club who wear club shirts in the town centre but don't necessarily go to the games. Can be found in an armchair or watching a dodgy satellite feed at 3pm, but certainly nowhere near the stadium. See also *armchair fan*.

2. *Player.* The prefix of real helps to highlight the true ability of a footballer. *"I was talking to Shay Given in the week and he says Afellay looks a real player."*

Real performance
Most likely demanded of teams with something to prove, as ex-Doncaster manager Paul Dickov demanded of his side: *"We were desperate to put to bed the home form we keep being reminded about. But we had to forget about that and go to Swindon with a real performance because I regard them as the best footballing side in the division."* Big game players put in these performances when it matters too; this is because they rise to the occasion, or possibly because the main stand is packed with visiting scouts. Performances are often described as *real*, as it sets them apart from the fake performances of those considered *flash in the pan*, such as Amir Zaki's wonderful half season at Wigan followed by pretty much nothing else – except for multiple fines for returning late from international duty, and a refusal to join Portsmouth due to them signing *"an Israeli player and also… an Israeli football director. On top of that, no way could I play at Portsmouth with an Algerian within in their ranks."*

Reality
This comes in either *dose* or *check* forms for the buoyant side. Teams that have faced easier opponents and had designs above their station are put to the sword in a shellacking by a side of seasoned quality. *"Five-star Cambridge hand Oxford a dose of reality."*

Rearguard action
A heroic defensive effort. *Rearguard actions* rarely fail, partly because they are often described retrospectively to emphasise just how good a performance it was by a side. This type of action usually sees *all hands to the pump* for the majority of the 90. *"The Seagulls' rearguard action repelled wave after wave of attacks from the Cottagers' triumvirate of McCormick, Woodrow and Dembélé."*

Reception
Former players coming back to their old clubs can expect to receive one of two very different receptions. Those remembered fondly by the fans will receive a *great* reception, with applause as his name is read out during the line ups (he may even be permitted to wave to the crowd if he is a club legend). However, if the split has been acrimonious a *hot* reception and copious boos can be expected; not so much like getting into a warm bath, but taking sugared boiling water to the face. Trips to unknown foreign lands can also bring such an atmosphere: *"Hayes knows his side face a red hot reception in Macedonia but is certain Derek McInnes' men will keep the tie alive for the return to the Granite City."*

Reckless challenge
A tackle which shows no regard for an opponent's wellbeing; adopting the attitude *if he dies, he dies*. The challenger may have his studs showing, go over the ball or jump in with both feet. Reckless challenges *in this day and age* are deserving of a red card.

Red button facility
Provides welcome relief for TV viewers during the World Cup who have grown tired of Lawro's moaning and instead wish to listen to Alan Green on 5Live.

Red faced
Embarrassment, as opposed to being green with envy at the attacking riches (but never defensive riches) a side possess. *"Mike Duff was left red-faced on the hour mark as he diverted a cross from the left flank into his own net."* Players left *red faced* will often apologise to *the lads* in the dressing room afterwards, yet the manager will refuse to blame him publicly for the error – although what is said behind closed doors is another matter.

Red mist
1. The red mist descends – and in serious cases *completely* descends – on players and touchline staff who have lost control of their emotions. They may very well have to be restrained from confronting the referee and match officials about anything they perceive to be an injustice. *"Red mist then descended on Dempsey as he took the official's notebook out of his pocket, before ripping it up then throwing it on the ground in a crazy outburst."*
2. The choice of flare colour in a *cauldron-like* atmosphere.

Reducer
An ugly tackle which has *no place in the game*. *Reducers* are usually double-footed *horror* tackles that result in a straight red and condemnation from *all quarters*. The question *"Referee, what are you going to do?"* is invariably asked by the commentators. Ron Atkinson claims to have coined this phrase, telling his players to *"put the reducer on him"* when referring to a particularly skilful opponent.

Referee's match report
Something that is filed after every match, but only referred to if there has been a contentious incident. There are always question marks over whether the referee spotted the incident, and henceforth whether it will be included in the report. *"The FA will wait for referee Mike Jones' report before deciding on what course of action to take, if any."* Failure to mention something usually gives the *authorities* carte blanche to administer their own brand of justice. What type of terminology is used in the report is unclear, but it is unlikely to say *"Matt Dolan scored a lovely little*

goal for Yeovil, finishing with aplomb from ten yards – wanted to applaud but obviously couldn't."

Refusing to throw in the towel

No matter how bad a situation may be, managers and players always retain hope it might be *salvaged*. *"We're not going to throw in the towel, we'll keep on fighting to make sure that Rotherham United Football Club remains in the Championship."* It would be a seismic shock in the footballing world if a manager ever admitted to throwing in the towel despite it being mathematically possible to stay up.

Regulation

1. *Time.* Anything other than added on time. Also known as the *allotted 90.* Any passages of play outside this period are termed *additional minutes.*
2. *Victory.* A straightforward three points which never look in doubt.

Reject

1. Players can *reject* a move to another club.
2. Those players who have played for a hated rival are described by former foes as *rejects.* For example, Jason Roberts will always be thought of as a *Baggie reject* by fans of Wolverhampton Wanderers, who in turn think the same about Kevin Doyle.

Relegation

1. *Dogfight.* The gloves off, down and dirty *scrap* seen at the bottom of the table from April onwards. The niceties of tactics are forgotten when three points is all that matters.
2. *Mire.* That stodgy, muddy mix which teams find themselves in if they are unable to string any kind of form together. The term is trotted out after one team has a terrible result and others go against them. *"Well, after that 4-0 beating today, coupled with results going against them, Crawley find themselves right in the relegation mire."* Teams may also be said to be *bang* or *deep* in the mire, or alternatively up to their necks in it.
3. *Six-pointer.* Matches of utmost importance are often billed as such. Towards the *business end* of a campaign, they will assume huge significance as teams can take points off the other. Perhaps termed a six-pointer because of the potential of a *six-point swing*, depending on the result. *"The perennial six-pointer, what a game this is, and Thommo will be watching it for us this afternoon."* Title chasers can also be involved in six-pointers, however they do seem to take more significance in the lower *echelons.*
4. *Twelve-pointer.* As if the hype needs to be ramped up any more, six pointers may turn into *twelve pointers when* games are fast running out. The

fate of either side may rest on the outcome of this game as defeat may very well be the *final nail in the relegation coffin*.

5. *Trapdoor.* Sometimes known as the *dreaded* relegation trapdoor, as the season draws to a close, clubs may *inch* towards it, it can *loom large* or it can *slowly open*, provoking fearsome imagery to any of the assembled *basement boys*.

Renaissance

1. Occurring in football when a team experiences a dramatic upturn in fortunes brought on by the appointment of a (potentially) new and forward thinking manager. It suggests the style of football played will be more urbane, refined and attractive, including an increase in triangles, possession-based play and attempting to score the perfect goal. Careers may also enjoy a renaissance, such as Udinese's Antonio Di Natale, who has *bagged* over 150 Serie A goals after his 30th birthday; this is similarly the case with Hellas Verona's Luca Toni, who topped the goalscoring charts in 2014/15: *"The prize marks an incredible renaissance for the imposing frontman, who has always looked more like a Vatican bodyguard than he did international marksman."* See also *effect*.

2. Renaissance FC, a top-flight Chadian football team.

Repaying a sizeable chunk of his transfer fee

When a new player scores a particularly important goal for his club he repays a large proportion of the money paid for him. It is no more the case than someone who scores a winning goal in the £120m playoff final, when the words *"...and then some!"* is tagged onto the end by the commentator. On scoring in the first few games at his new club, a player may said to have *started* repaying the transfer fee.

Report card

These generally come in two forms, *festive* and *end of season*. *"When Paul Buckle was handed his end of term report card, with the Robins languishing at the foot of the table, it surely read 'must do better.'"*

Reputation preceding him

What commentators say about footballers with poor disciplinary records when trying to provide justification for a *studs-up* tackle, or some other on-pitch misdemeanour. *"Well the referee has pulled Wise up for that, maybe a little bit of his reputation preceding him there."* See Aleksandar Mitrović, El Hadji-Diouf and any Sunday League central defender over the age of 40.

Results-based business

There are two schools of thought on this mantra:

1. Football is a results-based business.
2. Football isn't a results-based business.

Some managers place results above all other factors: *"Sam Allardyce dismisses criticism of his playing style by some fans as 'nonsense', arguing that football 'is a results-based business'."* Managers shown the door after picking up three points out of a possible 36 should have no complaints about this commonly held mantra. However, Roberto Di Matteo's Champions League victory, Nigel Pearson's heroics at Leicester, and Mark Warburton masterminding an unlikely playoff appearance at Brentford would suggest they may hold a different opinion.

Retrograde step
A backwards move, seen in a few differing transfer situations:
1. Players who drop down the divisions for the money would be accused of making a retrograde step for their career just to benefit their bank balance.
2. Clubs who sign players not generally seen as up to the required standard could be accused of lacking ambition.
3. Players signing for a top club at the expense of *game time*, who find themselves playing 13 games in two seasons, severely stunting their development. *"Sinclair desperate to repair reputation after retrograde City move."*

If the signing is intended as a replacement for a star man, accusations of failing to *adequately replace* him are often made. See also *poor mans*.

Retrospective action
A player who escapes punishment after a challenge goes unnoticed by the referee may be the *subject* of *retrospective action* or *punishment* from the FA. *"He can expect a call on Monday morning, Martin."* The conviction rate in these circumstances is 99.5%, leading to accusations that the FA is judge, jury and executioner.

Rhombus foot
Defender blessed with a foot shaped in such a way that any boot upfield will fly off at all angles. A montage of Titus Brambles' career would highlight this affliction perfectly. Those in the front row should probably protect their meat and potato pies, as well as their young child's face, if they have a spare hand.

Rich vein of form
A *hot streak*, either as a team chalking up the wins or as a striker scoring goals. *"Wycombe's rich vein of form saw them transformed from League Two also-rans into serious promotion contenders."* See also *purple patch*.

Rifle

One of a plethora of verbs to describe the action of shooting, and often scoring. *"McKinlay squared it to Saunders who rifled home from eight yards."* To *rifle* in a shot implies a straight, fast and deadly effort, buried right into the corner. Robbie Keane also has a gun celebration, however it is more cartoonish gun toting following a half-cartwheel-forward-roll, as opposed to Edison Cavani's 'sniper' routine.

Rift

Rifts fuel *constant speculation* and can be caused by a number of things:

1. Disagreement between a chairman and manager over the direction of the club.
2. A *boardroom rift*, i.e. a struggle in the corridors of power.
3. A *dressing room rift*, rumours of which will always be denied, or possibly even *scotched.*
4. Two managers almost coming to blows on the touchline after a fruity challenge.

Rifts are, by and large, denied by a player or manager, as it involves some sort of internal politics. To acknowledge such would only fan the flames and provide more fodder for the third estate to feed upon. *"Javier Mascherano denies rift with Ever Banega after penalty miss."*

However, if the rift is between two managers, the stories may be encouraged as a form of *mind game* mischief. Wily operators such as Brian Clough would revel in this form of brinkmanship, but Jose Mourinho is the king of modern day rifts – falling out with Sir Alex, Manuel Pellegrini and Arsene Wenger amongst others.

Right to the wire

If a manager is involved in a title push, or relegation battle, they adopt a curious mix of absolute belief that they will prevail in their quest, but caveat proceedings by claiming they will go *right to the wire.* Also applies when clubs are desperately trying to get deals over the line before the transfer window *slams shut.*

Riposte

Often seen as the best response to a disappointing run, barb or rival club where there is a bit of history. *"Berg launches furious riposte against Venky's detractors."*

Road to

1. *Wembley.* When any club, big or small, begins their FA Cup *campaign* (although not the League Cup), they are on the *Road to Wembley.* It doesn't matter if it's Sheffield Wednesday in the third round, or

Stocksbridge Park Steels in the preliminary round, it's still the same because *all roads lead to Wembley.*

2. *Nowhere.* Running into traffic or a cul-de-sac on the pitch.
3. *Recovery.* A route which begins with a morale-boosting win or a late, scruffy, pilfered and quite probably undeserved equaliser. This route is often found parallel to the *goal trail.* When questioned on the nature of the leveller the manager states, *"We have needed a bit of luck as we haven't had any all season"*; this particularly applies to Steve Bruce, whose default touchline expression is to look like someone has just nicked his parking space.

Etymology: Road to… was a series of seven comedy films starring Bob Hope, Bing Crosby and Dorothy Lamour.

Robbed
The sort of total injustice in football that leaves the losers feeling robbed of what would have been a deserved win, especially as their opponents only mustered one shot on target all game. Upon the post-match handshake, the victorious manager almost always pulls a *shit happens* sympathy face. Also used by the *armchairs* despite only catching the highlights on the Monday evening edition of *North West Tonight.* Can also apply in situations where players have been denied the chance to take part in success. *"Being robbed of the chance to taste the highs of last season was Gary Harkins' darkest hour at Dundee."*

Robust
1. Used when a known *hard man* makes one of his *trademark* tackles. *"Terry Hurlock steams into the challenge in typically robust fashion; Mickey Norbury will be feeling that one tomorrow morning."*
2. *Defence.* Unequivocal backing given to a player or manager who is up against it. This staunch support is often followed by an *impassioned plea* for the fans to get behind the boys and be the *12th man.* Retrospective defences of a tenure are also made, particularly when things have gone badly. *"Ridsdale launches robust defence of his Bluebirds reign."*

Rock at the heart of defence
A reliable, no nonsense central defender who rarely lets any opposition number get the better of him. He organises the rest of the back four with authority and is the main reason for an enviable *clean sheet* record. *"Martin can be the rock at the heart of the Norwich defence for many years to come."* Sometimes just shortened to *rock*, where the rest of the phrase is left understood.

Rolling back the years

When a veteran produces something you would normally expect to see from someone much younger, fitter, agile or thinner. *"McNulty's overhead kick drew gasps from the watching Luton faithful."* It is the opposite of someone who produces a mature display which *belies his tender years*.

Romp

1. A *resounding* victory. Term assigned to a side which has built an unassailable lead, and look like they might score with every attack. Such teams are said to be *"really enjoying themselves out there"* (or perhaps even in a *"rampant mood"*), whilst the opposition are *praying* for full time.
2. Prominent reason why a footballer might feature on the front page of *the Sun*.

Roo

Affectionate media term for Wayne Rooney. Used incessantly in newspaper headlines as a convenient abbreviation, or criminally, to create a pun. Examples include *"Roo-turn"* as Rooney is apparently restarting negotiations for a move to Chelsea. *"Roo are joking!"* describing the time when Rooney was asked to play for Scotland by Berti Vogts, *"Roo boo hoo"* was a Daily Mirror effort after his World Cup 2010 tantrum and *"Rio de Janei-roo"* which was predictably about his exploits at the 2014 World Cup.

Rookie manager

A gaffer who has very little experience. He will have to try hard with the press to gain acceptance, but this may be difficult to achieve. Headlines appear in the press a couple of weeks after they are appointed about *demanding respect*, despite the fact they have done little so far to *earn* it from the fans, players and media alike.

Round trip

Trips of considerable distance are always counted in *round-trip* form, never from point A to B. *"Carlisle make the 780-mile round trip to Plymouth, hoping to head back up the M6 with all three points."* Defeat evokes sympathy towards the *hardy-souls* who have *come back empty handed*. Trips are also measured in time, for example *12-hour round trip*.

It is exclusively used to signify the enormity of the journey; Bolton would not make the 78-mile *round trip* to Huddersfield, but may make the *short hop* across the Pennines.

Rout

A comprehensive beating; although there is no actual number specified for a game to be defined as a rout it is certainly no less than a four goal *reversal*.

Etymology: Military terminology which refers to the disorderly retreat and defeat of troops on the battlefield, and the subsequent loss of morale and/or discipline.

Route-one

Direct style of play, and the opposite of playing the right way. There is no *panache* to this particular tactic, just a desire to *pump the ball long* to the *big man*. Is a style which is frowned upon, but is effective and can define a manager's *ethos*. *"Wimbledon's route one ploy leaves them with few friends, but with the human wrecking ball in Efan Ekoku it is certainly effective."* Teams in the *last chance saloon* may disregard the gameplan and resort to this tactic.

Etymology: From the 1960s television show Quiz Ball, where route-one was the quickest way to scoring a goal.

Roving

Players are able to contribute to more than one phase of play, and are given *licence to roam*, perhaps in a *free role*. *"Dynamic stuff from the Hatters; their roving midfield has covered every blade of grass out there today, putting City under constant pressure. They haven't afforded them even half a yard of space."* Although seen as a positive term, the actual definition of *rove* is to wander about at random, and is therefore more comparable to *running around like a headless chicken*.

Rumour

1. *Mill.* The *rumour mill* is operated mainly by the tabloid press and football agents, looking to fill column inches and encourage movement for their clients. During the two transfer windows the mill will go into *overdrive*, churning out an endless stream of unsubstantiated stories, tedious conjecture and gossip which leave many football fans saturated. Terms such as *"mega deal"*, *"world exclusive"* and *"11th hour hijack"* are used. As time passes, increasingly exaggerated language is employed in an attempt to sell newspapers. It is in *constant operation*.

2. *Mongering.* The preserve of many a newspaper and broadcaster who trade in baseless or largely discredited stories. *"Real shock world of football by launching £150m bid which will SMASH world transfer record."* Rumours are almost exclusively tripe.

Run in
1. Of particular note when a side is facing six of last season's top seven in their final matches of the campaign, yet are three points from safety and their main goal threat has just snapped his cruciates.
2. When a manager encounters his former chairman at a top London restaurant following a much publicised and incredibly bitter fall out.

Run ragged
A team who have been dominated to such an extent that they appear to have been trampled by a herd of cows: *"The lightning Lowestoft attack ran the depleted Curzon Ashton back line ragged."*

Runners
"Rochdale don't need a Xavi in there, they just need enough willing runners to ask questions of the opposition defence." Possessing pace, stamina and reading the game extremely well, runners usually originate in the midfield and must be prepared to put in a *real shift*.

Running down the clock
A cynical attempt to waste time at the end of the match. The tempo will be slowed right down, and during stoppage time the ball will go straight into the corner; of course this tactic is a dangerous one if the hot-headed and frustrated opposition midfielder decides to steam into a challenge, wiping out the player, corner flag and linesman in the process. Teams who have a shock lead are jokingly said to do this at a much earlier point in proceedings: *"He's not going for the corner flag already is he Martin?!"* See also *beeline*.

Running on fumes
An energy-sapping match leaves very little fuel left in the tank, or indeed nothing in the legs. As such, these players are running on fumes. *"Well we've reached the halfway point in extra-time now and some of the Morton boys look out on their feet. Bobby Barr is just running on fumes and Connor Pepper looks like he's got the dry boak on the touchline."*

Rush of blood to the head
A *rash* decision. Usually followed by the question *"what was he thinking?"* It quite often results in catastrophe for the offending player's team, such as an embarrassing own goal or red card. Goalkeepers are particularly prone to this, coming for crosses they have absolutely *no right* to go for. *"Warner's decision to stray from his line was a total rush of blood to his head and it had dire consequences."* This will lead to apologies in the dressing room afterwards.

S

... 's answer to...

"Macclesfield might not have Lionel Messi in their side, but in David Gonzalez they certainly have Cheshire's answer to him." This is a player who has a similar impact on their side as the Argentinian wizard does on Barcelona, but not quite the ability.

Sack race

Akin to embattled top-flight gaffers fighting it out at a Premier League summer sports day, the sack race in football is not any sort of race a manager would wish to win. It normally concludes in September or October, but has been known to last until Christmas, much to the delight of the bookies.

Sacked

There are many terms to describe a manager who has been removed from his role. He could be *dismissed, relieved of his duties*, or in rare cases *placed on gardening leave*. Other methods include: being *shown the door, ushered towards the exit*, or sometimes the departure is *by mutual consent*. Managers usually ignore, refute or angrily hit out at rumours of the sack, answering any post-match questions with a five-second silence, accompanying death stare and the comment: *"Does anyone have any proper questions they want to ask?"*

Sacrifice
1. The unfortunate consequence of going a *man down* is for one of the strikers to be substituted in order to shore up the defence. Often described as the *unlucky one*, it is no reflection on his own performance.
2. Ploughing a lone furrow up top for the cause. *"Plaudits for Lambert today, he's run himself into the ground for his side, with little reward."* Someone who sweats blood for his teammates.
3. Grandiose claim by lower/non-league footballers to justify playing at an inferior level. *"Luke Chadwick says he was happy to sacrifice the glitz and glamour of League One football in order to pull on the shirt of his hometown club."*

Safe pair of hands
1. Trusty, erstwhile goalie who keeps clean sheets in his sleep.
2. The manager who can be trusted to steer a side away from danger, getting the most out of his players; you won't get fireworks, but such sides will be difficult to break down, are well organised and have an unerring ability to grind out results. *"Tony Pulis is the ultimate safe pair of hands at this level. If you want to maintain your Premier League status, he's your man."*

Safety first approach

A cautious, possession-based set up which teams tend to *adopt*. It is a development of the *keep it tight* theory during the first 20 minutes, where the only objective is not to concede. Instructions include *"no nonsense, play the easy ball, keep it on the deck, no overlapping runs, rigid positioning and most importantly TALK to each other." Safety first* suggests a team have come for the draw, despite all managers having a belief in the ability of their charges to pick up three points, even if it is a *backs to the wall* job.

Salvo

The most popular form is the *double-salvo* where two goals are scored in *quickfire fashion*. Indeed, such instances may *turn the game on its head*. *"The Woking double salvo knocked the stuffing out of a depleted Wrexham side."* Rare occasions may see a treble-salvo.

Etymology: Nautical term to denote the firing of weaponry in quick succession, particularly on warships.

Same direction

The way in which all clubs profess to *pull*.

Saw his name in lights

Rash decision to go for *glory* instead of spotting the pass *square* to a teammate in a *glorious position*. It is a common mistake of the player who has failed to get his *head up*, or is suffering from a severe case of *tunnel vision*. Exclamations by the commentators are usually long, loud and sneering. *"Dear oh dear oh dear! Beardsmore saw his name in lights, but he's made himself look rather foolish there."* May also be a *bold attempt* at a shot from 35-yards, which was more of a threat to the floodlights than the goalkeeper.

Scalp

A regular phrase during cup competitions, lower league teams will dream of getting one of the big scalps. *"Hereford, at ball number 57 have a history that doesn't need repeating. Edgar Street as we all know is a graveyard for big clubs."* At this point Ronnie Radford usually gets a mention, and will no doubt have been asked by BBC local radio to be waiting by the phone.

Scenes

Can be prefixed in a multitude of ways from *absolute* through *jubilant* to *agonising* depending on the situation, or simply as standalone *scenes*. With no further explanation or context, the mention of mere *scenes* by a commentator clearly conveys the idea that there is *"absolute pandemonium"* in the stands.

It is worth noting they can be as glorious as they can be ugly. However, the term is usually reserved for either a last gasp goal, or an against-the-odds David and Goliath-style victory causing a real *champagne moment*. Less than savoury moments lead to enthusiastic coverage in the press: *"Shocking scenes as fans clash with police in hot-tempered Midlands derby."* Such scenes include pitch invasions, knocking down advertising hoardings and ripping out seats.

Schemer
Crafty, wily and with bags of experience, these midfield artisans are not averse to a dirty trick or two to engineer a situation in their favour. *"Birmingham City schemer Andy Shinnie hails Robert Tesche quality and welcomes competition for places."*

Schoolboy error
An elementary and often ludicrous mistake unbecoming of a player at any level. Schoolboy errors are the object of much ridicule from all in the footballing world. Some of the more *street* pundits like Jamie Redknapp might say that a player has *committed a schoolboy*. Very similar to *having a 'mare out there* and *dropping a clanger*. There are occasions when it will refer to an amalgamation of defensive mistakes, rather than one specific incident: *"The defending for Stoke's first was a dereliction of duty, but the way Gleghorn was allowed to dance his way through the defence for the second was quite simply schoolboy stuff."*

Score the perfect goal
The ultimate aim of a superb *passing outfit*. Teams who *string* numerous balls together, in a superlative display of *artistry* are said to be *trying to score the perfect* goal. Teams attempting this are often accused of trying to *walk the ball into the back of the net*. *"Oh lovely stuff from the Jags! What was that, 35, 40 passes in a row? But maybe it was just one too many in their quest to score the perfect goal. Mathis Pogba should just have hit it."*

Scoreboard man
Individual who operates the scoreboard at a stadium. Original role involved putting cards into slots, but now the job is largely electronic. Referred to on rare occasions during commentary when there has been a *glut* of goals which will undoubtedly be *"keeping the scoreboard man busy"*. He would also need to occasionally dodge particularly *wayward* shots.

Scoreline doesn't tell the whole story
A result which doesn't reflect the true nature of the game or do it justice. For example, Brighton may have beaten Charlton 2-1, but this doesn't tell the whole story because:
1. They had to *see out* the final 35 minutes with 10 men.

2. They lost two *key players* to injury early on.
3. Charlton blazed a 94ᵗʰ minute penalty kick into *row Z*.

Scotch rumours
1. The rendering of a story as utter tosh.
2. The suggestion that a player has turned up still drunk from the night before.

Scramble
1. Exclusively to be found in the goalmouth, this type of play produces some of the most exciting moments in a game. It is somewhat of an irony that it is perhaps the scruffiest too, with no player able to properly put a stop to the *pinball* in the penalty area. *"Aaron Cresswell's free kick from the left touchline was almost turned in by Cheikhou Kouyaté in a goalmouth scramble, while Amalfitano's effort was also saved."*
2. The FA Cup Final every May sees the traditional *scramble* for tickets once the 25,000 corporate allocation has been made.

Scrapbook
1. A particularly good strike is said to be *one for the scrapbook* as it is worth saving for prosperity in the book of goals. Alternatively, goals from a rare source are also considered to be this. Scrapbooks may also have less than desirable connotations; *"Fabian Delph's move from Aston Villa to Manchester City has found a place in the all-time transfer sagas scrapbook."* See also *collector's item*.
2. Collection of newspaper cuttings kept by (mainly) children of their favourite games and players. Stories within would recall memories of players of yesteryear, featuring superb strikes by players like Ron Harris, Mike Trebilcock and Gordon Jones. Tales of seven goal *thrillers* at bygone grounds such as the Dell, Springfield Park and Underhill, with its sloping pitch, would be kept for prosperity and bought out to show the grandkids.

Screamer
A long-range piledriver. *"Take that! Anya with an absolute screamer as he announces his arrival with a moment of pure quality."*

Scuppered
A move for a player will be *scuppered* (or possibly *torpedoed*) by an unwilling selling club, or perhaps by a greedy player with sky-high wage demands. Greg Dyke's *B team* idea was *scuppered* by many within the game, as was Richard Scudamore with his *39ᵗʰ game* folly.

Etymology: The deliberate sinking of a ship.

Scythed down

Mark Lawrenson likes to call this a *yellow-and-a-half*; more than a yellow, but not worthy of a dismissal. However, the bench might not agree. *"That tackle on Kightly has caused the dugout to jump up in fury! Look at Dyche on the touchline, he's telling Steve Cotterill exactly what he thinks!"*

Seasoned pro

These veterans bring a wealth of experience to a side, and are able to offer a calm vision in the face of challenging circumstances. Like the oldest fisherman on *Deadliest Catch*, their immense experience has steered them through many treacherous campaigns. Not only do they know every trick in the book, they have probably written a chapter or two as well; they won't get nutmegged, know how to see a game out with five minutes to go, and in 50/50 challenges he will take everything out (ball, man, referee etc.) to make sure they win the tackle. *"In short, Romain Vincelot is a seasoned pro, and the fans are going to love him because he gives 110% every time he steps onto the pitch."*

Second ball

In *nip and tuck* encounters, the side who win this may well emerge victorious. It is a common gripe of managers that their sides *failed* to *win enough* second balls or the opposition were *quickest to* it, and indeed is advanced as a reason for losing the match. Sometimes the more creative of pundits may refer to the third ball. *"If you want to compete at this level Clive you have to show the desire to get to the second and even the third ball."* It is unclear what the *third ball* actually is.

Second bite of the cherry

Such bites are a fortunate occurrence for the attacker. On smashing home the rebound the player will often pick the ball up and boot it as high as he can in the air for no apparent reason.

Second gear

Something clubs will not *get out of* in the following situations:
1. Those having a stroll in the park, such is the ease of their victory. *"Ki and Gomis bagged the goals for a Swansea side who rarely threatened to get out of second gear."*
2. A side mentally *on the beach* with nothing to play for at the end of the season.
3. A team which has failed to motivate themselves for a match and as such has been comfortably beaten; no doubt their striker is more concerned

with promoting hair products on his Twitter feed than watching the assistant manager move magnets around the tactics board.

Second-season syndrome
Making a dash for the Europa league spots one season, yet propping up the table a year later; this type of behaviour has all the hallmarks of a side suffering from *second-season syndrome*. Often known as *the dreaded*. Perhaps the most difficult task for a team that blossoms in their maiden season is to repeat the trick the next. There have been numerous examples down the years, including Ipswich, Bradford and Middlesbrough. Can also apply to players in *red hot* form one season but who could not hit a cow's arse with a banjo the next.

Seen enough
Enraged at the *ponderous* and *ineffectual display*, players may be *unceremoniously* hauled off by their gaffer. *"Jim Bentley has seen enough from Kenyon, and I'm not surprised. He's telling McCready to get stripped and ready."* Fans have also *seen enough*, particularly those who feel the need to beat the traffic and leave on 85 minutes.

Seen them given
That *penalty shout* where the referee has a long, hard look before shaking his head. Leads commentators and pundits to opine *"I've seen them given [Gary, Clive, Martin, Gabby, Jonathan, etc.]"* Examples of what have been given are never ventured, however if a pundit said *"in the 1996/97 season Gary Martindale scored from the spot in Notts County's 3-3 draw with Wrexham, when I definitely saw that one given"* then it may provide a little clearer context.

Selection headache
This can carry both positive and negative connotations. An injury crisis, leading to a lack of cover in one or more positions is a *selection headache*. On the other hand, a manager may have a number of players in form; he therefore faces some tough choices. *"It is a nice problem to have and speaks to the commitment of the terrific squad we have that so many of the lads are forcing their way into contention."* Headaches are as bad as it gets though; there is no *selection migraine*, although a manager might need a striking crisis like a hole in the head.

Servant
The term servant normally implies some sort of second-class role; however, *servant* in the footballing sense carries much more lofty connotations. Many years dedicated to a side makes the player in question a *great* or perhaps even *wonderful servant* to the club who would *run through a brick wall* for the cause. It may extend even further though, as players who have taken on some de facto ambassadorial role are *fantastic servants* to the game in general; clearly there will be no floor

mopping for these lads – although they do remember cleaning boots as an apprentice. *"Bayern Munich and Paris Saint-Germain have an ongoing interest in Dani Alves, who has been a loyal and rampaging servant to Barcelona since signing for them from Sevilla seven years ago."*

Service

1. Alternatively known as *ammunition* or *assists*, *service* comes in various guises: crosses, through balls, set-pieces, *slide rule* passes and balls over the top to name a few. It is usually provided by the creative heartbeat of the team, who will take the flak if it is not provided. *"Alaixys Romao just hasn't provided the kind of service Lucas Ocampos was used to at Monaco."* There are accompanying culinary references here, such as *putting it on a plate* for the striker.
2. Usually counted in years, and will always be described in positive terms: *"Steve Cherundolo has been a wonderful servant to Hannover, racking up 15 years loyal service with die Roten."*
3. On signing for a club, managers will invariably be *delighted* to *secure the services* of a player.

Set out their stall

The stall is set out by a side that has the sole intention to play a certain way. When a side sets out their stall to defend, it has exactly the same meaning as - but is conversely the complete opposite of - *shut up shop.*

Setting their satnavs

The privilege of teams who have achieved promotion is to put the destinations of the teams in a higher division into their satellite navigation devices. *"What a season for Shrewsbury and Micky Mellon's men! Their promotion means they will be setting their satnavs for places such as Oakwell and the Keepmoat stadium next season."* Clearly the Shrewsbury bus driver would get lost without its guidance and should be advised that the postcode for Oakwell is S71 1ET.

Shades of...

An inferior player who produces skill that is above their station may be showing *shades* of a world-class player who showcases it on a regular basis. Sergio Torres may be able to produces *shades of Messi* on occasion, but it's what he does for 98% of the rest of the time which explains why he never quite made it to the very top.

Shake

1. *Things up.* Act intended to inject some sort of pizzazz into a *flagging* side whose current system is ineffective. It can also be an experiment such as the three-at-the-back trial, or inviting the entire first team squad to stay at

your house as an alternative to a pre-season tour, as Martin Allen once did.

2. *Up.* These come in two principal forms:

   a) *End of season shake up.* Those vying for promotion or a title will hope to be in this mix; and will necessitate a *rallying cry.* *"While Luton could theoretically still join them in League One next term, it would take a freak result next week against Stevenage, themselves guaranteed a place in the end of season shake-up."*

   b) *Boardroom shake up.* Seen when the director of football has signed complete trash from the continent and as such needs to be replaced.

Shelf stacker

Players who have come from nowhere to make it in the Premier League always find their previous non-footballing jobs referenced to highlight their rags-to-riches story. Kevin Phillips was the *shelf-stacker from Hitchin,* while Rickie Lambert plied his trade in a beetroot factory on the Wirral to make ends meet; meanwhile Papiss Cisse was an Ambulance driver in his native Senegal.

Neville Southall was a dustbin man who, as commentators would always say, looked like he had just finished a shift before the game kicked off; meanwhile Dean Windass was scouted whilst working as a bricklayer's labourer in Bradford. Throughout his career, pundits would use industrial words to describe his footballing traits, in particular *grafting* for the team or putting in a *hard shift.*

Footballers might also think about *throwing in the towel,* with Matt Gilks famously saying he very nearly gave it all up to become a banger-racing mechanic, and Jordan Seabright really did chuck it in to become a car salesman.

Shellacked

A phrase originating in the US meaning to administer a comprehensive beating, usually by three or more goals if the away team and four if playing at home. *"Robert Lewandowski popped up with his late treble, ensuring Poland top their group even after Germany shellacked Gibraltar in routine fashion."*

Etymology: Shellac is the resin secreted by the lac insect, and is commonly applied to nails as a varnish. Perhaps in footballing terms, this therefore means one team plasters the other with goals.

Shepherd

When under pressure from an attacker, the defender must show strength and no small amount of balance to usher the ball out of play, being careful not to concede a corner – or worse fall over to let the opposition in. *"Taggart's 'Bambi on ice' impression allowed Soltvedt to cross, with Tessem doing the rest."*

Shift

Apparently comparable to clocking 60 hours of minimum-wage hard labour, this accolade is awarded to men who put in 70+ minutes of competitive exercise once or twice a week. *"To a man, the subs that came on as well, they put in a real shift today. It's the one thing I'd say since we came in the door that the players have really grasped - hard work gets you results."* Comments about such a *shift* will be made as a player is trudging off the pitch to *warm applause*, or when on the floor receiving treatment for cramp. Accusations could also be made that a player only bothers to put in a *real shift* when the visiting scouts come to watch.

Shimmy

A piece of trickery that has moved from the dance floor to the football pitch. *"An intricate move on the edge of the box saw Chris Clements shimmy away but home keeper Artur Krysiak was equal to his low, angled effort."* The player in question will move his shoulders whilst keeping his feet relatively still in order to try and fool his opponent into thinking he's going one way when in fact he's going the other. Jay Jay Okocha was well known for his shimmy celebration; however a dance off never did ensue between himself and Martin Keown.

Shipping goals

To concede in bulk. Teams can be said to have been *shipping goals* all season, or with an *alarming frequency* of late. Players either not up to the standard or who are trouble-makers will be *shipped out* at the earliest possible opportunity, usually on loan.

Shirtful

The wily defender might get away with taking this from his opponent. Indeed this happens all too often in the box but inexplicably goes unpunished. *"Blatant impeding by Hangeland! He had an absolute shirtful of Mirallas there."*

Shocker

1. To put in a rancid performance – i.e. to *have a shocker*.
2. A disgraceful challenge.

Shoestring budget

Funds available to minnows of a division whose manager is expected to perform miracles. Potential signings come from a number of areas:
1. The bargain basement.
2. *Bosmans.*
3. Veterans looking for one last pay day.
4. *Bad boys* looking for another chance, i.e. *last chance saloon.*

Shooting boots

The accessory which really shouldn't be left at home, but all too often is. Strikers who forget their shooting boots are likely to have very little success in front of goal, and will be reminded as such: *"Emile, next week, remember your shooting boots okay?"* Alternatively, if they do manage to lace themselves up, a goal glut may follow, leading to assessments that a player *"definitely has his shooting boots on today."* There are no *heading hats* or *saving gloves*, however.

Shop window

Players use the *shop window* in order to advertise their talents to other clubs. Perhaps the best shop window of all is a World Cup or European Championships, where scouts from far and wide will be looking to unearth the new Mario Gotze, or Roger Milla. *"He's really put himself in the shop window with that strike, hasn't he Alan?"*

Shopping list

The list *drawn up* by managers as if *targets* can be found in aisle six next to the cat food. At the end of every season, it is completed in consultation with the board and if there is one, the director of football. However, whether it is realistic is another matter, and some requests are easier to swing by the holder of the *purse strings*. Steve Sidwell would be a store cupboard staple such as baked beans, however Paul Pogba would be more like a deluxe chocolate roulade. Of course if the Frenchman is top of the range it probably makes Charlie Adam *Sarah Lee Gateaux*.

Shot

1. Aside from it being the act of goalscoring, players who attempt to exacerbate a tackle in order to con the referee will *go down like they have been shot*; it leads to accusations of a sniper in the crowd. Didier Drogba carved an unenviable reputation for this type of behaviour.
2. At *glory*, which may very well be the last. *"Gerrard desperate for one last shot at domestic glory with Liverpool."*

Shot stopper

Complimentary term for a goalkeeper, as it carries the assumption he has the ability to halt any strike on goal. Shot stopping is seen as the ultimate yardstick as to a custodian's ability; they would, for example, not be called a *cross catcher* or *defence organiser*.

Shoving match

Touchline version of *handbags* which managers become *embroiled* in. Famously propagated by Arsene Wenger, this kind of *altercation* will undoubtedly make the headlines on a Sunday morning. It is one of four grades of *touchline spat*, which (in order of seriousness) are: words, finger pointing, shoving match, headbutt.

Showdown

A clash between two bitter rivals or title contenders. In reference to the former, it may be a *high noon showdown*, with the police moving the kick off to prevent the locals from necking too many cans of Carlsberg pre-match, therefore fanning the flames of animosity between the two warring factions.

Showdown talks

The kind of discussions which take place when the situation has reached *crisis point*. The secretary may well be preparing the P45.

Sickening

An incident which makes players, fans and pundits wince. There can be a *sickening collision*, where a player collides with either opponent or object. Perhaps the most well-known involved David Busst, who suffered a broken leg playing for Coventry against Manchester United. This incident is referenced extensively whenever a player suffers a similar (but always less severe) injury. There can also be a *sickening clash of heads*, when two players *go for the same ball*, leaving at least one requiring the smelling salts, or the *magic sponge*.

Sighter

Initial shot early doors from the striker, in an attempt to *find their range*. *"Armand Gnanduillet fires the shot in, but it's just a sighter, with Forde seeing it all the way."* Also known as a *signal of intent*.

Signalling to the bench

Acknowledgement by a player that his game is over. When a signal is made to the bench it is normally accompanied by a shake of the head and the circular substitution hand motion players seem to make; either that or following the established doctrine of hamstring-holding.

Silky skills

This attribute is very often in the possession of a *luxury player* who loves to *dance around defences*. Examples of silky skills include the *lollipop*, the *Cruyff turn* and the *pirouette*. It does not include doing keepy-ups with the knees. *'Luke Beckett's dynamic pace plus silky skills, multiplied by an all-important end product equalled quite a mouth-watering equation which inevitably made him a fan favourite.'*

Silverware

The type of finery which belongs in the *trophy cabinet*. Clubs *chase, hunt, set their sights on* or *dream of* silverware. *"Known as Le President, Laurent Blanc is building up an impressive personal haul of silverware."* It should be noted that the FA Vase is also included under this banner. One may think it is most likely to be made from glass, however it is actually forged from metal.

Simulation

Official FIFA term for diving. Players accused of simulation will be rewarded with a yellow card. In Germany, the word is *schwalbe*, which means *swallow*, like the diving bird. Some players carve out a reputation for simulation, and as such are chastised for it, being touted as *the new* Tom Daley.

Sitter

A miss of epic proportions. The kind of chance which has the crowd on its feet only for thousands of hands to be collectively placed on heads and the question *"how did he manage to miss that?"; "Oh I say! With goal gaping Raphael Rossi Blanco blazes it wide... what an absolute sitter!"* Players never score a *sitter* (or a *gilt-edged* chance) for that matter.

Six of one and half a dozen of the other

Challenge or incident in which the commentators are not able to distinguish the aggressor, and subsequently where to apportion blame. *"Could possibly be a bit of handbags for me Clarke, but it's six of one and half a dozen of the other."* I.e. he grabbed him by the throat, but the other guy slapped him in the face and trod on his foot. The advice to the ref is to have, at least, a *stern word*.

Sixes and sevens

A defence found to be wanting is often in this state. The irony is if a side had six or seven at the back they probably wouldn't have conceded. *"Alan Julian and his Bromley defence were at sixes and sevens and the goalkeeper only just grabbed a Stuart Lewis cross to the far post."*

Skinned

Quaint, 90s term for *beats his man*. A player may *"see himself get skinned all too often."* Usual suspects who get skinned are *labouring*, ageing centre halves, who have – in the words of Lonnie Urquhart in *Mike Bassett: England Manager* – *"all the pace of an Austin Allegro."* The phrase has become less common over the last few years, with use restricted to 7-year old *playground tricksters*, who go on to slot the ball inside the jumper-cum-schoolbag goalposts before embarking on a 40-yard celebration.

Skips

1. *Past his man.* Player who makes light work of a defender's challenge, quite possibly as *if they weren't there.*
2. *Training.* Action of the *bad boy* who *plays for himself.*

Slap

1. *A fine.* Managers relish nothing more than being able to hit their players with a fine. It is alleged that during his pre-Nietzsche twitter quotation years, Joey Barton's face was red raw, with the sheer number of fines he had been *slapped* with.
2. *A hefty price tag.* This occurs when clubs are looking to deter potential bidders. *"Blackburn slap a hefty price tag on Rhodes, saying only a ridiculous offer would prize him away from Ewood Park."* One step away from being *not for sale at any price,* but the *initial hands off warning* might still be issued.

Sleeping giants

A marginally more complimentary version of *perennial underachievers,* the phrase still implies there has been a paucity of trophies in recent years; often asked *"can they awaken from their slumber?"*

Sleeve

The following keep things up here:

1. Tricky *wing wizards.*
2. A potential game-changing player who gets on the ball for the first time since entering the fray.
3. The dead ball specialist when standing over a free kick 25-yards out. *"Hakan Calhanoglu stands over the ball just outside the D. What has the mercurial Turk got up his sleeve?"*
4. It is also a place for managers to keep *super subs.*

Slide rule pass

A pass of such accuracy it could have been made using this instrument. Slide rules are therefore seen as the benchmark of accuracy, and are known to *split* defences. Used predominantly by the *architect* of a move. Other words of exactitude are used to highlight what a fine art this form of ball is: *"Sam Corne's slide rule pass through to Akinde was measured to absolute precision."*

Sluggish

The period of lethargy may last all game long, but it is usually applied to how a side begins the match. Whatever the outcome, teams will *pay* for or *fail to recover* from it. Teams who have endured a gruelling journey to the continent for the Europa league could also be excused for having such a malaise about them. *"After their mammoth 8000-mile round trip to Kairat Almaty, it was no surprise to see the men from the Granite City get off to a sluggish start at Tannadice."*

Smash and grab
An opportunist's dream, analogous to breaking a shop window and making off with the till. Originally, this was the work of two strikers; The Bristol Rovers duo of Alan Warboys and Bruce Bannister were architects of many acts of *daylight robbery*, with the former being known as *smash* and the latter *grab*.

Nowadays, it is a collective team effort. Bobby Zamora's dramatic late strike for QPR versus Derby in the playoff final of 2014 was a prime example of a modern day *smash and grab raid* by a side that had spent the previous 89 minutes with their *backs to the wall;* they posed so little threat the Derby's Lee Grant was sat back *smoking cigars.*

Smash their own transfer record
The act of putting in a *mega bid* for a player; of course, it is relative to what the current record is. During transfer silly season, tabloid journalists will use this phrase in abundance. *"Arsenal are hoping to blow away the competition for Real Madrid striker Gonzalo Higuain by smashing their own transfer record in order to bring the Argentinian goal-getter to North London."* Such rumours are often said to be *wide of the mark.*

Smother the loose ball
An action which is the sole preserve of the goalkeeper. *"It was pinball as the initial effort by Euell was blocked before Spink smothered the loose ball."* It may result from an initial *fumble*, and will be *gathered up at the second attempt;* a *flashpoint* may arise if an attacking player *leaves his foot in* during the *melee*, causing *ugly scenes.*

Snap
1. *Up.* Talented players available on a *Bosman* are a pretty rare thing, yet they are prime candidates to be *snapped up*, having no doubt a number of suitors chasing their signature. It is a marginally less aggressive version of *hoovering* talent, especially when the intent is to simply farm them out on loan again.
2. A vicious, damaging tackle. See also *leg breaker.*
3. To have the *red mist* descend. *"Oh look that this, have you ever seen anything like it! Alloa's number nine has just snapped!"*

Snapshot
1. An unexpected and opportunistic strike. *"Hernandez with a snapshot on the turn, but Green was unlikely to be troubled by that."*

2. A singular event which is indicative of a wider state of affairs within a club. *"The 15-minute second-half collapse by Yeovil was a real snapshot of their season. All that hard work undone in one crazy spell."*

Snatching victory from the jaws of defeat
A turnaround in the dying minutes snatches victory from the jaws of defeat. Examples include:
1. Manchester United's *quick fire double* which stunned Bayern Munich in the Champions League Final of 1999.
2. James Coppinger's title-winning goal for Doncaster against Brentford in April 2013 after the home side had missed a penalty seconds earlier. Had Marcello Trotta not crashed his effort against the crossbar then it would have been the Bees who would have clinched promotion.
3. In a similar scenario, Watford's 95th minute *heartbreaker* versus Leicester in the 2013 playoffs which sent them to Wembley at the Foxes' expense and caused Johnny Phillips to go into meltdown.

The opposite is to snatch defeat from the jaws of victory, and go home *empty handed*.

Snookers
Term used to denote just how deep in the mire a side is: *"Hyde are totally cut adrift at the bottom; we're only just into January and they are already in need of snookers."* Of course, this is a literal impossibility in football, with the term only used to highlight the desperate situation.

Snub
To firmly rebuff. In transfer terms, this isn't just a rejection, it's a firm no. Snubs may also take their forms in a refusal to do something. *"McClean's snub to England's flag branded a disgrace."*

Snuffed out
A pass, attacking move or set play may be *snuffed out* if anticipated by the defending side. *"Daniel Powell seemed to be Dons' most likely player to spark a comeback, but he fired over one shot and saw one threatening cross snuffed out by the Getafe defence."* The term can also refer to title aspirations or drawn out transfer *pursuits*.

Solo effort
Such efforts are normally *superb* or *magnificent*. For it to be solo, at least two players must be beaten or a large distance covered. The commentator will often pinpoint exactly how far the scorer has travelled; *"Barrie McKay added a third 12 minutes after*

the restart when he decided to go it alone with a fine solo effort from the halfway line." Solo efforts are considered *virtuoso goals*, and a shoo-in on the player's own *highlights reel*.

Somebody must have said something at half time
A team who turns in a transformed second half performance may have been on the receiving end of a half time *rollicking*, or words of encouragement that inspired a *comeback*. Either way, *somebody must have said something at half time*. Often stated by commentators a few minutes into the second half, with the team unrecognisable from their *woeful* first half display; they show all the verve and passion required to take something from the game. It can also be used retrospectively in the post-match analysis. *"Ersun Yanal clearly said something at halftime as Fenerbahce tore out of the blocks, but the Gunners delivered a sucker-punch goal just four minutes later."*

Soul searching
An unexpectedly heavy defeat will often bring about this phenomenon, particularly if the fans have undertaken an arduous *round-trip* journey (which is likely to be retrospectively refunded – the ultimate indignity for the players). *"Mackay begins bout of soul searching following latest reverse."*

Special one
A moniker for Jose Mourinho. Often prefixed with *the self-styled*; the term has been somewhat broadened out to refer to all managers who believe themselves to have the *X-factor*; indeed it may even be used as an insult. *"Lusitans boss Xavi Roura has accused Slaven Bilic of believing he is the 'special one' in a stinging attack."* Jurgen Klopp simply referred to himself as *"the normal one"* at his first Liverpool press conference – reducing half of the gathered press to tears with the quip.

Etymology: In Jose Mourinho's first press conference as Chelsea manager he stated, "I am not one of the bottle, I think I am a special one." Five European semi-final defeats later, many do believe that Jose is indeed one of the bottle.

Specialist
1. There are many types of specialists in football, including *free kick, corner, penalty, draw, in failure* and *deadball*, which combines a number of *situations*.
2. Obtaining a potentially serious injury will often see a player sent to a specialist. Groin strains, bruised shins, thigh strains et al are the domain of the magic spray and the firm hands of the club physio. However knee ligament damage will see the player in question jetting off to Colorado to pay Dr Steadman a visit. The news is almost entirely bad, being described as a *"bitter blow."*

Speculation

Speculation is the lifeblood of the transfer market, particularly in the *transfer window*. *"Karim Benzema fuels speculation he will leave Real with cryptic Instagram post."* It can be *welcomed* by a player angling for a move to one of the *big boys*; similarly, it can be *laughed off* by a manager, eager to dismiss unfounded rumours. *"Westley scoffs at 'crazy' transfer speculation."*

Speculative

Shot on goal the attacking player harbours no great expectation for. Coming in a variety of forms, including effort, shot, lob, attempt etc., they will not often *trouble* the keeper; however when they do, they will likely have been caught out by an absolute *peach*, with no blame apportioned: *"Nothing Mike Hooper could do about that Clive."*

Spending spree

Affluent clubs often embark upon rapid investment in their playing squad, particularly for sides recently subject to a multi-million (or billion) pound investment, known as a *transfer splurge*. The committed yet limited British midfielder (who has been with the club since aged nine) will be *consigned to the bench* by a mercurial and prodigiously talented foreign import. Rival managers will often complain of unfair domination of the market and there will be *question marks* about whether the buying club will meet their *financial fair play obligations*.

Spine

Consisting of a minimum of four players but may be:
1. 1 x safe pair of hands.
2. 1-2 x colossus centre backs.
3. 1 x midfield *maestro* and/or 1 x *enforcer*.
4. 1 x 20-goal a season man and/or 1 x *foil*.

Teams are often lauded for having a *solid* spine, while *powder puff* sides will be criticised for a *lack* of one. Possibly one of the most recognisable spines in English football is the one boasted by Manchester City consisting of Hart, Kompany, Toure and Aguero; although if one is missing, the Citizens' weaknesses are laid bare.

Spiritual home

Despite having moved on from the club, a player who has given many years' service, or enjoyed a particularly strong rapport with the fans will describe the club as his *spiritual home*: *"My body belongs to Tottenham but my heart is in Barnsley"* etc. Brazil is known as the spiritual home of football, presumably because they play the *beautiful game* the way it was meant to be played and not in the manner you might see down the local rec on a Sunday morning.

Spoil the party
The footballing equivalent of a quite deliberately acted out faux pas. It is the footballing equivalent of stealing the champagne, cutting the wedding cake or getting unacceptably drunk and passing out on the lawn.

Sportsman's dinner
Source of income for ex-pros. Usually billed as '*An audience with...*' these evenings are popular at local venues up and down the UK, and feature many of the leading lights of the bygone days of football. There is now somewhat of an established circuit, with former players and managers such as Dave Bassett, Jan Molby and Des Walker lifting the lid on what *really* happened in the dressing room. Hilarious stories may include the one about Michael Booger's caravan, which player insisted on watching Willy Wonka and the Chocolate Factory before each game (the original version), and who really did defecate on Crystal Palace's dressing room floor.

Sportsmanship
The bastion of footballing morality, sportsmanship tends to fall within the spirit of the game rather than the laws. It covers a wide range of actions, including (but not limited to):
1. Not making the most of a tasty challenge; something which is *always nice to see*.
2. Returning the ball to the opposition after an injury.
3. Combatting racism with handshakes.

Spray
1. The act of firing off passes left, right and centre with gay abandon, the midfield *anchorman* looks to dictate play at every opportunity. These passes are most commonly *sprayed around the park* by a confident playmaker in midfield. *Ball playing* defenders can also spray balls from the back.
2. Vanishing spray. The latest invention for referees to make sure the wall is back the *full complement*. *"Neil Swarbrick brandishes the vanishing spray in the direction of the Aston Villa defence; he's laying down the law to Jores Okore and co."*

Spread himself well
A 'keeper of real quality can smother a striker's *gilt-edged* chance by making himself big; looming over the onrushing goal threat, narrowing the angles and *snuffing out* the danger. *"Braham-Barrett was a constant threat down the left for the visitors and worked*

an opening for himself on 17 minutes but was denied by Barry Roche, who spread himself well to save." The *Big Dane* Peter Schmeichel was world-renowned for this trait. Another way in which 'keepers look to cover as much of the goal as possible is by producing a *sprawling* save.

Squeaky bum time
The twitchy end of season period in which nerves begin to jangle. Articles appear on the BBC Sport website every April featuring articles on this phenomenon. Originally referring to a period of the season, it can also apply to an individual match – or *squeaky bum encounter.*

Etymology: The phrase was coined towards the end of the 2002/03 season by Sir Alex Ferguson to articulate the mounting tension between the Red Devils and Arsenal in their title race. While it was initially synonymous with Ferguson himself, like so many other phrases in football it has come to apply to other footballing situations – and indeed society in general.

Stake
1. *A claim.* Those on a fine goalscoring run may stake their claim for a first team berth or a *spot on the plane.* Similarly, interim managers may oversee good form which leads to them staking a claim to get the top job on a full time basis. *"The job Chris Ramsey has done in such trying circumstances down Shepherd's Bush surely means he's staked a claim to get the QPR hot seat on a permanent basis."* It is one step away from *throwing his hat into the ring.*
2. *High stakes.* The type of situations where dreams are made and mercilessly crushed.

Stalemate
Turgid goalless draw. The kind of game most likely to be *last on Match of the Day.*

Etymology: Chess term to describe a player who is not in check, but who is unable to make a move. In such instances, a draw is declared.

Stalling over a new deal
Players who are unsure about whether to *put pen to paper* on *an improved contract* may very possibly be *stalling over a new deal,* perhaps looking to test the waters and seek admiring glances from elsewhere. Are said to be *keeping their options* open but their current club will be keen not to *lose them on a Bosman.* This kind of behaviour can fuel the rumour mill and send the tabloids into a frenzy. *"Shreeves slams contract rebel Quinn for persistently stalling over a new deal."*

Stalwart
Stalwarts usually have a long association with the club and are held in high regard by everyone from the tea lady to the chairman. A loyal and reliable player, he is someone who *wears his heart on his sleeve* and would, without question, die – metaphorically – for his teammates.

Stand up and be counted
A form of *rallying cry* to the troops, to remind them of their responsibilities and the expectation that will be on them from the fans. The phrase forms the basis of many newspaper headlines: *"John Ward says his side must stand up and be counted."*

Standard bearers
"Chelsea are the standard bearers for the Premier League in Europe now." Those nominated to lead the charge for a side or nation are often described as such. John Terry may be elected Chelsea's *standard bearer*, displaying a commitment, drive and passion which all others should aspire to, particularly when parking across two disabled bays outside *Pizza Hut* – and then again outside that kebab shop.

Staring relegation in the face
A team who is down, but not quite out. The side facing the drop are usually the ones to blink first and the dreaded trapdoor *swings* open. It can also be used to denote just how far a side has come. *"A mere 12 months ago the Chairboys were staring relegation in the face, but now Ainsworth's charges have a very real chance of breaking out of League Two."*

Starlet
A *wonderkid*, with the ability to make it at the very top. He will however require careful nurturing and development in order to harness their boundless potential. Is often used as a trumped-up term for a player who happens to be at one of the big boys; if he plays for Margate he is simply *"the small kid in the reserves, but has been here since he was 12."*

Etymology: The term originates from Hollywood, describing young actresses or singers going through the star system.

Star-studded
Usually a *line up*, although when looking ahead to a match featuring many world-class talents, commentators will be *drooling* at the prospect of a *star-studded cast*.

Starting berth

Unfortunately, for the perennial *bench warmers* out there, only 11 starting *berths* exist in any team. No matter if a player is happy to play in any position just to get a game; he must prove his credentials in order to secure it. *"It's six and two threes whether Joe Royle plumps for Gunnar Halle or Craig Fleming at the back."*

Stellar half time entertainment

When Whitehawk FC have inexplicably booked the Rolling Stones while the crowd *blow on their Bovrils*.

Stick

1. Informal name for the goalposts. The term is used in a variety of ways, such as *between the sticks*. Big Ron's *Ronglish* lexicon saw the phrases *front stick* and *back stick* come into use, such as *"I'll tell you what, the lad's left the back stick unguarded there and van Nistelrooy, predating as usual has gobbled up that chance."*
2. *Dog's abuse*. Those players who are totally out of form will undoubtedly come in for their fair share of *stick* from the *terraces* and *armchairs*. Their name may be booed as it is read out before the game, or ironic cheers may be heard on their substitution.
3. *Stuck one on him*. A nasty tackle causing an injury unlikely to be remedied by a sticking plaster.

Stiffs

Uncomplimentary name for a team's reserve side, or as known in today's day and age, the *development squad*.

Stifling tactics

A game plan that is likely to produce little attacking intent, and a back line so tight and well organised that it is almost impenetrable. Stifling tactics are used a) by a side who know that they are unlikely to get a win, so will look to *nick* one on the break or b) sides who have a first leg advantage, and therefore do not need to attack. The *onus* therefore is all on the opposition. Accusations that only one team came to play football may be meted out, however managers may be *lauded* when they utilise a man marking scheme to render a quality opposition player ineffective. *"He kept the lid on Luke Freeman all afternoon."*

Sting

During periods of play when the danger is substantially heightened, it would be wise for the defending team to try and take the *sting* out of the game. On the other hand, when a side concedes a goal they perhaps didn't expect to, they will be *stung into action*. Alternatively, the team hit by a late *sucker punch* will have been caught by the *sting in the tail*, or finally a killer goal might remove it. *"We peppered their goal, dominated the game but their second really took the sting out of the tail."*

Stinker
Something the referee usually has, but this can also refer to players who have put in a rancid performance too. *"Monk fury at Oliver stinker."*

Stonewall
Term used to describe a *stick on* penalty. Colloquially called an *absolute stonewaller*. *"When Ken Monkou scythed down Darren Eadie in the box even the most ardent of Saints wouldn't be able to deny it was a stonewall penalty."* Other descriptions include *cast iron* and *ironclad* penalties. It should be noted they are not always given, leading to complaints about having to rob grannies in order to get one. *"He could have shot him and the ref would have waved play on."* There is, therefore, plenty to discuss for fans of both sides – who usually synthesise their arguments with the platitude *decisions even themselves out over the course of the season.*

Storm
A number of situations can cause a storm:
1. An onslaught by a team may lead to questions about whether the opposition can *weather* it?
2. A story which the press finds contentious. *Twitter storms* perhaps, about an ill-judged or unauthorised photograph. Ezequiel Lavezzi caused such a storm after posting a compromising picture of him in a policeman's hat.
3. On being asked a question they simply do not care for, the more temperamental manager may *storm out* of a pre- or post-match briefing, causing somewhat of a sensation. *"Nigel Pearson calls reporter an 'ostrich' then storms out of press conference."*
4. In extreme examples, fans might storm the pitch in protest or anger because of something they have witnessed.

Straight down the 'keepers' throat
A shot straight at the goalkeeper. It is viewed differently depending on the esteem in which the shooting player is held. For example, a shot straight down Manuel Neuer's throat might be deemed *world class*, but a similar shot at Tim Deasy is just *meat and drink*.

Stranded
Over-zealous 'keepers who come for crosses run the real risk of finding themselves in *no man's land. "Oluoch was left stranded by Kipre Tchetche's free-kick in the 67th minute after John Bosco had put his side ahead early in the first half."* It is worth

pointing out that events outside of their control might also leave them as such; for example, a wicked deflection off a wall.

Streak
1. *Winning.* The run all sides want to embark upon.
2. *Losing.* The run all sides want to avoid.
3. Streaker. One of two things the TV cameras cannot show; the other being a particularly nasty injury.

Etymology: Streakers are certainly not unique to football; indeed the act of parading naked in front of a crowd is something which has occurred for many years. Perhaps Lady Godiva was the pioneer of the act as she rode naked through the streets of Coventry in the 11th Century; however in a sporting context the first person to streak at a major event was Michael O'Brien at Twickenham in 1974 who accepted £10 to run onto the pitch naked at half time.

The word streaker has only been known in its current form since the early 70s. Before this, its meaning was 'to go quickly, to rush, to run at full speed'. There have been other variants too; John Arlott once referred to a 'freaker' at the second Ashes test at Lords in 1975, noting 'he's getting a very good reception... a fine performance but what will they do about finding his swimming trunks?'

Streetwise
The adroit, *wily operator* is bestowed with this tag. With a *wealth* of experience in the game he's seen it all. He won't be fooled by a *disguised pass*, nor will he *crumble* under pressure. *"Maddix has committed a tactical foul there, stopping the Bolton attack before it starts... quite clearly Fabian de Freitas will have to get up a lot earlier in the morning to outwit this streetwise defender."* Alternatively, the assertion is often made if teams had been savvier, their quest for points might have been successful. *"East Fife 0 Clyde 1: Fifers not streetwise enough".*

Striker's
1. *Dream.* The *dream* of every striker is to have a *set piece specialist*, or supremely talented crosser of the ball out wide, to provide the kind of service they only encounter in their sleep. Strike partners might also provide the *perfect foil*. *"It's every strikers' dream to have a player like Jamie Devitt popping cross after cross on your head every week Colin."*
2. *Tackle.* A tackle that wouldn't look out of place at the local *rec* on a Sunday morning. Akin to a mechanic trying to make choux pastry or a man walking in high heels for the first time.
3. *Union.* Mythical union referred to on a regular basis by Michael Owen. Current campaigns include better access to *goalscoring opportunities*, an increase in the *4-4-2* system and an abolition of the *false nine role*.

String
1. Stringing a number of passes together is an attractive way to play. Common when playing *total football*. Conversely, it may be used to highlight a poor performance: *"Pjanic expressed his embarrassment that Roma 'couldn't string three or four passes together' as they were thrashed by Bayern."*
2. *Second string*, i.e. the reserves. The senior side is never referred to as the *first string*.

Stripped and ready
Comprised of two parts:
1. *Stripped*. Removing tracksuit top and bottoms, briefly being topless in front of the entire stadium, before finally putting a shirt on.
2. *Ready*. Taping up rings, having boots checked, swigging from a water bottle, moving the head in a circular motion and getting a last minute *pep talk* from the gaffer, possibly about occupying *the hole*.

Studs up
The kind of tackle no one wants to see. Showing studs is majorly frowned upon in footballing fraternities; considered a *coward's challenge*. Despite the change in technology from the 90s, it is never known as *blades up*.

Stuff
1. *Strut his*. To show off a skill or ability. *"It's a real coup for the Railwaymen, and is a signing that could push them to the next level. No doubt the fans can't wait to see Rodney Jack strut his stuff in a red shirt."*
2. *Stuffed*. To be soundly thrashed. *"I'll be the first to admit it, we took a good stuffing today Gabby."* The phrase is often used around the festive period. *"Magnificent Cobblers serve-up stuffing to hapless turkeys Hartlepool."*

Stunned the football world
Sides who pull off the unexpected by notching a seemingly impossible victory may very well *stun the football world*. The result would make a mockery of one of Lawro's standard 2-0 home win predictions. It can apply to many footballing scenarios however: *"Sven Goran Eriksson sweeps into Meadow Lane to stun the footballing world."*

Sublime finish
A glorious finish where the crowd collectively thinks: *"Pick that one out."* There are also *sublime* moves of one-touch passing.

Sucker punch
Having had the best of a side but not being able to find that crucial goal, a team can be hit with an unlikely goal in the dying seconds that *KOs* any chance of victory. *"Jannik Vestergaard dragged wide as the Danes pushed, only to be hit by a sucker punch after Alexander Scholz was adjudged to have bundled over Isaac Kiese Thelin."* A goal which nobody saw coming, but will end up *costing them dear*.

Sudden death
A cruel way to lose. Curious term to describe the nail-biting end to a penalty shootout; although the sudden death is more instantaneous if the opposition do not need to take their penalty in order to win the shootout. These periods are hugely tense, with one team certain to be left on the floor at the end, and can often lead to calls for FIFA to change the rules to come up with a fairer alternative than the *lottery* of the penalty shootout.

Suicidal
Adjective preceding *backpass* or *defending*. The term insinuates that such a terrible ball was intentional, when of course it was not.

Suitable finale
The type of finish that a *big occasion* deserves. *"The Gills came up with a suitable finale in the pulsating Johnstone's Paint quarter final."*

Summer clearout
The overhaul of playing staff, which for many clubs occurs annually. Those who are out of contract or deemed surplus to requirements will be *jettisoned* in favour of fresh blood. Like Keith Curle going into the loft to take his box of unwanted strikers down to the *British Heart Foundation*.

Superlative
An exaggerated form of expression which can be used as an umbrella term for just how good a shot, goal or other passage of play was. *"What a superlative effort from the diminutive Italian Giovinco!"* Pundits may also find they are *running out* of superlatives to describe a player or team.

Super-sub
The ultimate *impact player*, such as baby-faced assassin Ole Gunnar Solksjaer. Sure to strike fear into the hearts of the opposition when he is getting *stripped and ready* – although strangely it is the manager who will take the bulk of the credit should they make the difference. David Fairclough was the original super-sub, being used as Bob Paisley's *secret weapon* on many an occasion. See also *impact player*.

Supply lines
The lines which a side will look to cut to the *front men*, in an attempt to *starve* them of any decent service.

Etymology: Military terminology, particularly in siege warfare.

Supremo
Head in charge of a footballing entity, taken from Spanish, meaning – unsurprisingly – supreme. Managers are sometimes described as *supremos*, but it is a term generally reserved for those in real power, such as *FA supremo* Greg Dyke.

Surprise omission
Previously a *nailed on* first teamer, the absence of a player's name from the team sheet makes them a *surprise omission*, especially if they are not thought to be on the *treatment table*. May lead to speculation in the media about what exactly did go on during that unauthorised night out, suggesting that there is substance to the rumours about being photographed smoking in the VIP area at 2.30am.

Surprise package
Usually the bookmakers get things pretty spot on. The hot tips for league success come from a select band of elite clubs; the only reason why some sides are listed at 2000/1 is because some *diehard* will always lump a tenner on it. However when a team does break into this cabal for a certain period of time, they are labelled the division's *surprise package*. Usually they fade away, however some do last the distance; Ipswich Town's *odds-defying* charge to the UEFA Cup in 2000/01 gave scant regard to the leading lights of the division, although their relegation the following season was something of a wake-up call.

Surrendering possession
Giving the ball away without much, if any, fight. Suffixed with *all too easily*, typically.

Survivor
Players who played a corresponding fixture in previous years are *survivors* of that clash. Similarly, those who have played under a manager from bygone years are also considered *survivors* of their tenure. *"Lewis Stevenson is the sole survivor from John Collins' time at Hibernian."*

Suspect
Criticism of goalkeepers who have questionable attributes. Catching, kicking, shot stopping, command of the area and general ability can all be placed under the *suspect* banner. Weak links in the side may also stand out as *suspect*, as do displays

in general. *"Mike Newell's boys turned in somewhat of a suspect performance against the Daggers."* On conceding a shocking goal, the most culpable player may be identified as such: *"The fourth Leicester strike was due to diabolical defending by Sunderland, with Kaboul the prime suspect."*

Swap shirts
For reasons unknown, this is a practice frowned upon at half time but encouraged once the hostilities are over. Many footballers like to collect famous shirts, with Messi, Neymar, and Tevez regularly the subject of post-match bunfights between opposition players. Players may not necessarily want Shola Ameobi's shirt hanging in their trophy room however.

Swashbuckling run
A daring run which gets the crowd *on their feet*, particularly if it is the game's first moment of *real quality*.

Sweat
1. The amount that players sweat during matches of high humidity is often referenced, particularly during the summer months of the World Cup. Jan Koller, for example was rumoured to have lost half a stone during one of Czech Republic's games at the 2006 tournament. It is unclear what unit of measurement will be used in 2022.
2. While footballers literally sweat, clubs metaphorically perspire over the fitness of a player ahead of what is a potentially *pivotal* match. Images of Barry Fry furiously dabbing himself with a hankie in a sweltering office spring to mind.
3. *Blood.* To describe players who have given it their *all.* Perhaps has *toil* and/or *tears* mixed in. *"I am ready to sweat blood for this club. I want to create and score goals and I know I can be part of a trophy-winning team this season."*

Sweepstake
The event which takes place every two years around the start of a major international tournament. All the office, from the receptionists to the MD draw teams out of the hat, but there's always one person who gets Brazil and one who has to get Iran.

Sweet left foot
A foot of considerable ability, capable of producing superb through balls, incisive passes and *unerring* finishes. *"Yarmolenko operates on the right wing, often cutting inside to strike at goal with his sweet left-foot."* Is a variant of the *cultured* left foot, but the *sweet* form can be possessed by players from the home nations too, whereas *cultured* cannot. Right feet tend to be portrayed as more run-of-the-mill, being qualified as

trusty or *dependable*; something there to be *swung*, but from which you wouldn't expect *fireworks*. *"Robert Molenaar clubs the ball away with his right boot; it's not pretty but it is effective, because as a result Leeds are now on the counter."*

Swipe

Something returned for *barbs*. Managers may question whether the opposition are good enough to achieve what is expected of them, with the response being less than complimentary. *"Watson takes swipe at FC Halifax promotion credentials."* In serious cases, they will *let fly*, often at *former charges*. *Jibes* will be met with similar short shrift.

Swoop

Used with greater frequency than *pounce*, clubs *swoop* for other teams' prize assets. Varieties include *double, audacious* and *record breaking*; additionally, *sensational summer swoops* are spoken of annually during the dog days of pre-season and will usually be qualified with *according to reports in....* Particularly bold enquiries are often *laughed off*; alternatively managers could be accused of *living in a dream world*.

Symptomatic

Evidence which seems to sum up just why a side has *problems*. *"You know Chappers, I've seen some poor defensive displays but the difficulties Aston Villa have had offensively has been symptomatic of a pretty poor end of the season and shows why they've finished 17th."* Not, of course, that Robbie Savage would ever use the word symptomatic.

T

Tactics truck

Much maligned televisual device associated with ex-ITV pundit Andy Townsend. Oft ridiculed as the leading reason for the channel's ill-fated programme *The Premiership*. Has now been converted into a burger van.

Take nothing for granted

Despite having an advantage, whether it is a first leg lead or superior personnel, managers will always *take nothing for granted*. This is usually *out of respect* for the opposition. *"We've built a four goal advantage, but we will be taking nothing for granted when we travel to Brisbane Road next week."*

Take that!

Exclamation screamed by excited commentators when an absolute *howitzer* of a goal is scored. An alternative is *"How about that!"* Like the band, these phrases seem to have been in their heyday during the 90s.

Take the positives

These positives are usually *plenty* in number. A sentiment that the fans are unlikely to share; the assertion that *"we won the second half"* will not cut the mustard when the team was two down after half an hour.

Take the rough with the smooth

The Zen approach to football management, usually reserved for mid-table football or those with no great expectations. This gaffer doesn't get too excited or carried away, but neither will he push the *panic button*. *"We've had some great times at Stockport this season, but we knew we'd lose sooner or later. We just have to take the rough with the smooth."*

Take to Twitter

The go-to medium to garner footballer's opinions on a range of subjects. Nicolas Anelka might inform his followers as to why he is leaving his latest club, Joey Barton will tweet to comment on the fruity tackle he's just seen live on TV, and Gary Lineker might express his 140-character thoughts on the latest developments in the Syrian crisis. See also *storm*.

Taken as far as he can

The manager who has been in charge for a number of seasons and either a) has achieved nothing or b) achieved something yet looks like going no further, will fall into this category. A departure by *mutual consent* is very likely in these circumstances.

Taking each game as it comes

A classic press-conference quote. It is a phrase used by the gaffer post-match to project a sense of pragmatism and security regarding his team's prospects, because to do anything else would mean getting *carried away*. *"Our focus is on the Queen's Park match; we're taking each game as it comes and come May what will be will be."* Along with a few other well aired examples (such as that *cold wet Tuesday in Stoke*), the individual in question will always acknowledge the fact that they are trotting out a massive cliché.

Taking home the match ball

The honour of the *hat-trick hero*. At the end of the game, TV cameras rush to get the killer shot of him striding off with the match ball tucked firmly under his arm.

In the days of the *multi ball system* it is questionable whether the ball is the actual one that *found the back of the onion bag* on three occasions. Nowadays it perhaps doesn't carry as much significance; having a brown leather caser on the mantelpiece must have been a much more satisfying interior design choice than current official ball of the Premier League, the *Nike Ordem 3*.

Talk

1. *Fighting.* *"Reid comes out fighting amidst squad rift rumours."* Whilst managers will come out and defend a player against criticism, this type of chatter might have fanciful connotations. *"Chairman David Sharpe aims to smash 100-point barrier with Wigan."*
2. *Takeover.* Not quite *advanced talks*, but these are certainly stronger rumours than mere conjecture. Such reports will prompt the gaffer to say they are *"not worried"* about their own future, should any deal go through.
3. *Title.* The sort of chatter which swirls through the air during the early to mid-stages of a season, particularly if a side has exceeded expectations. Is commonly heard on Merseyside between the months of June and September, but it is not until the turn of the year that a side can be considered *genuine* title contenders.

Talking a good game

A manager or player who sings from the right hymn sheet for the fans, but often fails to implement lofty ambitions; indeed anyone can talk a good game, but it is generally accepted that any talking of note will be done *on the pitch*. Also known as *fighting talk*.

Tapping-up affair

Clandestine meetings at a top London hotel, an illicit rendezvous at Newport Pagnell services or the Smoking Terrace at the Club at the Ivy; these locations all lend themselves to one of football's biggest taboos: a tapping up affair.

What constitutes tapping up another side's player is very much a grey area; indeed this dark art of football may well be more prevalent than many would like to admit. Brian Clough once famously said he had *"tapped up more players than the Severn-Trent water board."* It is interesting to note that players of clubs can often try to tempt players they'd love to see join the side without rebuke, however managers or club officials would without doubt receive, at the very least, an *FA rap*.

Etymology: The practice was brought to wider attention by the 1953 film 'The Great Game' starring Thora Hird, Diana Dors and James Hayter. It revolved around an illegal approach of a football club chairman and his subsequent ban from the game.

Target

1. *Man.* An old fashioned centre forward. Teams lump the ball long because he's *good in the air.*
2. The *onion bag. "Try as they might, Leroy Rosenior's men couldn't hit the target for love nor money."*
3. A player the opposition will look to hit – and hit hard. He is perhaps a mercurial *speedster* who relies on his pace, and therefore a well-placed *early doors* dead leg *reducer* is the aim. Such instances will lead the manager to call on referees to afford more protection. The target can also be the *hothead* of the team, continuously *hacked* to try and coax him into a reaction.

Tatters

A Player or team so bereft of belief they are unsure where the next victory is coming from. Confidence can be reduced to *tatters* through a bad run of defeats, or committing a glaring individual error. Is the opposite of a player in *sublime form.*

Dreams are reduced to *tatters* for many managers every season, as are reputations after a less-than-successful spell in charge of a side. Similar to being in *ribbons.*

Taxi

A miss of such embarrassment, it will require the offending player to hail a taxi to transport him away from the ground. *"Taxi for Heskey!"*

Tea lady

The oft-referred to employee at a football club. It is vitally important that nobody upsets the tea lady, because she will no doubt have been there for nigh on 40 years and as such is part of the *fabric* of the club. She is seen as the connection with the real world, and is the yardstick for measuring club harmony; *"Everyone from the tea lady to the chairman is pushing in the same direction."* She is also loved by the players, with stories of *the lads* clubbing together to buy her a new urn or pinnie as a sign of their affection.

Teacups flying

Euphemism for a *complete bollocking being dished out. "Knowing Adams as I do, there'll be teacups flying in the dressing room right about now Gary."* So furious is the manager at what he has just seen he is willing to forego his cup of PG Tips to use it as an aid with which to demonstrate his displeasure.

Team meeting

These are never held in positive circumstances. Team meetings take place due to a dreadful run of form or a particularly brutal beating. Held at the training ground during the week, issues ironed out include the following:

1. Who was at fault for the fourth goal.
2. Why the defence is so porous.
3. The exact problem between the club captain and the left back.

This is subsequently publicised to the media, with assurances that discussions were *"positive"* and *"the lads are raring to go for Saturday"* with a possible addition of *"we believe in ourselves."*

Team talk

The classic motivational tool with which a manager hopes to inspire the troops to victory. Pre-match team talks are full of encouragement whereas half time team talks carry a much greater risk of risk of shouting, swearing, finger pointing and threats. See *Mike Bassett: England Manager* at half time vs. Mexico, or indeed Steve Bleasdale whilst in charge of Peterborough United; *"When it's a battle, you f****** battle!"* Opposition players or managers who unleash *barbs* ahead of a game are often thanked for doing the team talk for the manager.

Full time team talks do not exist, per se. In general, however, interactions include the manager swigging on a bottle of Lucozade, telling *the lads* they gave it *their all*, or perhaps having a quick word with his assistants before nipping off to pay the ref a visit. Alternatively, he might decide to *lock his team in the dressing room*, which will likely keep the gathered journalists waiting.

Teasing cross

A flirty ball in to the middle which screams out *"get on the end of me."* Hangs around just enough to keep the attacker interested.

Technical area

Many believe this is the box in-between the dugout and the pitch. However, according to the *Laws of the Game*, it includes the dugout, bench and the rectangular area on the touchline. This is where *technical* stuff happens such as whistling, remonstrating with a harangued fourth official, and making the 4-4-2 gesture with an accompanying *get it forward* motion. Strict rules prevent managers from *encroaching* onto the field of play, with sanctions handed out for flouting the rules. For example, managers may be sent to the stands to sit with their Bluetooth headset and the opposing chairman's son.

Telegraphing

A pass easier to read than a book. This occurs either across the face of a player's goal or when mounting an attack which comes to an abrupt end. In defending situations, it is customary for the player to sink to his knees in despair, wanting the ground to *swallow him whole*; in attacking situations the forwards are usually pretty hacked off, gesturing pointedly at their feet. *"The telegraphed pass by Kiwomya was suitably punished by a ruthless Ruel Fox."*

Tempo

The pace at which a match is played is the most reliable indicator as to the entertainment levels on show, and both teams will attempt to control it. A *furious* tempo implies excitement, drive and a desire to win; whereas a slower tempo is the hallmark of a game which is crying out for a goal, a *snoozefest* or one which won't live long in the memory. *"The tempo of this game suggests both teams wouldn't be too unhappy with a point Clive."*

Tender years

The period of a professional footballer's career when he is wet behind the ears. Showing *composure* is not something he is expected to do, but when he does it *belies* his tender years. *Cool heads, decision making abilities* and *brute strength* are attributes only developed from the mid-20s onwards. Speed, however, might diminish. See also *raw*.

Etymology: Tender years originates from a legal doctrine which assumed said years were the age of four and below; clearly the age range has altered slightly in reference to footballers.

Tensions running high

This game is about to boil over, the mood is turning and the referee is on the verge of losing control; particularly when the talisman of a side has just been snapped by the opposition enforcer and no sanction has followed. Commonly found in *heated* derby atmospheres.

Test the 'keeper

Something every striker should *at least* do from a decent range, but quite often has *failed* in their aim. A *test* for the keeper ranks higher than something considered *bread and butter, meat and drink* or *regulation*. The inference can be made that a side drew or lost because they did not do this. *"The Tartan Army's failure to properly test the 'keeper was the reason why they drew a blank."*

Testimonial

Reward for a player who traditionally *amasses* ten years of service for his club. Used to be the case he could keep all the gate receipts of the tie, perhaps due to impending unemployment. However, since the advent of multi-million pound contracts this is increasingly rare, with charitable causes the most likely beneficiaries. Matches might have 70,000 in attendance (like Roy Keane's testimonial), 1,300 hardy souls as was the case at Darren Wrack's, or a 17-man mass brawl (as seen at Julian Dick's benefit match).

THAT
Word usually capitalised by newspapers to make sure the meaning is crystal clear to the reader. *"Deschamps refuses to discuss THAT challenge… and no wonder why"*; *"His reputation, still in tatters after THAT incident in the Prague hotel room."*

That night in Barcelona
Phrase used by Clive Tyldesley at least 25 times every time Manchester United play in European competition.

That wasn't in the script
When something unexpected happens. The comment is usually laced with a patronising glaze, especially when European *minnows* take the lead against one of our beloved English giants. Those who turn up to spoil the party may *tear up the script* in defiance of the expected procession of goals. Alternative to: *you couldn't write a script like this.* On scoring such a goal, it may be described as *"the goal the script demanded."*

That's better
Term used by Andy Townsend to get across his pleasure at seeing a team remedy some of the faults he has previously identified. Normally takes about ten minutes for it to be cracked out, possibly because one of the sides in action has *"started nervously".*

The … half of the city
Cities that have more than one team are traditionally split into two halves. So in Dundee, United fans would form the *orange half of the city* and Dees the *blue*.

The beautiful game
Similar to *the game* but is used when emphasising the fact that football is the greatest game on the planet. *Proponents* of *the beautiful game* include Olivier Giroud, Sebastian Larsson and Dirk Kuyt. When an uncompromising, one-dimensional or agricultural style of play is adopted, it may be said a side *"has turned the beautiful game ugly."*

Etymology: The true origin of the term is disputed, however it features in the title of Pelé's book 'My Life and the Beautiful Game' in 1977.

The decisions even themselves out over the course of a season
Assumption made my pundits who believe every team will have an equal number of decisions go for and against them in a campaign, although where they get their evidence for this is another matter. Referees may also even things out during a match when analysts accuse them of knowing they have got a decision wrong. *"Well, he owes Brighton one after that penalty in the first half, a case of evening things up perhaps Jon?"*

The game
1. Informal name for football.
2. *'The Game.'* Actor, rapper and Dr Dre protégé, real name Jayceon Terrell Taylor.
3. Nickname for WWE superstar Hunter Hurst Helmsley.

The game needs a goal
Remark by commentators running out of things to say during particularly *turgid* affairs. They have already discussed the injury to the second-choice left back who hasn't made the trip, the fact that the foreign number 10 is wearing gloves in September and that the press box has stopped serving chicken Balti pies; *'The lad from Kestrel FM was raging.'*

The hole
The space between midfield and attack. It has obtained a somewhat mythical status over the years, having been *occupied* by some of the leading lights of the game such as Diego Maradona, Jari Litmanen and Enzo Scifo. The hole is also something star strikers will dig themselves out of with a match-winning performance.

The mark of true champions
Firstly, these teams serve up performances to remember, and secondly there is no *choking* when it comes to *the crunch*. True champions are *serial-winners* who have a *bulging trophy cabinet*, rather than a team who have been recently bankrolled by a wealthy foreign owner and could go bust when he *pulls the plug*. True champions may also grind out the *one-nils* when playing *well below par* and *winning ugly*, or turn a two-goal deficit into three points.

The men from...
Term used when talking about geographical areas, rather than actual towns or cities. For example, Wolverhampton Wanderers would be *the men from the Black Country*, Stoke *the men from the Potteries* and Norwich *the men from East Anglia*. You would not hear *the men from Doncaster*, for example. It disregards the fact the

starting eleven will probably hail from Transylvania, the coastal lowlands of Venezuela and Castle Donington.

The Messis and Ronaldos of this world

"Well Jim what I would say is Inter cannot be considered true favourites this year because of what Barca and Real possess. It's the ability of the Messis and Ronaldos of this world that set them apart." Similarly, it may be used to provide context to a player's talent, or lack thereof. Averaging more than a goal a game is something the *Messis and Ronaldos* of this world are capable of, but it is highly unlikely to happen in the *Ryman League.* Also known as *your Messis…* and *your Ronaldos…*

The number nine

Term for the Eastern European striker the commentator cannot remember the name of in a Champions League tie against stellar English opposition. *"The number nine has turned his man really well there, Clive, and he's unlucky not to score."*

The one glaring omission from his CV

Many great players have graced the game, yet have found it impossible to add one particular trophy to their personal medal collection. A Premier League winner's medal is the *one glaring omission* from the CV of Steven Gerrard for example. Frank Lampard (and many other England stars) will harbour regret over a lack of international *honours* having achieved everything domestically. It might however be more than one glaring omission; Matt Le Tissier is often cited as the man who sacrificed the chance to get a shot at any major silverware to remain a *one club man* throughout his professional career.

Appearances in competitions are also noteworthy by a player's absence; George Weah is notable for never appearing in a World Cup Finals. Managers too can be affected by this; the one *glaring omission* from Brian Clough's CV was a failure to win the FA Cup.

The pitch is a good leveller

Ability is the best indicator of what sets two sides apart. One team may be 108 places above the other on the *league ladder* but when they make the trip down to Giant Axe on a Sunday afternoon in the FA Cup first round they are likely to find a mud bath in the centre circle, more sand than grass, and a penalty spot which has had three applications of whitewash. *"These pretty boys haven't played on a real pitch in years!"* the boys from *Bailrigg FM* might cry as the ball stops dead in the midfield quagmire. In these circumstances is it fair to say that *the pitch is a good leveller.*

The post-match bottle of red
The practice is associated largely with Sir Alex Ferguson, who would invite managers to his office afterwards by way of courtesy and solidarity. The media revelled in the assertion that any manager he had clashed with in the past would not be offered the chance to share in one of his choice *Clarets*, or perhaps a '99 *Montepulciano*. The denial of the opportunity was always seen as a *snub*.

It is also not known how long the session would last; would the team bus be held up to allow the manager to quaff his way through a Shiraz, fit in a quick game of *Ring of Fire* with Sir Alex and Mike Phelan, before climbing aboard half cut at 7.30pm? The answer cannot be known with any certainty. It is also unclear what beverage other managers offer; however Neil Warnock might offer builders' tea, Alex Neil stocks a fine malt, whereas Peter Reid dishes out the *Sambucas*.

The real winner is football
Forget the fans of either side, in a rip-snorter of a game the true victor is the sport itself. *"Well Gary, someone might have won, someone might have lost today. But you know what? The real winner is football."* A phrase unlikely to offer any comfort to disappointed fans.

The referee today is from
Snippet of information provided about the matchday referee. *"Today's referee is Mike Dean from the Wirral."* Before officials became professional, it was the case that the occupation of the referee would be given too. So Howard Webb was known as *"a policeman from Rotherham"*, Graham Poll was a *"sales manager from Tring in Hertfordshire"* and of course David Elleray, the *"schoolmaster from Harrow."*

The Relegator
Iain Dowie.

Theatre of dreams
The informal home of Manchester United, coined by Bobby Charlton. The term has helped to promote a mythical aura around the club, turning the Red Devils' home into something of a fortress; a place which teams fear to tread, that is until David Moyes took over.

There for the taking
The phrase probably started out life referring to the three points on offer, but it has developed to mean a team too. It is often accompanied with a condescending use of *lot*. *"Come on lads, get into them! This lot are here for the taking!"*

They've scored too early
Seen as the worst time to score for an underdog as it may mean up to 90 minutes of defending. The best time to grab a goal is generally thought to be on the *stroke* of half time (aside obviously from the last kick), because managers may have to *tear up their notes*, but for the opposing manager *"the team talk will have just become much easier."*

Three points is the important thing
No matter whether a player has hit a superb treble and set up two others in a *5-0 romp*, modesty dictates *that three points is the important thing*. On halting a run of defeats, it is important that teams *stop the rot*. On the other hand, a losing striker might be pleased to get on the scoresheet but *"obviously, I'm not happy with the result."*

Thriker
A *belter* of a shot which stands very little chance of being saved. The phrase was invented by Alan Partridge in his World Cup Countdown of 1994; other offerings included *"liquid football"* and *"he must have a foot like a traction engine."*

Thriller
A barnstormer of a match. It is quite often mentioned in conjunction with the location: *"As you might have heard, it's been a thriller at Bloomfield Road today, here's Juliette Ferrington with the details."*

Throwing the kitchen sink at it
When time is most definitely not on their side, a team will throw the *proverbial kitchen sink* at the opposition's goal in a desperate attempt to score. The last five minutes of a match is informally known as *kitchen sink time.*

Etymology: The phrase in its original use was to throw everything but the kitchen sink at a situation, however in football parlance it includes the Reginox Butler Classic 600.

Thumping
1. *Header.* Very often produced by the centre back. Such attempts may *thunder* off the crossbar with a delightfully onomatopoeic *thwack*. *"The thumping header from Kevin van Veen left the crossbar shaking for a good 10 seconds."*
2. *Victory.* A big win. To hit a side *for six* in a particularly *one-sided affair.*

Thunderbolt
A 30-yarder which *crashes* into the net. See also *howitzer, screamer, pearler, worldie,* etc.

Thursday nights on Channel 5

Somewhat dubious award for Europa League participants, despite the fact it is now on ITV4. The chant *"Thursday nights... Channel 5"* is a taunt by opposing fans to a team who have failed to achieve Champions League qualification, or who have been knocked out at the initial group stage.

Ticker

Breaking news ticker. The yellow bar (which is normally red) when an important hot-off-the-press story has broken on Sky Sports News. However, so much news breaks nowadays that the bar is hardly ever any other colour but yellow.

Tight lipped

Managers will rarely give anything away regarding transfers. Firstly, they do not want to *alert* other clubs to their interest in a player. Secondly, they do not talk about other club's players *out of respect* for their current team. Unless, of course, you are someone who makes a point of *not talking about other teams' players*.

Tightrope

Two types exist in football, *managerial* and *disciplinary*; both are to be walked.

Tiki-taka

A short passing, high tempo style of play pioneered amongst others by Pep Guardiola. It showcases the intricate style of play for which those on the continent, in particular, have become renowned. Spain has been credited with their dominance of the World and European stages over the last few years by implementing the tiki-taka style. This era obviously came to an end after the 2014 World Cup though. It is a style of play befitting some of the great teams, however any manager can have ambitions to play it: *"Colin Cameron keen to implement tiki-taka style of play at Berwick."*

Etymology: It is generally thought the late Spanish commentator Andrés Montes helped to popularise this term whilst describing Spain's style of play in the 2006 World Cup. It is a phrase which had been in use for a number of years prior to this, however.

Time

1. Full time. Referees *decide it's time, blow for time, call time*, etc.
2. *Needs time*. Without exception, upon any managerial appointment in the top flight, the footballing community will come out and say the new gaffer needs time at his new club. Similarly, when a manager is sacked, many will come out and say the dismissed boss needed more time; indeed the manager may even say it themselves due to their unshakable belief they *"would have got it right eventually"*.

3. *If ever there was a time.* The optimum or final chance to effect influence upon a match, normally during an important fixture. *"If ever there was a time for England to score, this is it, or it is the Three Lions who will be exiting the World Cup."*

4. The opposite of *"man on!"* this is the collective shout by the crowd to one of their players when they are in space. Akin to shouting *"don't drop them!"* to a man carrying three pint glasses, it is most commonly heard close to the pitch at lower and Sunday league games. The player in question will have plenty of room to assess his options yet is screamed at from a distance of three yards by the well-meaning yet misguided fans.

Timely

Something welcoming for a team or manager.

1. *Timely reminder.* Usually provided by a player in a rich vein of form. *"He's provided Massimiliano Allegri with a timely reminder ahead of the Champions League Final."*

2. *Timely boost.* The *return to action* of an injured player to *bolster the ranks* of a *beleaguered* side. *"The return of Max Clayton is like a new signing for Wanderers."*

Tinkerman

A manager who is constantly searching for his best eleven, or is simply well-versed in keeping all the Armani-clad players happy in expensively assembled *outfits*. Claudio Ranieri is perhaps the most famous of all *tinkermen* (and now called *the original tinkerman*); he is the advocate of a *rotation policy*, and someone who is extremely unlikely to name an unchanged side for any more than one game. Accusations of not knowing their best starting XI have long been levelled against those who employ this philosophy. A *storming* 4-0 *romp* one week may still mean *wholesale changes* the next.

Tipped

Many things in football can lead to something being *tipped*:

1. A youngster with a potentially bright future could be *tipped for the top*.
2. An out of work manager may be *tipped* to take up the reins at a club who are looking for a new boss.
3. Players who are expected to make an impact in a forthcoming tournament. *"Black Stars tipped to shine at AFCON 2015."*

Tips can also be found down the pub from the man who has apparent insider knowledge of club goings on. Tapping his nose, he will tell the regulars to *"Get your money on Moyes to be Newcastle boss by Monday"*.

Toe poke

Less technical version of catching a ball *on the laces*. While it is no less effective, it is still frowned upon by *purists* who see the *toe poke* as a departure from the traditional method of shooting. Also known as a *toe punt*, and may produce a *trundler*.

Too good to go down

No team would ever be foolish enough to exclaim that they are *too go to go down*, however many were believed to be so. Examples of teams thought too good to go down, yet who did so, are West Ham in 2002/03 and Middlesbrough in 1996/97. Perhaps this was because there was a large quantity of *prodigious talent* in both squads, such as Fabrizio Ravanelli, Emerson, Juninho, Lee Bowyer, Les Ferdinand, Joe Cole, David James, Michael Carrick, Nigel Winterburn, Trevor Sinclair, Jermain Defoe, Frederic Kanoute, Don Hutchison and Paulo Di Canio. Conversely, a manager will never say his side are *"not good enough to stay up."*

Too hot to handle

A player who just cannot be shackled. Such players *prove* to be this way. *"The full back needs oven gloves today Jon."* Also refers to the overall attacking potency of a whole team.

Too small

Being too small is one of the reasons that many players are rejected at a young age. Examples include Pat Nevin, Peter Beardsley and Alan Wright. These stories are usually regaled on an evening football magazine show on the radio, where said *reject* talks about being a *"skinny lad, not much more than five feet four inches tall getting kicked from pillar to post in the youth team."* Non-league goalkeepers always seem to come on the small side, which is possibly the reason why they never made it as a pro. However, non-league centre backs are always giants, standing 6"5 and built like a wardrobe.

Top drawer

Play of a very high standard; goals, skills and general sublime play can be *plucked from* or *taken straight out of* here. *"Top drawer stuff from the Stags. It's the kind of performance level that's been the hallmark of their rise to the top of the league this season."* Is the opposite of a *second-rate* performance.

Top flight status

The kind of status which must be *preserved* at all costs. There is no *middle flight tier status*, but there is *Championship status*, and subsequent ones down the leagues.

Top job
1. Refers to the hot seat at any football club. Something coveted by many out of work managers and *perennial number twos*.
2. The kind of praise Harry Redknapp gives a manager who is performing well in his role, or alternatively, the kind of job he coveted (i.e. the England one).

Tormentors
An absolute *shellacking* will be handed out by the unfortunate side's *tormentors*. If one player proves a particular thorn in the side by either scoring or having a hand in the goals, he will be known as the *tormentor in chief*, but often only of an individual player: *"Ashley Ward has absolutely tormented Sagi Burton today."*

Total football
Style of play associated most closely with the Dutch National side of the 1974 World Cup, and the Ajax team before this. Undoubtedly a style of play for the classically trained footballer, it is completely fluid and mobile, and each player is expected to contribute to more than one different *phase of play*. Johan Cruyff once commented: *"simple football is the most beautiful. But playing simple football is the hardest thing."* In Holland it is known as *totaalvoetbal*.

Touch
1. *First*. These are usually *great*. Can range from a *feather* to something rather less savoury.
2. *Scoring*. The perennial *lost touch*. It is the attribute which always goes missing and must be *found, rediscovered* or *regained*.
3. *Tight*. Marking close enough to stand on a few toes from a corner, however the referee will normally turn a *blind eye*. *"Well it is six of one and half a dozen of the other for me Gary so the ref is right not to give it"* reports the co-commentator as the replay shows Branislav Ivanovic executing a flawless vertical *suplex* on Nikica Jelavic inside the six-yard area. Most situations are *touch tight*; otherwise it's *slack marking* to the extent you couldn't even call it *zonal*.

Touchline spat
Very public and often unsavoury clash between two opposing managers, Arsene Wenger and Alan Pardew have particular form both with each other and generally in this field. On some occasions, members of the backroom staff may get involved and the incident will go on to define their presence at a club. Ally McCoist had an infamous *spat* with Neil Lennon whilst *number two* at Rangers in 2011.

Tough taskmaster
A real *hard liner*. A manager who demands *110%* from his players both in training and on the pitch. *"Tough taskmaster Allan Johnston watched his side thump Brechin then insisted: We weren't at our best."* Other examples include John Lambie, who was more fire breathing and 'f-bombs' than tactics, and Felix Magath, who would fine a player for letting a ball bounce in front of them. See also *disciplinarian*.

Tout
1. Agents will tout their clients' names about in an attempt to find them a new club and in the process earn themselves a *lucrative* payday.
2. Less than reputable men standing around, outside the ground, asking if *"anyone needs a ticket for the game?"* or *"tickets, anybody got any tickets?"* The kind of person who spends half his time outside Wembley stadium and the other half on an EDL rally.
3. Players are often *touted as the next* by the media.

Tracksuit manager
Resplendent in white trainers, baseball caps and a firm belief in 4-4-2, these are the *proper football men* of tomorrow. They are the polar opposite of a continental manager bedecked in a slim-fit suit, with their pass-and-move philosophies. Arriving at the training ground at 6am, they have polished off their full English, chatted with Maureen the cleaner, and laid out the cones before the lads arrive in their assorted luxury cars two hours later.

Trademark
The sort of play a footballer has become known for and, as such, is their *calling card*. Rory Delap was synonymous with his trademark throw-ins; possessing arms like windmills, while Facundo Sava famously donned a Zorro mask every time he scored.

Trailing leg
The type of appendage left hanging out, ripe for an attacker to fall over. Defenders usually *stick out* a trailing leg, although in reality said leg is *left in* rather than *stuck out*.

Training ground
1. *Bust up.* An incident very often leaked to the press. There seems to be a standard way of dealing with them, which includes managers saying something along the lines of *"These incidents are ten a penny really,"* when in reality the police were called and statements taken. *Bust up* is always the description of choice, although it may be slightly diluted by calling it an incident, and will always be *played down, laughed off* or *dismissed*.

2. *Move.* A plan born on the training ground and put into action on the pitch. Training ground moves are almost always showcased from dead ball situations, particularly free kicks from just outside the area. The fact that it is a training ground move is always noted by the commentators; one of the best-known was Argentina's goal versus England at the 1998 World Cup which caught the *Three Lions* totally off guard.

Transfer embargo
Transfer ban *slapped* on a club which has committed some sort of infraction. The ramifications may be far reaching, particularly in the top flight where it is generally accepted you need to spend money just to stand still. *"Financial fair play infraction means Forest transfer embargo."*

Transfer kitty
The amount of money a manager has to spend in a window. He will of course hope it is *sizeable*, however it is usually the piggy bank version of a *war chest*. *"After their splurge on Thauvin, Steve McClaren might find there's little left in the transfer kitty until January."*

Transfer window slams shut
It is tradition that the window must *slam* shut. It's never closed quietly, but in a way to signal finality to proceedings. Except, of course, when the fax machine is playing up and special dispensation is provided by the FA.

Transitional period
The period of time a club goes through to explain why they have failed to live up to expectations during a season. A transitional period is never sought out by a side but does happen if in a state of flux, possibly because of the loss of a key part of the squad, or the manager. The question remains, will this signal the start of longer-term lethargy? Also used to explain temporary shortcomings: *"Paul Cook admits his side are in a transitional period following the departure of striker Eoin Doyle to Cardiff City."*

Travelling fans
The away *contingent*. Road travel is usually given as the transport of choice: *"The travelling Shakers fans in fine voice, making the short trip across the M66 for this derby game."* Larger numbers will be described as *hoards*, whereas when there are relatively few, it is a *batch*.

Treating it like any other game
Assertion made in an attempt to play down the importance of an upcoming match. This is usually in response to the question *"Will you be doing anything different*

in the run up to the game?" Whilst the manager will profess to keep the status quo, in actual fact he will probably consult the horoscopes, urinate in all four corners of the ground and refuse to shave in the run up to the big day.

Treatment

1. *Table.* Semi-metaphorical table referenced when talking about a club's injury crisis or an individual player's situation. There is also a *treatment room*, which during times of injury crisis is said to be *full*, with a long line of injury victims keeping the physio busy. Treatment can also refer to on-pitch attention. *"John-Paul Kissock is down and requires treatment."*
2. Type of experience handed out to a chastened opposition player. *"Tadić felt the full-force of the Toure treatment."*

Trialist

The preserve of the Scottish lower leagues, it is a strange quirk that these players are not afforded the privilege of a name on the team sheet. Commonly found on Soccer Saturday, Jeff Stelling will assert they will become a *"household name"* before long; although old hand Derek Riordan's goalscoring appearance for East Fife as a trialist debunked the myth they are all *raw talents*. Of course, everyone knows someone who had trials at a club, but were rejected for either a height-related issue or a serious knee injury sustained in an under-12s match.

Trickle wide

Shots which trickle wide have often beaten the 'keeper. Things appear to be unfolding in slow motion before said effort goes *agonizingly* past the post. Watching managers may turn away in disgust on the touchline, cursing their luck. *"Paul Carden had his head in his hands as Louis Almond's snapshot trickled wide."*

Triffic lad

Harry Redknapps' favourite term to describe his number one transfer target; that and *top, top player.*

Trigger happy chairman

Head honchos who don't think twice before replacing the manager. They *wield the axe* so often they have developed repetitive strain injury. It is often an accusation which is denied: *"Tony Adams is entitled to his own view but I won't have it be said Blackburn Rovers are trigger-happy or that we are not prepared to give young British managers a chance."* Some chairman may be fairly candid in their assessment of team affairs; Christian Constantin, owner of FC Sion once described a performance as: *"Awful, awful awful. For this game every adjective is applicable, as long as they are negative. It was pathetic. The players should be ashamed of being paid."* Constantin has been through almost 40 managers since he bought the club in 2003.

Triple substitution
Act of desperation by a manager chasing the game in a bid to boost his side's *flagging fortunes*, usually after he's *seen enough*. Using all three subs at once is a rare occurrence which gets the commentator excited; *"Look at this! A triple substitution"* followed possibly by the opinion that it is a *"bold move"* and they would now have to be wary of *"picking up injuries with more than 30 minutes on the clock."*

Trophyless
Term applied to sides which have undergone a *barren period* where success has been hard to come by. It can be a trophyless season, which has been endured by a side *tipped* to challenge for honours. Alternatively, it could be a much lengthier spell for a success-starved side, such as Newcastle United's *trophy limbo* which stretches back to 1969.

Trudge down the tunnel
Slow, ponderous and most definitely despondent walk back to the dressing room after a particularly poor performance and defeat or a niggling injury which has forced an early exit. *"The Blues fans applaud him as he eventually trudges off down the tunnel – but how serious is that injury?"*

Turn back the clock
A veteran showing considerable agility and dexterity will produce something only thought possible by a much younger player, such as a scarcely believable goal from an impossible angle, like Bobby Zamora's *worldie* against West Brom.

Turn of pace
To be able to *hit the burners* quickly.

Turnaround of fortunes
A situation once bleak, which now appears rosy. It is quite often triggered by a change of manager, the introduction of a *marquee* signing, or the need to play due to an injury crisis. *"Coquelins' recall from Charlton sparked a remarkable turnaround of fortunes from the one-time Arsenal cast-off."*

Turncoat
Often with the added *dirty*, every football fan in the country knew one of these at school. In professional football, it refers to one who has turned his back on the club he has professed to love. *"When one thinks of Robin van Persie, a few terms come to mind; genius, maestro, predator, game-changer and winner. Or if you're an Arsenal fan, the words would most likely be replaced with traitor, sell-out, turncoat, defector and scoundrel."*

Etymology: Thought to possibly refer to Barons who switched allegiances from one side to another, thereby 'turning' their coat of arms.

Turned on a sixpence

The quintessential sublime turn. It is a very useful manoeuvre when trying to shake off an opponent or get out of a tight space. It originates from the pre-decimalisation days, so perhaps a more appropriate modern term would be *turned on a fivepence*, which offers a considerably smaller turning circle.

Turning point

1. Of a match. This could be a contentious decision, a red card or a goal. *"Up until that point it was plain sailing for the Baggies."*
2. Of a season. *"The implementation of three at the back was the turning point for Southgates' men."* Is slightly debateable as the turning point can only be used in hindsight, however many managers profess their sides to have turned the corner when, in actual fact, nothing has changed; although this is probably said more in hope than expectation.

Twelve men

1. When the referee makes a series of bad calls perceived to benefit one side over the other the crowd may make accusations of partiality. The chant *"Twelve men! You've only got twelve men!"* is a common one throughout the land.
2. The crowd, which is usually referenced by the team captain post-match following an away win. *"I think I speak on behalf of all the lads when I say how brilliant the fans were today; they really were the twelfth man out there"*.

Twilight years

The latter years of a player's career. This period is indicated by increasingly aching joints, a marked slowdown in pace and an increase in appearances on the Match of the Day sofa. *"Gianfranco Zola could have opted for a much easier way to see out his twilight years than the challenge of trying to haul Cagliari in his native Sardinia out of Serie B and back into the top flight."*

Two banks of four

Advocates of the traditional 4-4-2 will set their side up displaying two solid banks of four. This style is seen as harder to break down than a more dynamic formation, however it has also had to suffer accusations of being archaic and inflexible. Footballing dinosaurs are huge believers in this style of play, unless you are Terry Venables with his Christmas tree formation.

Two feet

Jumping in with two feet is generally seen as the classic method in which to get a *straight red*. These days the addition of studs showing and players leaving the ground add weight to the argument. *Jumping, hacked down, scythed down* or *lunged in with* are all variants of the two-footed challenge. Most players will never admit to purposefully doing this, however Phil Neville once said on seeing a cheeky reverse ball: *"If that was a training session and somebody did that I'd be first over there and I'd probably look to two-foot him or take him out of the game. If somebody did that in training to me, winding me up, I would be straight in there. I'd smash them."*

Two-horse race

Some leagues have two-horse races every year, or at least did, such as Celtic and Rangers and Barcelona and Real Madrid (until Atletico Madrid gatecrashed the top table). Debates are had year-in year-out about how many horses are in the Premier League title race, with answers ranging from one to six; now affording itself the title *"The most competitive league in the World."*

Two-legged

The only type in football is the *two-legged* affair. There is no one-legged tie or indeed three-legged match. They would be knockouts, and some sort of round-robin type scenario respectively.

Tycoon

Foreign, wealthy and with a passion for the beautiful game; this is the sort of individual many supporters wish would take over their club. More often than not, however, this man will go through six managers a season, be indicted in another county on match fixing charges, and insist on picking the team from his private resort in the Cayman Islands.

U

Ugly

1. *Challenge.* The kind of tackle which usually has a *calling card* attached, along with at least six stud marks. Is a precursor to *ugly scenes*.
2. *Side of the modern game.* Aka diving. *"Well we don't like to see that Gary, it's really the ugly side of the modern game which we're seeing more and more of nowadays."* Footballing *dinosaurs* will have you believe this is a foreign invention.

Unbelievable Jeff!

Chris Kamara-ism. What was initially a method to describe a piece of play that was difficult to fathom or almost impossible. *"Unbelievable Jeff! You'll not believe this, Patrick Roberts, all five foot five of him has just floored his own teammate, the man mountain Dan Burn. Accidentally of course but the boy – he went flying."*

Uncharted territory

The position that a club has never been in, or hasn't for a number of years. Progressing to the latter stages of a cup competition is such ground for many lower league teams (see Chesterfield in 1997/98). This can lead to ideas above their station, such as Blyth Spartans declaring they can *"go all the way"* after reaching the FA Cup second round. Similarly, if a club reaches *lofty heights*, this may be *uncharted territory* too, for example Fleetwood's rise to League One.

Etymology: Territory not found on nautical charts.

Unconventional clearance

Clearance made by any means. Examples include heading the ball away while on the deck (or any sort of clearance while prone, in fact), overhead kicks from underneath the crossbar, and with any part of the knee, heel or hip. *"Glentoran's John Devine produced an unconventional clearance whilst on all fours. It was certainly unorthodox but nonetheless effective."* Some players are more prone than others to producing these, such as Phil Jones and Nyron Nosworthy.

Under siege

1. Defences which are under an inordinate amount of pressure and as such have battened down the hatches, put on their tin hat, and assumed the brace position. Siege mentalities will also be adopted when a manager believes the whole world is against their team, or if they are preparing for a relegation *scrap*.
2. Series of films starring Steven Seagal as former Navy SEAL and cook Casey Ryback.

Under the cosh

Relentless pressure imposed by a side, which often lasts for *long periods*.

Etymology: To be under the cosh is to be beaten by a stick. The word comes from the Romany term koshter.

Under the floodlights

Term applied to night matches. *"We are back at 7.30 on Wednesday where we'll be at the Recreation Ground, with Aldershot taking on Forest Green under the floodlights. What a match-up that promises to be, so do join us then."*

Under wraps

Concealment or suppression of a transfer deal to ensure rivals are not put on *red alert*. *"The lad agreed terms, I thought the chairman had got it over the line but we've obviously been gazumped, despite our attempts to keep things under wraps."*

Underdogs

Tag to be applied to a side whose chances look slim. Conversely, a manager will always look to use this to his advantage. *"Howe shrugs off Cherries underdog status."* Antonym of *top dogs*.

Underemployed

The goalkeeper who has had an easy afternoon between the *sticks*. *"Butland unfolded his deckchair and popped his sunglasses on as there was no risk of him being called into action."*

Understudy

A role which is generally the preserve of the back-up 'keeper. On a domestic level they are known as the understudy, however on the international stage they would be called *[England's/other nation's] number two*. Domestically, they will be rolled out for Capital One Cup games and are usually of an inferior standard; but given the chance it will be seen as an opportunity to make a name for themselves – hopefully for the right reasons. It is a role which many will only be willing to perform for so long, however: *"Serial-understudy Joe Murphy ready to quit the John Smith's Stadium in search of first team football."*

Undisclosed

The most common fee to be found in transfer dealings; this face-saving mechanism is in place in part to shield the fact that a club has paid over the odds for a bang average player. It doesn't stop the media having a pop at what they *think* might be the final fee, which often brings about a slight difference of opinion: *"Wickham signs for Palace in £6m deal."; "Eagles snap up Sunderland hotshot for £7m."; "Ex-Tractor boy in £9m transfer gamble."* Some journalists may account for *add-ons*, and some may not.

Unfashionable club

These clubs usually hail from a number of categories and are fully aware of their status:

1. Drab northern towns or *footballing backwaters* whose fanbase is hoovered up by the behemoths down the road.
2. Clubs who have a reputation for being serial *basement dwellers*.
3. Grounds which serve pies instead of artisan sausages in the concourse.

Unknown quantity

1. The player from obscurity who has escaped the attentions of scouting networks far and wide, and, as such, most teams are in the dark. *"No one really knows a great deal of him,"* remarked Alan Shearer on French international and *seasoned* Champions League player Hatem Ben Arfa. A hot streak in front of goal may mean a player is the *name on everyone's lips*.
2. The newly-promoted team who may go down without a whimper, but who do possess a striker that bagged 25 goals the previous campaign, and as such should be *afforded respect*.

Unleashed

1. The *super sub* from the bench. *"By this point Martin Allen had seen enough and unleashed Muggleton into the action."*
2. A returning star of the team, who has been hampered by injury and is *champing at the bit* for a return to the action.

Unlock the defence

Metaphor to describe the attempt to – or breach of – a back line. *"Try as they might, Motherwell could not find a way to unlock the stubborn Callie defence."* It isn't necessary to try this with some teams, who will simply *leave the back door open*.

Unmentionables

Audience-friendly term for the tender reproductive organs a player often receives the football in, leading to an extended period on *the deck*. Commentators will state the rather obvious *"that one is likely to hurt"* or if feeling particularly risqué *"new balls please"*, with an additional *"rather him than me"* for good measure from the chuckling co-commentator. During the winter months, it is common to hear *"on a cold day like this, that's the last place you want the ball to hit you."*

Unorthodox

The non-conformist footballer who prefers to perform a diving header on the deck than clear the ball with his feet. When a player is fielded out of position he is described as being an *orthodox* something (as in an orthodox centre half), even though he is playing in the defensive midfield position. *"Not a role he's familiar with, isn't that right Robbie?"*

Unplayable
1. *Player.* The opponent who is such an *enigma* he cannot be predicted. He sees things others (fans included) don't, e.g. Eden Hazard. *"Sam, when he's in this kind of form, there's no defender in the world who could stop him."* No player will be unplayable every time they step onto the pitch however; in fact many have two default settings: unplayable and anonymous.
2. *Pitch.* In these circumstances, the game is very unlikely to go ahead, perhaps even being called off at the *eleventh hour*, after the travelling fans have arrived at the ground. TV pictures relayed back to the studio show the referee attempting to kick a ball through a puddle of water from underneath a huge umbrella, with little success. *"There was a mini swimming pool forming on the pitch at Richmond Park yesterday."*

Unsportsmanlike behaviour
A classic way for a player to find his way into the referee's notebook. Examples of unsportsmanlike behaviour include:
1. Kicking the ball away at a free kick.
2. Not going back the *full complement* of ten yards (in a wall situation this is rarely enforced, however it is when a lone player doesn't retreat back the required distance). This has become somewhat obsolete with the introduction of vanishing spray.
3. Diving to try and con the officials.
4. Removal of the shirt during celebration of a goal. This is justified apparently because it might rile the opposition fans and lead to unrest.

A more old-fashioned term is *ungentlemanly conduct*, which *nobody likes to see.*

Unveiled
Upon the capture of a new player, a press conference is called where the signing will be *unveiled*, most probably after *jetting in* (if they have come from abroad). Such media calls are also termed *unveiling ceremonies. "David Villa touches down for unveiling ceremony in New York and is determined to be the first fan favourite of new era."*

Up in the gods
Clubs who have no regard for the travelling *contingent* place them here. Commentators are sure to remark if they are making plenty of noise, however. *"You have to give it to the QPR fans, making the long trip up north to find themselves 4-0 down just after the hour mark… yet they are in absolutely magnificent voice."*

Uphill
The *task* clubs face when attempting to overturn a multiple-goal deficit or keep hold of their prize asset. Managers will not usually attempt to hide the magnitude

of such a challenge: *"Ange Postecoglou pulls no punches over size of Socceroos' uphill task."* A sending off or key injury may mean that from that point onwards achieving a result became an *uphill task* – although if the manager feels a dismissal was harsh, he may describe it as an *"impossible task"* to emphasise the injustice.

Urgency

Commonly found when the clock is fast running down. Also occurs when a side has spent a large proportion of a match chasing shadows, only to come to life at a certain point: *"If Gregory's team had shown the same urgency in the first half, they could well have come away with something."*

Ushered

1. On some occasions, more so in bad tempered affairs rather than the majority, a bad tackle can lead to a *mass brawl.* This in turn sees the referee produce at least one red card, leading to further chaotic scenes. After a lengthy break in play, which sees the offending player(s) *ushered* down the tunnel, proceedings can resume. Accompanied by the exclamation *"he's refusing to go!"* or possibly *"he's having to be escorted off the pitch!"*
2. New eras are *ushered* in by big-name managers after they take the reins.

Utility man

The perfect squad player, he can be trusted in a variety of roles. Known as *Mr Versatile*, examples of utility men include Sean Gregan, David Livermore and Kevin Großkreutz. Whether he turns up to training donning a tool belt, with accompanying pencil tucked behind the ear is unknown.

U-turn

Merciful and fair-minded managers know that their differences with a player should be set aside for the good of the team as a whole. The willingness to welcome said player back into the fold after being *out in the cold* signals a U-turn and possible thawing of relations between the two. Players may *perform* this too, with headlines accompanied by the necessary trumped-up lexicon: *"Delph stuns Villa in shocking Man City double U-turn."*

V

Valuable

1. *Point.* Points picked up where none were expected, such as away at a top four side. However, it may also be the case that managers will attempt to

justify not winning a game by saying that *"you never know - the point could be valuable come the end of the season."*

2. *Lesson.* Naïve defensive displays will always lead to an elder statesman of the side proclaiming how *"lessons will be learnt"* from the horror show.

Value for money
Term used to equate whether a player has been worth the outlay. Players who have dubious scoring records, despite their price tag, are measured on a cost-per-goal basis and as such are *poor* value for money. In the era of megabucks TV deals, it is a common complaint that *"there isn't much value for money in the transfer market these days."*

Verbals
"A bit of verbals happening over on the touchline, both benches disagreeing over the legality of Peter Fear's tackle on Bernard Lambourde." Otherwise described as *exchanging pleasantries, verbals* are essentially a frank exchange of views. May also occur in the dressing room with accompanying *finger pointing.*

Versatile
He is a jack of all trades, but master of none. Versatile players, without doubt, have their place in a side though. John O'Shea for example is famous for having played in every position for Manchester United, except in goal. Sides which cause problems for the opposition can be categorised as such: *"The versatile nature of the Oxford forward line gave the Exiles a headache which lasted all afternoon."*

Veteran
The elder statesman of a team. Veterans offer experience, gravitas and a wise old head to bring calm to proceedings, especially when operating across the back four. *"Noble lavishes praise on veteran Collins."* The term can be used to highlight how a player or manager will produce results. *"A veteran of five FA Trophy triumphs, if you want to go far in the competition, Geoff Chapple is your man."*

Etymology: From the Latin word vetus, meaning old.

Vicious foul
A nasty challenge which draws a collective cry of anger from the crowd. Players commonly find themselves sent off for fouls of this ilk, it being a rare occasion when there is real *intent* to cause injury (despite the inevitable protestations that they are *not that kind of player*). Often said *"he has to go."*

Victory
These are many and varied in type, including:

1. Resounding *romps*. Also known as a *cruise*, or if particularly easy, a *waltz*.
2. Scrappy, hard fought affairs, i.e. *winning ugly*.
3. Regulation or routine.
4. Come-from-behind.

Video nasty
To denote either:
1. A shocker of a challenge.
2. An uncomfortable re-run of 90 minutes of hell at the training ground on a Monday morning. *"Parkinson steels himself for video nasty post-mortem after chastening defeat."*

Etymology: The term was popularised in the 1980s by the National Viewers' and Listeners Association. The passing of the Video Recordings Act 1984 was heavily influenced by social activist Mary Whitehouse, who apparently coined the phrase.

Vidiprinter
The traditional method by which football fans across the land would follow Saturday afternoon football, save for being at the actual match, of course. It has taken many forms in the past but is possibly best known for its fetching blue format during the *Grandstand* years under Des Lynam, and latterly Steve Ryder. Scores were accompanied by a very audible clicking noise, as if someone was typing away just out of shot. (In reality, it is an outsourced service provided by Opta for a number of media outlets).

There are a number of strange yet well-loved quirks about the vidiprinter. Perhaps the best-known (or worst, depending on how you look at it) was the necessity to type out the number of goals scored if seven or more were scored. For example Newcastle United 7 (seven) Tottenham Hotspur 1. However this no longer seems to happen.

Vintage
Wine analogy. A golden period of time referred to, amongst others, by Clive Tyldesley. Vintages commonly discussed are Manchester United's Champions League winning side of 1998/99. Also referred to as the *class of 99*. This compares favourably to the 2013/14 batch, which by all accounts was corked. Players display their own vintage abilities on occasion too: *"The run and finish was vintage Dalian Atkinson."*

Virtual spectator
When the goalkeeper is so underemployed due to a total lack of potency from the opposition. *"Kevin Pressman's smoking cigars out there, he's been a virtual spectator for much of this match."*

Virtuoso goal
A goal of verve, panache and immense skill. Often a *superb solo effort.* *"Oooh that is just what he is capable of! Lee Trundle does it again with a virtuoso goal! This boy is the toast of Vetch Field!"*

W

... were at number 1 the last time...
Strange practice of the media informing anyone who will listen who was at number 1 the last time an event happened before now. *"The last time Spurs won at Stamford Bridge, Margaret Thatcher was still in power and Sinead O'Connor was at number one."*

It may also refer to some popular culture of the time: *"The last time Newcastle United players took to the field at Turf Moor, Bonnie Tyler topped the charts with Total Eclipse of the Heart while on TV's Coronation Street Deirdre Barlow had just dumped Mike Baldwin to get back with husband Ken."*

Wage
1. *Bill.* In reality, for most top level sides it is not so much the type of bill which would be presented at the end of a meal in a restaurant, but more like a series of huge numbers which will make even the wealthiest oligarch's eyes water. Failure to meet the PAYE deadline can have serious consequences, including a winding-up order or eventually a call to the administrators. Strangely, bailiffs never seem to visit football clubs to claw back unpaid debt. Presumably because they won't have transportation for goalposts, or much use for an assortment of faded plastic seats. Rumours of the Glazers being spotted at the Eccles branch of *Cash Converters* with 47 boxes of 2003 Tampa Bay Buccaneers jerseys turned out to be unfounded.
2. *Packet.* The form of remuneration for most footballers judging by this term is the handing over of a bunch of rolled up twenties in a brown envelope. Where clubs have paid over the odds for someone, he is said to have *"cost an absolute packet."*

WAGs

Acronym used to refer to wives and girlfriends of international standard footballers. They first came to prominence during the 2006 World Cup in Germany when the British press seemed more interested in where Posh Spice was going to get her manicure done than what was happening on the pitch.

Etymology: The 2006 World Cup saw intense media coverage of the partners of the England squad; so much so that the football became a virtual sideshow. However, the first apparent recording of the term was in a Daily Telegraph article in 2002 which attributed the term to staff at the Jumeirah Beach Club.

Wake-up call

A sharp dose of reality. Teams are given a wake-up call, or alternatively a *rude awakening* following a particularly heavy or unexpected defeat. *"It's a real wake-up call for us. First half we acquitted ourselves fairly well, but really if we want to be in and around the playoffs, a big improvement is needed."* Of course if this is not heeded, the fans are said to be *living a nightmare* following their team every Saturday.

Wallop

A shot hit with some zest. It definitely has a *bit of mustard* on it. *"There wasn't much grace or style about Gavin Swankie's wallop towards goal, but it was effective as Forfar edged ahead."*

Want-away

An *unsettled* or unhappy player; he is likely to hand in a transfer request in order to *force through* a move to another club. When players openly admit they want to leave, their relationship with the fans will undoubtedly become *strained,* particularly because no player is bigger than the club. *"The want-away striker left the pitch to a chorus of boos, without stopping to look at his manager as he stormed off down the tunnel."*

War chest

Likely to be a large amount of funding given to a manager in order to secure, for example, a *20-goal a season man.* Often used in football because it likens the game to a battle. In the Premier League, this is a mandatory requirement as the doctrine of spending to stand still is generally accepted. *"Van Gaal to be backed with whopping £200m cosmic war chest to bring title home."* Note this is never less than £15m, in which case it is more likely to be a *transfer kitty* to aid a lower league *promotion charge* or top-flight survival *scrap,* and plenty of shopping in the bargain basement.

Etymology: A war chest originally referred to the container located in barracks or home of a soldier where they kept their armour or weapons.

War of words
Managers either start these, or refuse to be drawn into them, perhaps decrying *barbs* as *"not worthy of a reply."* Such stunning ripostes when managers do choose to reply are *"he should concentrate on his own team"*, that their opposite number should *"keep his mouth shut"*, and Stan Ternent's memorable *"I would rather cut my grass than talk about Neil Warnock."* This was after Warnock said he *"wouldn't cross the road to piss on him."*

Warhorse
An old, wily, trustworthy and (above all) experienced footballer. Well past his testimonial years, he doesn't conform to the modern day fads of rubbing *Vicks* on his chest before a match, pulling socks above the knees and wearing odd coloured boots. He probably wears his shorts high up over his waist, keeps his socks up with electrician's tape and has the ability to produce a sublime snot rocket.

Warm the bench
Those who partake in this activity are known as *perennial bench warmers*. Goalkeepers for obvious reasons have particular form in this area, with many being signed as *cover* and therefore finding themselves forever waiting for the number one to dislocate his finger or the like. They will never admit to being openly pleased when their colleague picks up an injury, however, even though this means game time for them.

Wary
No matter what the gulf in class between two sides, the one expected to win comfortably will always be *wary* about the threat their opponents will show, lest a *banana skin* situation develop. Compliments about their style of play or recent results (which provide justification to their danger) will be made. *"Crawley might have had a tough season, but as many of the top sides have come unstuck against them, we must be wary."*

Watertight defence
Impenetrable back line. *"The Tykes are defending like beavers Jeff."* Opposite of *porous*.

Waved in
Goals given a helping hand by a generous custodian. *"It wasn't a day for Roman Berezovsky's highlights reel; he waved in goal after goal out there."*

Way
Clubs in possession of a rich and successful history often deign it upon themselves to have a *"way."* This isn't just the style of play, but the ethos of the

club and the way it conducts and projects its image across the globe. Selling the way is a useful technique when attempting to sign a new player. *"I'm sure he'll be interested in playing for us, he's exactly the sort of player who buys into the Manchester United way."* To some, however, it is a characteristic seemingly only applicable to the very best teams. Sir Alex Ferguson remarked in his autobiography *"I hope that before I die someone can explain the 'West Ham way'… I never came up against a Hammers side who played football I was afraid of. They were always surviving, or lucky as hell against us."*

Wayward

Shot which has more chance of troubling the stewards than the goalkeeper. A tut and a roll of the eyes is usually the prefix as a row Z specialist – who *saw his name in lights* – blunders one into the stands. What follows are ironic cheers from the opposition fans and thinly-veiled comedy *barbs* from the commentary team, unless they are one of the *big boys* as *"he buried them in training every day when we played together."*

We can beat the drop!

Exclamation issued by player or manager ahead of a key set of fixtures that will go a long way towards deciding their *fate*. Usually teams are well *adrift* at this point and the next game could very possibly be a *last throw of the dice*. *"There's plenty of belief still in the dressing room Chappers."*

We don't need to tell you what they're thinking

During high stakes or unbearable tension, the TV cameras show the anguished expressions on the faces of fans in the stadium. The shot is almost always accompanied by the observations *"We don't need to tell you what they're thinking."* What the fans are thinking of course depends on the circumstances, but it can range from *"how the hell are we not winning this"* to *"how much longer left, ref?"* In the latter example, commentators also like to remark that the amount of time remaining will be the longest period of such time they have ever experienced. *"This will be the longest ten minutes of their lives Sam, the seconds will literally tick by."*

We tried almost too hard

One of the commonly-held principles of the game is that of being able to give more than 100%, i.e. *110%*. On the contrary, some situations can lead to a side trying too hard, and henceforth this being cited as the reason for defeat. 111% may be the threshold, but it is yet to be tested. Musings that *"the occasion got the better of the boys"* may be made by the gaffer. New signings might also be *"too desperate to impress and forget the basics."*

Well-travelled
More complimentary term for *journeyman* or *mercenary*. *"Well-travelled Cambiasso reignites Champions League dream at Olympiakos."* To be well-travelled suggests a player is in demand with clubs, no matter what the level, and he has generally been successful throughout his career; he's sunned himself on some of the finest beaches in the Mediterranean, but has also mixed it up in the freezing rain at Bradford on a cold December evening.

Wembley
1. *Stadium.* The English national stadium and headquarters of the Football Association (where they carry out their numerous, ever-promising investigations). All who play or manage in the game dream of walking out on the *hallowed turf*, perhaps the most famous of all footballing stages. Commentators will ask which of the 22 players on the pitch is *"ready to make themselves a hero and write their name into footballing folklore on the most famous day in its calendar?"* Victory is, of course, one to *tell the grandkids about.* A defeat, though, could mean a sizeable serving of Wembley *heartache.*
2. *Singles & doubles.* Playground game of football where it's either *every man for himself* or *two-a-side.*

Wenger boys
Any team Arsene Wenger takes charge of. A play on Dutch Eurodancers *Vengaboys*, who enjoyed numerous hits in the 90s and early 00s; presumably they travel to games on the *Wenger bus.*

What playing in the Premier League is all about
'What it is all about' ranges from turning over the big boys to having to recover from a *drubbing.* However, trips to Old Trafford, Stamford Bridge, the Etihad, Anfield and the Emirates are usually the first things newly promoted clubs look for when the fixture list is released, and as such it can be assumed this is the primary factor. Playing against heroes is also a driving force. *"I've watched Philippe Senderos since I was 10 years old, and now I'm lining up against him."*

Wheels away
Always *in celebration, delight* or other triumphant form. Nine times out of ten this continues, however if an unseen *linesman's flag* is raised, these celebrations will be embarrassingly *cut short.* *"Tony Colliver's at Colchester - Macauley Bonne is looking a bit red-faced isn't he?"*

Whipping boys

These lads are usually *perennial whipping boys of the division*, and are given a sound beating most weeks. *"Ronnie Moore's men have been given the tag whipping boys, and judging by this performance, who can argue with that?"*

Etymology: Originating from the 16th century, a whipping boy was a child assigned to a Prince who was whipped every time he misbehaved during his education.

White line

In its literal sense, the markings of a football pitch. However, in crossing it there are a number of unspoken considerations to acknowledge:

1. Friendships go out the window. *"When the teams cross that white line, our friendship will be forgotten. We'll no doubt share the post-match Chablis though."*
2. Players will, or are expected to, show absolute commitment. *"When the boys cross that white line, I demand nothing less than maximum effort from them because it's the fans that pay their wages."*
3. Players may be able to claim managers cease to have an effect in a way to deflect criticism. *"As players, the gaffer can only get his message through in training and pre-match. When we cross that white line it's down to us."*
4. The only thing that matters is football.

The line was also 'snorted' by Robbie Fowler as part of a goal celebration amid unfounded allegations of cocaine use.

Wholesale changes

1. Subjective term which can mean as little as a complete use of the substitute allocation, and as much as the entire squad. For a cup tie perhaps, or more likely because *the lads* have let their gaffer down with an insipid performance in the last outing, i.e. the sort of display which would leave no one assured of their place. Changes may also be *rung*. *"Steve Clarke's underperforming side will know the no-nonsense Scot won't be afraid to ring wholesale changes next time out."*
2. Managers may also profess not to make wholesale changes to a squad which has served them so well the previous campaign, particularly if promotion has been achieved; they prefer to see if some of the individuals in the side can make the *step up*.

Whopping

When trying to put emphasis on a huge, probably inflated transfer fee, this adjective is trotted out. Also refers to contract offers. *"Barca look to tempt Neymar with whopping £500k a week wage packet."* It ranks above *sizeable*, *lucrative* and arguably *mega* in the sliding scale of magnitudes.

Wicked
1. *Cross.* The sort of cross which *fizzes* across the area at pace. Wicked crosses *scream* out for an attacker to get anything on it, because surely that would be the *vital touch* which results in a goal.
2. *Deflection.* The cruellest of all ricochets which invariably wrong foots the goalkeeper. *"Tony Roberts could do nothing about the third, however, as the ball took a wicked deflection off Mark Aber and crept inside the near post."*

Wide open at the back
A defence where you would be forgiven for thinking the centre backs had never met. *"York's centre backs simply looked like a pair of strangers."*

Wilderness
1. Those who have had a fall out with their manager run the very real risk of being *banished* here. There are only two ways in which a player will be allowed to return. Firstly, a change of manager, or secondly if this doesn't happen, the *persona non grata* must get their head down in training, not complain and give it 110%. If not, a loan move to a lower league's *doldrums* may *beckon*. Sympathetic clubs may also bring players in from the cold: *"Shaun Wright-Phillips bought in from wilderness to begin stateside adventure."*
2. *Small Time: A Life in the Football Wilderness* by ex-footballer Justin Bryant.
3. Wilderness Rovers FC, of the TSDL Premier Division.

Will play in any position just to get a game
Line trotted out by a *fringe player* who has been given a *taste* of first team action, and without a doubt is *hungry* for more. As such, they will play in any position to get a game, including in goal. *"I just want to get on the pitch to help the team. I'll play anywhere the gaffer asks me."* Some players take less kindly to being played out of position, such as the striker who much prefers a *central role* being shunted out onto the wing.

Willing
Euphemism for *tries hard but isn't good enough.*

Winning formula
The manager's theorem. They will spend many years *searching* for this and is something along the lines of:

$$\frac{\text{(Commanding Centre Back + Midfield General)}}{\text{Natural Goalscorer}} \times 442 = 3 \text{ points}$$

Additionally:

Dubious Businessman + nefariously acquired hefty cash injection = Champions League at Least

See also *magic formula.*

Winning ways

The sort of *way* which teams are desperate to get *back to.* Always seems to be an aspiration rather than a reality. *"We've had a few bad results on the spin now, but let me tell you, Barnsley will return to winning ways very soon."*

Winter break

The *winter break debate* rears its head every Christmas as a *chorus* of managers bemoan the hectic festive schedule where teams are required to play two games in three days. There is no doubt these demands will stretch a thin squad to its limit, with little or no time to recharge the batteries in preparation for the season's *run in.* Identical headlines of *"[Premier League manager] adds to the call for PL winter break"* adorn the back pages. The deals made with the broadcasting powers stipulate sacrifices must be made; not eating too much turkey at Christmas lunch is unfortunately one of them.

Winter of discontent

The period around December and January which has been particularly chastening for a team. This is commonly due to ructions within the squad: outspoken players criticising training regimes, fans calling for the manager's head or results that have taken a significant *turn for the worse* are such examples. Known as the *bleak midwinter.* Qatar's 2022 World Cup has often been called the *Premier League's winter of discontent.*

Etymology: Taken from the first line of Shakespeare's Richard III.

Witch hunt

Mass hysteria in the media against an individual or team, in the perceived hope they will fail. Indeed, at major tournaments some England staff are almost constantly the subject of such a hunt by the fourth estate; at least that is what those inside the camp will tell you. *"Neville bemoans Hodgson witch hunt."* Managers of players whose reputations precede themselves will say they are also subject to a witch hunt by the media and the authorities.

Wizardry
Superb skill from an accomplished dribbler. *"Ooooh, fantastic skill from Kinkladze! What a maverick the little Georgian is. Alan Ball's team talk must consist of 'Give the ball to Georgi.'"*

Wonderkid
A must-have signing on *Football Manager*. Real world projected results may vary, however. Vincent Kompany realised his potential... Tonton Zola Moukoko did not. Scouts from all the *big boys* will make the long trip up for a reserve fixture in some footballing backwater on a cold Monday night just to report back on this copiously talented youngster.

Etymology: Taken from the German word Wunderkind.

Word
To be *had*, usually in a disciplinary capacity. Various offences necessitate a word – particularly from the referee; however it is never more necessary than when the offence is diving, in which circumstances a player will be *reminded of his responsibilities*. *"Berahino should be embarrassed by that. I hope someone at West Brom has a word with him, because it has no place in the game."* Conversely, the same action is not called for when the offence in question is a *reducer*.

Workmanlike
A *performance* that is lacking in the *finesse* department, but contains a lot of *grit and determination* in order to get the desired result. The footballing equivalent of donning hard hats and digging up the roads; it's not pretty but it is necessary. *"Tommy Wright admitted his side's Europa League win in Belarus would not have won points for beauty."*

World Cup credentials
Once every four years those in with a shout of a place in a national side's *final 23* will do all they can to prove their World Cup *credentials* to secure their place *on the plane*. Tough tests prior to selection will provide a good idea as to where a particular player is at.

Worldie
Another phrase favoured by Paul Merson, to emphasise just how good a goal is. Worldies are usually from distance, out of the blue and found in the top drawer. *"Jeff, Nathan Redmond with an absolute worldie, from 25-yards right on the postage stamp!"*

World's oldest cup competition
As commentators are never sick of telling the audience, the FA Cup has this distinction. Undoubtedly, it adds to the *romance* of the cup.

Writing on the wall
Such writing usually sounds the death knell for a manager and reads in big bold capitals *"you're sacked."* I.e. *P45 time.*

Written his name into the history books
The kind of moment reserved for special players. Images of Wayne Rooney scrawling his name into *'The Big Book of Record International Goalscorers'* come to mind.

Written in the stars
Defining moment (usually a goal or result) destined to happen; something most definitely *in the script.* *"It was written in the stars that Le Tissier would score the final goal at the Dell."*

X Y & Z

X-factor
1. Extra, often unknown, quality belonging to the supremely talented. Phenomenal prospects have this attribute. *"There's no doubt the kid has the X-factor... we can safely say the lad from Cork will be tearing up defences for many years to come!"*
2. Worldwide singing *talent* show.

X-rated
A tackle or incident which requires immediate *censure* from the referee. They come with an 18+ certificate and possibly a health warning. *"The X-rated challenge from Robinson almost started a full-on war between the opposing benches."* When serious injury is inflicted, TV cameras may decline to show a replay. X-rated activities on the pitch can be categorised as follows:

- U – A clean, fair challenge.

- PG – Contains scenes of mid-peril; tackles leading to a collision with the advertising hoarding perhaps.
- PG12 – *"You'd have to be accompanied by an adult to see that at the pictures, Clive."* The sort of tackle which is more than a bit naughty; a cynical trip.
- 12 – Choice language picked up by pitch-side mics, such as Wayne Rooney's decision to tell the nation to *"f*** off"* in to the TV cameras at Upton Park. Such instances lead the commentator to apologise if *"any of our viewers were offended by that."*
- 15 – A clear yellow card, or borderline red, leading to extensive treatment from the physio and accompanying *magic sponge*.
- 18 – Challenge banned in some countries. A *knee-high, studs-up leg-breaker.* A *video nasty.*

Yard of pace
The crucial bit of speed which gives a player a distinct advantage over his opponent, i.e. that *"he's got that extra yard of pace"*, often with the additional *"and he can finish too".* Alternatively, it may be lost over the years. *"Well Yorke has lost that yard of pace, and as such he's had to covert himself into an orthodox central midfielder."* For *speed merchants* this could spell the end of their careers.

Yardstick
The point of reference which teams measure themselves against. *"John Coleman wants to use Accrington's Memorial Stadium heroics as the yardstick for future performances."*

Yo yo club
The age old poser over what fans would prefer: celebrating every weekend or being humped with alarming regularity. In Holland, these teams are known as *heen-en-weer club* or *back and forth*, in Germany the term is *fahrstuhlmannschaften* or *the elevator team*, whist in Poland they are called *wańka-wstańka*, which is the Polish name for a roly-poly toy.

You don't save those
Phrase pioneered by Andy Gray. Ranking amongst his top commentary moments, it is repeated throughout England in shameful Scottish accents. There is often a subsequent invitation for the scorer to *"take a bow, son"* as he has given the 'keeper *absolutely no chance.*

You don't shoot you don't score
Common footballing phrase. *"A couple of his goals were heading for the corner flag before they got deflections, but the gaffer is always saying if you don't shoot, you don't score."* The statement fails to account for other eventualities, for example when a player *diverts*

a cross past his own 'keeper which very much suggests you can score without having a *dig*; in fact it is a source of much excitement to commentators when teams are in the lead without having a shot on target.

Young guns
1. The *development squad*.
2. A team that has a high number of sprightly youngsters in its ranks. Much will be made of their average age, and pundits will no doubt hark back to Alan Hansen's ill-fated *"you don't win anything with kids"* remark. Note the average age will be broken down into months, as well as years. *"Aston Villa, their team which has an average age of 24 years and three months out there today, will have to work hard to restrict a resurgent Spurs. Their young guns are facing quite the test Clem, I can tell you that."* The opposite of *old guard*.

Young man
Second most common thing Ray Wilkins says, behind *my word*; describes any footballer below the age of 35. *"He really is quite a special young man."*

Yuletide gift
Mistake by a defender which comes *gift-wrapped* during the Christmas schedule. *"Barkley blunder presents Colback with yuletide gift."*

Z, row
Often the final resting place of *wayward* shots. It has since been succeeded by row ZZ at many grounds, particularly those with two tiers. *"Emmerson Boyce has just wellied a shot at least twice as far back as row Z."* The phrase has developed of late with the introduction of padded seats which afford the best view; as such *"Emmerson Boyce put it in the posh seats"* might be more likely, or alternatively *"the directors are ducking for cover."*

Zenith
The pinnacle. *"The European Cup triumph was the zenith of Djimi Traoré's career."* It is the opposite of *nadir*. *"That back-heel against Burnley was the nadir."*

Zinger
1. *Thunderous effort* which often *stings* the palms or fingertips of the 'keeper. *"Oof! Thunderous effort there from Hitzlsperger! That was a real zinger which flashed past the post. Goodness me he can hit them."*
2. Pithy barb by a player or manager. *"What Carew can do with a football, I can do with an orange,"* said Zlatan Ibrahimovic of his former international teammate John. Furthermore, he described out-foxing ex-Liverpool

defender Stephane Henchoz as such: *"I went left, and he went left too. I went right and he went right too. I went left again and he went to buy a hot dog."*

Other Books from Bennion Kearny

The Bundesliga Blueprint: How Germany became the Home of Football by Lee Price

In this entertaining and superbly-researched book, sportswriter Lee Price explores German football's 10-year plan. A plan that forced clubs to invest in youth, limit the number of foreign players in teams, build success without debt, and much more. The Bundesliga Blueprint details how German fans part-own and shape their clubs, how football is affordable, and the value of beer and a good sausage on match days. The book includes interviews from Michael Ballack, Jens Nowotny and Christoph Kramer, and the movers-and-shakers behind Germany's leading clubs including Schalke, Dortmund, and Paderborn. Particularly appropriate now that Jurgen Klopp has joined Liverpool.

Worst in the World: International Football at the bottom of the FIFA Rankings by Aidan Williams

The fate of sporting underdogs has long stirred the passions of many a follower. There is something pleasing about watching apparently 'ordinary' people taking on the sporting elite. Teachers, accountants, fishermen and waiters – they play for the love of football and the pride in their nation.

For footballing countries ranked at the bottom of FIFA's world rankings life can be hard. Sporadic fixtures against far better equipped teams can be a soul-destroying enterprise – frequent defeat, sometimes bordering on humiliation, is the regular outcome for these teams and their players. But when that positive result finally arrives, it can mean so much: unbridled joy, national glory, and even… redemption.

In *Worst in the World*, Aidan Williams looks at the national teams at the wrong end, so to speak, of FIFA's rankings. In doing so, he brings attention to those nations whose footballing aspirations lie not in trophies or even qualification, but simply in the love of the game and the pride of representing their country.

Lightning Source UK Ltd.
Milton Keynes UK
UKOW06f1942091215

264451UK00017B/819/P